Indian Basketry

By

GEORGE WHARTON JAMES

BEN DOVER PUBLICATIONS, INC.
NEW YORK

Published in Canada by General Publishing Company, Ltd., 30 Lesmill Road, Don Mills, Toronto, Ontario.

Published in the United Kingdom by Constable and Company, Ltd., 10 Orange Street, London WC 2.

This Dover edition, first published in 1972, is an unabridged and unaltered republication of the fourth edition of *Indian Basketry*, published by Henry Malkan in 1909.

International Standard Book Number: 0-486-21712-4
Library of Congress Catalog Card Number: 72-81280

Manufactured in the United States of America
Dover Publications, Inc.
180 Varick Street
New York, N. Y. 10014

CONTENTS.

❧ ❧ ❧ ❧

ILLUSTRATIONS.

A PAINTI EXPERT AT THE TULE RIVER RESERVATION.

PREFACE.

❧

What would be the civilized man of to-day without the art of weaving—the soft art that surrounds his home with comforts and his life with luxuries? Nay he deems them necessities. Could he do without his woven woollen or cotton underwear, his woven socks, his woven clothing? Where would be his bed linen and blankets, his carpets, his curtains, his portieres? His every day life is so intimately associated with weaving that he has ceased to think about it, and yet it is all owing to the work of primitive, aboriginal woman that he is thus favored. For there is not a weave of any kind, no matter how intricate or involved, that the finest looms of England or America produce to-day under the direction of the highest mechanical genius, that was not handed down to us, not in crude form, but as perfect as we now find it, by our savage ancestry in their basketry and kindred work.

Interest in the arts and industries of our aboriginal tribes has grown so rapidly in recent years, that whereas, twenty years ago, illustrative collections of the products of these arts and industries were confined to the museums of scientific societies, to-day they are to be found in scores of private homes. This popular interest has created a demand for knowledge as to the peoples whose arts these collections illustrate, and of the customs,—social, tribal, medicinal, religious,—in which the products of their arts are used.

One of the most common and useful of the domestic arts of the Amerind* is that of basketry. It is primitive in the extreme, is universal, both as to time and location, and as far as we know has changed comparatively little since the days of its introduction. It touches the Amerind at all points of his life from the cradle to the grave, and its products are used in every function, domestic, social and religious, of his simple civilization.

To give a little of such knowledge as the intelligent collector of Indian baskets desires to possess is the purpose of this unpretentious book.

Its field is limited to the Indians of the South-west, the Pacific States and Alaska. It is an incomplete pioneer in an unoccupied field of popular literature, and later writers will doubtless be able to add much, and correct more. It is the result of twenty years personal observation and study among the Indians of our South-west, much correspondence and questioning of authorities, and the reading and culling from every known source of information. Everything that I could find that seemed reliable has been taxed. Necessarily, no one individual could possibly describe, with accuracy, the basketry of

---

*This is a new coinage by Major J. W. Powell, of the U. S. Bureau of Ethnology, to designate the North American aborigine.

this entensive territory unless he were prepared to travel over the vast regions of the North-west and South-west, and personally visit each tribe of basket-makers, watch them gather the grasses, collect the dyes, prepare both for use, dye the materials, and go through all the labor of weaving, then study the symbolism of the designs, learn all about the ancient methods of manufacture, and, finally, visit all family, social and ceremonial functions where baskets are used.

Hence, it is evident that such a work must be, as this confessedly is, largely a compilation.

If collectors find it at all helpful or suggestive; if it aids in popularizing knowledge on these interesting products of our aboriginal peoples, and leads to a study of the peoples themselves I shall be more than repaid for the time and labor expended in its production.

For material aid, I wish most cordially to thank Major J. W. Powell, Dr. J. Walter Fewkes and Professor F. W. Hodge, of the U. S. Bureau of Ethnology, and the Hon. S. P. Langley, Professors Otis T. Mason, W. H. Holmes and Dr. Walter Hough, of the Smithsonian Institution, together with Dr. J. W. Hudson, of Ukiah, Cal., and Rev. W. C. Curtis, of Norwalk, Conn.

The engravings of the Government have been placed at my disposal, and many of the detailed descriptions of the baskets are taken verbatim from Professor Mason's papers which appear in the reports of the Smithsonian Institution.

My thanks are also extended to Mr. W. W. Newell, of the American Folk Lore Society, Dr. J. H. Kellogg, Editor of Good Health, Appleton's Popular Science Monthly, and the Traveler, San Francisco, for the use of cuts and especially to F. S. Plimpton, Esq., of San Diego, Cal., who has kindly made it possible for me to illustrate several most interesting specimens of his excellent collection.

GEORGE WHARTON JAMES,

PASADENA, CALIFORNIA.

CHAPTER I.

INTRODUCTION.

A few hundred years ago our own ancestors were "aborigines,"—they wore skins for clothes; wove baskets; lived in wicker and skin huts or in caves; ate nuts, herbs, acorns, roots and depended upon the fortunes of the chase for their meats, just as the Amerind of the present and past generations are doing and have done. Hence, as Indian baskets are woven by human beings, akin to ourselves, and are used by them in a variety of relations of intensely human interest, we are studying humanity under its earliest and simplest phases,—such phases as were probably manifested in our own ancestral history—when we intelligently study Indian Basketry.

The earliest vessels used by mankind undoubtedly were shells, broken gourds or other natural receptacles that presented themselves

A HAIDA INDIAN AND HER BASKET WORK.

opportunely to the needs of the aborigine. As his intelligence grew and he moved from place to place, the gourd as a receptacle for water when he crossed the hot and desert regions became a necessary companion. But accidents doubtless would happen to the fragile vessel and then the suggestion of strengthening it by means of fiber nets arose and the first step towards basket-making was taken. It is easy

A YOKUT WEAVER AND HER SON.

to conceive how the breakage of a gourd thus surrounded by a rude sustaining or carrying net led to the independent use of the net after the removal of the broken pieces, and thus nets ultimately would be made for carrying purposes without reference to any other vehicle. Weaving once begun, no matter how rough or crude, improvement was bound to follow, and hence, the origin of the basket.

In Indian basketry we may look and find instruction as to the higher development of our primitive people. There is no question that baskets preceded pottery-making and the close and fine weaving of textures, so the ethnologist finds in "the progressive steps of their manufacture a preparatory training for pottery, weaving and other primitive arts."

Basket-making was a common industry with all the Indians of the American Continent. In the North, baskets were, and still are, made, and we know of their manufacture by the Indians of Carolina, Virginia, Georgia and Louisiana. Baskets have also been found among the remains of the Mound Builders. In the ruins of Southern Colorado and that interesting region of Arizona and New Mexico, some of the prehistoric graves contain so many baskets as to give their occupants the name of "The Basket Makers."

"There are no savages on earth so rude that they have no form of basketry. The birds and beasts are basket-makers, and some fishes construct for themselves little retreats where they may hide. Long before the fire-maker, the potter, or even the cook, came the mothers of the Fates, spinning threads, drawing them out and cutting them off. Coarse basketry or matting is found charred in very ancient sepulchers. With few exceptions women, the wide world over, are the basket-makers, netters and weavers."—Otis T. Mason.

Of the antiquity of baskets there can be little doubt. Col. James Jackson, U. S. A., says:

"Pottery making and basket weaving are as old as the human race. As far back as there are any relics of humanity are found the traces of these industries, supplying no doubt a very positive human need. From the graves of the mound builders, from Etruscan tombs—far beyond the dawn of Roman power—from the ruins of Cyclopean construction, Chaldean antiquities and from Egyptian catacombs come the evidences of their manufacture. Aboriginal occupation of the American continents seems to be as old, if not older, than that of either Europe or Asia, and when we look upon the baskets and pottery gathered here we behold the results of an industry that originated in the very dawn of human existence and has been continued with but little change down to the present time. Our word basket has itself changed but little from its original, the Welsh "basgawd" meaning literally a weaving or putting together of splinters. The ancient Welsh, or Britons, were expert basket makers, and Roman annals tell us that the halls of wealthy Roman citizens were decorated with the beautiful and costly produce of their handiwork. Made from whatever substances were most appropriate or convenient they have been shaped by the needs and decorated by the fancy or superstitions of barbaric or semi-civilized peoples, and have served all purposes from plates to dwelling houses."

"Among primitive arts, basketry also furnishes the most striking illustration of the inventive genius, fertility of resource and almost incredible patience of the Indian woman. They collected the fuel, gathered the stores of acorns, mesquite and other wild seeds; they dried the grasshoppers for winter use. In times of scarcity they searched every hiding of fat grub or toothsome bulb; or with a tough stick drove the angle worms from their holes and with the addition of a few wild onions and acorn flour converted the mess into an appetizing soup. They made petticoats of tule and other wild grasses for summer use, and winter garments of rabbit and squirrel skins. And

MERCED NOLASQULY, A PALATINGWA BASKET WEAVER, SOUTHERN CALIFORNIA.

while all these accomplishments added to the market value of the women, it was invariably the most expert in basketry who brought the highest price, viz.: two strings of shell money, or one hundred dollars."—Mrs. Jeanne C. Carr.

Indian basketry is almost entirely the work of Indian women, and, therefore, its study necessarily leads us into the sanctum-sanctorum of feminine Indian life. The thought of the woman, the art development, the acquirement of skill, the appreciation of color, the utilization of crude material for her purposes, the labor of gathering the materials, the objects she had in view in the manufacture of her baskets, the methods she followed to attain those objects, her failures, her successes, her conception of art, her more or less successful attempts to imitate the striking objects of Nature with which she came in contact, the aesthetic qualities of mind that led her to desire to thus reproduce or imitate Nature—all these, and a thousand other things in the Indian woman's life, are discoverable in an intelligent study of Indian basketry.

One has but to study the history of all industrial, as distinguished from military, occupations, to see how honored a position woman has won by her indomitable energy, constant industry and keen wittedness. Those fools of the male sex who sneer at the "uselessness of woman" merely reveal their supernal ignorance of what man owes to woman in the industrial arts and sciences. Her work, from the very earliest ages of human history, has tended towards the health, the comfort, the knowledge and the culture of mankind. She has not been merely the wife, the mother, the nurse of man, but the teacher in many arts which man now proudly and haughtily claims as his own "sphere."

And one of the foremost of these industrial arts is that of weaving— purely a product of woman's wit and skill. As Dr. Otis T. Mason has eloquently written: "A careful study of the homely occupations of savage women is the best guide to their share in creating the aesthetic arts. Whether in the two Americas, or in the heart of Africa, or among the peoples of Oceania, the perpetual astonishment is not the lack of art, but the superabundance of it."

"Call to mind the exquisite sewing of the Eskimo woman with sinew thread and needle of bone, or the wonderful basketry of all the American tribes, the bark work of Polynesia, the loom work of Africa, the pottery of the Pueblos, of Central America and Peru. Compare these with the artistic productions of our present generation of girls and women at their homes. I assure you the comparison is not in favor of the laborers' daughters, but of the daughters and wives of the degraded savage. In painting, dyeing, moulding, modelling, weaving and embroidering, in the origination first of geometric patterns and then of freehand drawing, savage women, primitive women, have won their title to our highest admiration."

Compare the basketry of women with that of men. Go into any basket shop of the modern civilized world and pick up the ugly and homely, though useful, objects called baskets, and place them side by side with the products of the savage woman's art and skill. Every lover of beautiful work, of artistic form, beautiful design and delicate color cannot fail to be struck with the highest admiration at the sight of the latter, while the former are tolerated only for their usefulness.

To the uninitiated a fine Indian basket may possess a few exterior attractions, such as shapely form, delicate color and harmonious design, but anything further he cannot see. On the other hand the initiated sees a work of love; a striving after the ideal; a reverent propitiation of supernatural powers, good or evil; a nation's art expression, a people's inner life of poetry, art, religion; and thus he comes to a closer knowledge of the people it represents, a deeper sympathy with them; a fuller recognition of the oneness of human life, though under so many and diverse manifestations. Fine baskets, to the older Indian women, were their poems, their paintings, their sculpture, their cathedrals, their music; and the civilized world is just learning the first lessons of the aboriginal melodies and harmonies in these wicker-work masterpieces.

What Victor Hugo strikingly expressed about the cathedrals of Europe when he exclaimed "The book has killed the building!" could be truthfully applied to the Indian in the expression "Civilization has killed the basket." For as the Indian woman finds that she can purchase for a few cents the pans, pots and kettles used by her civilized sister she loses the desire to spend weary days, and even months, in making the baskets, which, in the past, served alone as her domestic utensils. Consequently basket making as a fine art among the aborigines is rapidly dying out. True, there are still many baskets made, and on a recent trip to the High Sierras of California I found a number of first-class basket makers at work, and, more pleasing still, some of the young girls were learning the art. But in almost every case the basket maker of to-day is dominated by a rude commercialism rather than by the desire to make a basket which shall be her best prized household treasure as the highest expression of which she is capable of the art instinct within her. Hence the rage for old baskets. A true collector does not wish a basket made to sell, and as the old baskets were comparatively limited in number, the opportunity to secure them is rapidly passing away, if it has not already disappeared. By this, of course, I do not mean that old baskets may not be purchased. Collections now and then are for sale, which are rich in rare old specimens of the weaver's art; and occasionally, but, now, alas, very occasionally, the indefatigable collector may pick up an ancient basket in some far-away Indian hut.

CHAPTER II.

BASKETRY THE MOTHER OF POTTERY.

That the art of basketry antedates the art of pottery is generally conceded. In an interesting monograph published in the reports of the Bureau of Ethnology, Mr. Cushing urges that pottery was sug-

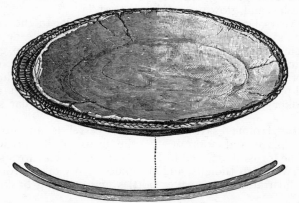

FIG. 6. HAVASUPAI CLAY-LINED ROASTING-TRAY.

gested by the clay lined basketry of the Havasupai Indians in Arizona. In 1887, when he visited them, he found them doing the cooking of their seeds, mush, meat, etc., in wicker baskets lined with sandy clay, and thus describes the method followed:

FIG. 7 BASKET-BOWL AS BASE-MOULD FOR POTTERY.

"A round basket tray, either loosely or closely woven, is evidently coated inside with clay, into which has been kneaded a very large proportion of sand, to prevent contraction and consequent cracking from drying. This lining of clay is pressed into the basket as closely as possible with hands, and then allowed to dry. See Fig. 6. The tray is thus made ready for use. The seeds or other substances to be parched are placed inside of it, together with a quantity of glowing wood coals. The operator, quickly squatting, grasps the tray at opposite edges, and by a rapid spiral motion up and down, succeeds in keeping the seeds and coals constantly shifting places, and turning over as they dance after one another around and around the tray, meanwhile blowing or puffing the embers with every breath to keep them free from ashes and glowing at their hottest."

A few years later when I made my first visits to the Havasupais I found the same methods still in vogue. It is readily apparent that the constant heating of the clay lining would cause it to grow hard, and instances would occur when it would become detached from the wicker work and a perfect earthen roasting vessel be produced. The occasional production of such a vessel, suitable in all ways and for all uses in cookery, would suggest the manufacture of similar serviceable utensils.

Professor Holmes says: "The clay vessel is an intruder, and usurps the place and appropriates the dress of its predecessor in wicker. The forms illustrated in Figs. 8 and 9 are clay forms, common with South Western Indians, and are undoubtedly taken from basketry shapes as illustrated in the water bottles and carrying baskets, shown elsewhere."

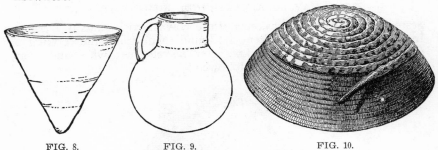

FIG. 8.   FIG. 9.   FIG. 10.

That basketry was intimately connected with two distinct methods of pottery-making is proven by the clearest evidence. In the Mississippi Valley, in Arizona, New Mexico and elsewhere in the United States thousands of pieces of pottery have been found which unmistakably show that the soft clay was modelled around the outside or within some basket form which gave the shape of the vessel. In all the museums these specimens of pottery may be found. It will be observed in studying them that they bear far more impressions of basketry and other textile arts than of natural objects, such as gourds, shells, etc. It is also observable that every basketry stitch or pattern known to the aborigines is found in these pottery impressions. Hence the natural inferences that basketry antedates pottery, and that the art of basket-making was in an advanced stage whilst pottery was still in its infancy.

How fascinating the work of the antiquarian and archaeologist. To pick up even the fragments of the pottery of a long past age, brush off the accumulated dirt and read thereupon the relation its manufacture bore to a sister art, and then, slowly but surely, to decipher every method followed by primitive artist; to tell how spinner, weaver, net maker worked, and with what materials, and then to discover that every stitch of plain weaving, diaper weaving, twined weaving and coiled weaving known to modern art was used by these ignorant and savage people of the dark ages.

Mr. Cushing thus describes the process of manufacture as he saw it carried on, and as I have seen it again and again, at Zuni, Laguna, Acoma and the Hopi pueblos.

Forming a rope of soft clay, she coiled it upon a center, to form the bottom. Placing it upon an inverted food-basket, bowl-shaped, she pressed the coils of clay closely together, one upon the other (Fig. 10), and as soon as the desired size was attained, loosened the bowl from the basket and thus provided herself with a new utensil. In consequence of the difficulty experienced in removing these bowl-forms from the bottom of the baskets—which had to be done while they were still plastic, to keep them from cracking—they were very shallow. Hence the specimens found among the older ruins and graves are not only corrugated outside, but are also very wide in proportion to their height.

FIG. 11. BASKET BASE MOLD FOR COILED POTTERY.

FIG. 12. FIRST FORM OF THE VESSEL.

The other primitive method followed was one that is still practiced by all the pottery makers of the South-west. It is an imitation of basketry methods; not a moulding upon baskets, but an application of coiled methods of weaving to the manufacture of pottery. Just as the basket weaver wraps one coil upon another, so does the pottery maker take her rope of clay and coil it up as shown in Fig. 11.

By and by the desire for ornamentation of pottery arose, and from this sprang the discovery of the fact that, while the clay was plastic, the exterior of the vessel could be smoothed with a spatula of bone or gourd, no matter what its size, if supported at the bottom in a basket or other mold so that it could be shifted or turned about without direct handling. See Fig. 7.

To smooth such a vessel inside and out required that it have a wide mouth, but, by and by, the potter determined that the mouth must be contracted as much water was spilled in carrying the full olla from the spring or river to the house. She still used the basket as a base for her pottery as shown in Fig. 12, and to this desire for a small mouthed olla Cushing claims we owe the beautiful shape of Fig. 13.

He says: "One of the consequences of all this was that when large they could not be stroked inside, as the shoulders or uttermost upper peripheries of the vessel could not be reached with the hand or scraper through the small openings. The effect of the pressure exerted in smoothing them on the outside, therefore, naturally caused the upper parts to sink down, generating the spheroidal shape of the jar, one of the most beautiful types of the olla ever known to the Pueblos. At Zuni, wishing to have an ancient jar of this form which I had seen, reproduced, I showed a drawing of it to a woman expert in the manufacture of pottery. Without any instructions from me beyond a mere statement of my wishes, she proceeded at once to sprinkle the inside of a basket-bowl with sand, managing the clay in the way above de-

FIG. 13. SECONDARY FORM   FIG. 14. FINISHED VESSEL,
    OF THE VESSEL.   SHOWING CONTRACTIONS
                                    IN DRYING.

scribed and continuing the vessel shaping upward by spiral building. She did not at first make the shoulders low or sloping, but rounded or arched them upward and outward. At this I remonstrated, but she gave no heed other than to ejaculate "Wa-na-ni-ana!" which meant "just wait, will you!" When she had finished the rim, she easily caused the shoulders to sink, simply by stroking them—more where uneven than elsewhere—with a wet scraper of gourd until she had exactly reproduced the form of the drawing. She then set the vessel aside in the basket. Within two days it shrank by drying at the rate of about one inch in twelve, leaving the basket far too large. It could hence be removed without the slightest difficulty. (See Fig. 14).

FIG. 15.   BASKETS IN THE PRIVATE COLLECTION OF W. D. CAMPBELL, LOS ANGELES, CAL.

CHAPTER III.

BASKETRY IN INDIAN LEGEND.

Considering the important place that basketry holds in the life of the Indian, it is to be expected that much legendary lore of one kind or another would be associated with it. And such is the case. Did one have the time and opportunity, he might accumulate a large volume of such legends. A few must here suffice.

MacMurray thus writes of the Cosmogony of the Yakimas as it was told to him by one of their great war chiefs: "The world was all water, and Saghalee Tyee was above it. He threw up out of the water at shallow places large quantities of mud, and that made the land. He made trees to grow, and he made a man out of a ball of mud

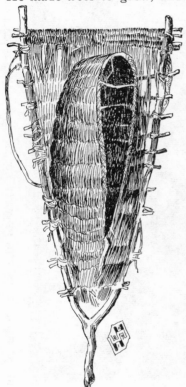 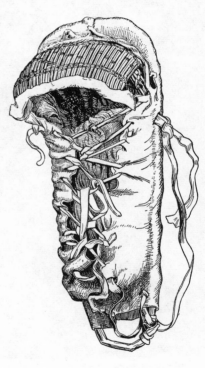

FIG. 16. INDIAN BABY BASKET.   FIG. 17. CRADLE OF NEVADA
     CALIFORNIA TRIBE.   UTES, SHOWING CALIFORNIAN
     CHRYSALIS PATTERN.   INFLUENCES.

and instructed him in what he should do. When the man grew lonesome, he made a woman as his companion, and taught her to dress skins, and to gather berries, and to make baskets of the bark of roots, which he taught her how to find.

"She was asleep and dreaming of her ignorance of how to please man, and she prayed to Saghalee Tyee to help her. He breathed on her and gave her something that she could not see, or hear, or smell, or touch, and it was preserved in a little basket, and by it all the arts of design and skilled handiwork were imparted to her descendants."

This Yakima chief then, in order that Mrs. MacMurray might be inspired likewise, presented her husband with a very ancient drum-shaped basket, about two and one half inches in diameter, which is now most carefully preserved among other baskets in the Mac Murray home at Princeton, N. J.

According to Washington Matthews the Navahoes have many legends with which baskets are connected.

Here is a description of the first baby baskets ever made. Surely none but a poetic and imaginative people could ever have conceived so wonderful a basket. Their gods of war were born of two women, one fathered by the sun, the other by a waterfall, and when they were born they were placed in baby baskets both alike as follows: The foot-rests and the back battens were made of sunbeam, the hoods of rainbow, the side-strings of sheet lightning, and the lacing strings of zigzag lightning. One child they covered with the black cloud, and the other with the female rain.

Another form of this story says that the boy born first was wrapped in black cloud. A rainbow was used for the hood of his basket and studded with stars. The back of the frame was a parhelion, with the bright spot at its bottom shining at the lowest point. Zigzag lightning was laid in each side and straight lightning down the middle in front. Niltsatlol (sunbeams shining on a distant rainstorm) formed the fringe in front where Indians now put strips of buckskin. The carry-straps were sunbeams.

It has often been stated that the Navahoes make no baskets, yet in the light of the following legend it would certainly appear that they were basket-makers from the earliest ages. Doubtless the art has suffered a great decline, and it is true that but few Navaho women now practice it. Yet I have myself seen them at work and while thus occupied have succeeded in photographing them.

This legend is of one of their maidens who made baskets. She was wooed by the Coyote, whose life principle was not in his chest where it would be easy to destroy it, but in the tip of his nose and the end of his tail. The Coyote had slain the Great Wolf but the maiden refused to marry him unless he had first been slain four times and four times had come back to life. Coyote allowed the maid to beat him with a great club until she thought him dead. Then she went to her basket-making. She was engaged in making four baskets at the time, but had not worked long before Coyote came back.

Again she beat him with the club so that his body was hacked into pieces, and again she returned to her basketry, only to find Coyote shortly by her side saying "Twice you have slain me and I have come back to life."

Once again she sought to slay him but failed to kill the vital principle and so she had only succeeded in taking a few stitches in the work when Coyote was back again.

This time she smashed him all to pieces and mixed him with earth and ground him to powder and then scattered the powder in every direction. But, after considerable trouble, Coyote managed to gather together his scattered corpus and returned to his basket making maiden, who soon thereafter became his wife.

From another legend, however, we learn that it was a family or clan called Dsiltlani, who joined the Navahoes in the early days of the nation's history, who taught their women how to make wicker water-bottles, carrying baskets, etc.

Yeitso, the tallest, fiercest, and most dreadful of the alien gods of the Navaho never travelled without carrying a basket. Yeitso was a singular being, born a monster at a time when the Navaho men and women were living apart. During this period of separation both sexes indulged in evil and vile practices and Yeitso was the fruit of the evil doing of his mother. He was slain by two mythical heroes who took his scalp and broken arrows to their home in his own basket.

The Navahoes have an interesting legend which they connect with the carrying basket, Fig. 18. In the early days of the world's history one of their mythical heroes was seized by a flying monster and carried up to a dangerous ledge on a high mountain in New Mexico. He suc-

FIG. 20.   PAIUTI WATER BOTTLE.
THE TUSJEH OF THE NAVAHO.

FIGS. 18 AND 19.   HOPI BASKET
AND METHOD OF WEAVE.

ceeded in killing the monster and its mate but was unable to get down from his perilous position. Just then he saw the Bat Woman (one of the mythical characters of the Navahoes) walking along the base of the cliff. After a good deal of persuasion she consented to come up and carry him down in her basket, but she required that he should close his eyes before she did so. Before he closed his eyes he saw that the large carrying basket was held upon her back by strings as thin as those of a spider's web. "Grandmother," he said, "I fear to enter your basket; the strings are too thin." "Have no fear," she replied, "I have carried a whole deer in this basket; the strings are strong enough to bear you." Still he hesitated and still she assured him. The fourth time that he expressed his fear she said: "Fill the basket with stones and you will see that I speak the truth." He did as he was bidden and she danced around with the loaded basket on her back; but the strings did not break, though they twanged like bowstrings. When he entered the basket she bade him keep his eyes shut until they reached the bottom of the cliff, as he must not see how she managed to descend. He shut his eyes and soon felt himself gradually going down; but he heard a strange flapping against the rock, which so excited his curiosity that he opened his eyes. Instantly he began to fall with dangerous rapidity, and the flapping stopped; she struck him with her stick and bade him close his eyes. Again he felt himself slowly descending, and the flapping against the rock began. Three times more he disobeyed her, and the last time they were near the bottom of the cliff, and both fell to the ground unhurt.

FIG. 21. THE HO-A-PUH OR CARRYING BASKET
OF THE HOPIS AND NAVAHOES.

As soon as they reached the ground the hero and the Bat Woman plucked the feathers of the winged monsters and placed them in the basket. Before the hero left the Bat Woman he cautioned her not to pass through two particular regions, one of which was overgrown with weeds and the other with sunflowers. The Bat Woman failed to heed the warning and as she walked along through the sunflowers she heard a rustling behind her, and, turning, saw the feathers changing into birds of strange appearance and varying plumage and all swarming out of her basket. She tried to hold them in, to catch them as they flew out, but all in vain. She laid down her basket and watched, helplessly, her feathers changing into little birds of all kinds, wrens, warblers, titmice and the like, all flying away until her basket was empty. Thus it was that the little birds were created.

In the Chaco Canyon in Northern New Mexico are a number of interesting cliff-dwellings or pueblo houses. In the early days they were inhabited by the Pueblo people. One day a war eagle was seen floating in the sky. The Pueblos much desired the feathers of the eagle, so they watched where the bird alighted. When they found the nest it was in a cleft on the face of a precipice and inaccessible unless one were lowered in a basket. None of the young men of the Pueblos was willing to risk his life in the attempt and they finally persuaded a poor Navaho, afterwards named Kinniki, to make the effort on their behalf. A great, strong carrying basket was made, somewhat after the style of Fig. 21, and the Navaho got inside it and was lowered to the eagle's nest. He was told to drop the eagles to the ground below, but the Wind whispered to him that the Pueblos were his enemies and he had better not obey their behests. He heeded the warning of the Wind and called out to those above: "Swing the basket so that it may come nearer to the cliff. I cannot reach the nest unless you do." So they caused the basket to swing to and fro and when it touched the cliff the Navaho stepped out leaving the empty basket swinging in the air.

FIG. 22.   HOPI BASKET, MADE OF YUCCA.

The Pueblos were very angry when they found out the trick that had been played upon them, and they tried to kill the Navaho by shooting fire arrows to the nest. For four days he stayed here starving, keeping himself warm at night by sleeping between the two young eaglets.

Then the eagles came home and they took him up to the upper world above the sky. He learned all the wonderful songs, prayers, sacrifices and ceremonies of the eagles, which are now practiced by the Navahoes in one of their great rites.

Now he returned to earth, and soon thereafter visited the treacherous people of Kintyel, upon whom he took a singular and appropriate vengeance.

Another typical hero of the Navahoes was Na-ti-nes-thani—He who Teaches Himself. He was a great gambler, and after he had gambled away all his possessions, he left his home for some far away country in the hope of bettering his fortunes.

After wonderful adventures he came to the home of a wicked wizard, who was a cannibal, and whose own daughter was also his wife. This vile creature introduced Natinesthani to his daughter as his son-in-law, for he wished him to stay, so that he might slay and eat him. The wizard insisted upon smoking some of his son-in-law's tobacco, but it sent him into a swoon which seemed so like death that his wife and daughter besought Natinesthani to restore him to life. Four times this occurred, then the wizard determined to get rid of his son-in-law. The former induced his daughter to take a sacred basket filled with mush, together with other food, to her husband, in which he had placed poison next to the a-tha-at-lo or finishing point on the rim. By craft the stranger avoided eating the poison, for the Wind People had warned him of it. When his wife presented the basket to him, she said: "When a stranger visits us we always expect him to eat from the part of the basket where it is finished." He replied: "It is my custom to eat from the edge oppposite the point of finish." He thus escaped the poison.

When the young woman told her father he saw that he must try again, so the next day he sent his daughter with a dish of stewed venison and a basket full of mush. But as the young man took it the Wind People warned him that there was poison all around the edge of the basket, so this time he ate freely of the stew, but, when he took the basket of mush he said: "When I eat just as the sun is about to come up, it is my custom to eat only from the middle of the basket." The following day both stew and mush were brought him, but as the Wind People whispered to him and told him that poison was mixed all through the mush, he said to his wife: "I may eat no mush to-day. The sun has already risen, and I have sworn that the sun shall never see me eat mush." On the fourth morning the wicked father-in-law poisoned both stew and mush, but being warned as usual by the Wind People, the young man said to his wife: "I do not eat at all to-day. It is my custom to eat no food one day in every four. This is the day that I must fast."

After such marvellous proofs of power the old man ceased his attempts for awhile; but by and by, he was again filled with desire to slay his son. Many were the ruses that he followed, the ambuscades that he planned, the treacheries he concocted, but Natinesthani evaded them all. Finally he succeeded in obtaining charms which altogether destroyed the wizard's power. Then he told the wizard how he had all along known of his nefarious designs, and how he had thwarted them. Fully exposed, the incestuous wizard confessed his wickedness and begged forgiveness and asked his son-in-law to cure him of all his evil. This was done and thus the Feather Chant and Dance were inaugurated which continue to this day as potent ceremonies for the confusion of all the wizards and witches.

In the legends which describe in detail the growth of the Navaho nation, the accession of one gens is thus accounted for: "It happened about this time while some of the Tha 'paha were sojourning at Agala, that they sent two children one night to a spring to get water. The children carried out with them two wicker bottles, see Fig. 20, in somewhat the same fashion as pictured in Fig. 23, but returned with four. "Where did you get these other bottles?" the parents inquired. "We took them away from two little girls whom we met at the spring."

answered the children. "Why did you do this, and who are the girls?" said the elders. "We do not know. They are strangers," said the little ones. The parents at once set out for the spring to find the strange children and restore the stolen bottles to them; but on the way they met the little girls coming toward the Tha 'paha camp, and asked them who they were. The strange children replied: "We belong to a band of wanderers who are encamped on yonder mountain. They sent us two together to find water." "Then we shall give you a name," said the Tha 'paha; "we shall call you To 'baznaazi— Two Come Together for Water." The Tha 'paha brought the little girls to their hut and bade them be seated. "Stay with us," they said.

FIG. 23. APACHE WOMAN   FIG. 24. POMA WOMAN CARRYING
CARRYING WATER IN BASKET BOTTLE.   LOAD IN CONICAL BASKET.

"You are too weak and little to carry the water so far. We shall send some of our young men to carry it for you." When the young men found the camp of the strangers they invited the latter to visit them. The Tha 'paha welcomed the newcomers as friends, and told them they had already a name for them, To 'baznaazi. Under this name they became united to the Navahoes as a new gens, and they are now closely affiliated with Tha 'paha.

One of the chief legends of the Hopi is that of Tiyo, the mythical snake hero, and with that is intimately associated the "Ho-a-puh," or carrying basket. (Fig. 21.) Tiyo's father lived on a mountain near the junction of the San Juan and Colorado rivers. The youth was thoughtful and studious and was much puzzled to account for the ever flowing away of the water of the Colorado river. After long reflection he decided to endeavor to solve the mystery. His father helped prepare a dry cottonwood tree, hollow it out and thus make a closed boat in which he could sail down the river to the discovery of its secret. To keep him from starving his mother and sister each gave him a po-o-ta, or basket tray made of yucca, (Fig. 22) heaped up with food.

It was a dangerous trip but he finally reached the end of the journey. Here he descried a small round hole in the ground, and, hearing a sound, he advanced and was saluted with the cordial greeting "Um-pi-tuh, my heart is glad; I have long been expecting you; come down into my house."

FIG. 25. HAVASUPAI MAKING BASKET.

Under the direction of the Spider Woman, Tiyo visited the underworld and learned all the secret songs, prayers, dances and other ceremonials that are now performed by the snake-antelope fraternity. Then they went to the Sun and learned much from him, and after several day's journeyings returned to the Snake Kiva, where the chief taught him many things and then bestowed upon him two maidens. Said he: "Here are two maidens who know the charm which prevents death from the bite of the rattlesnake; take them with you, and one you shall give to your younger brother."

Four days later Spider Woman made a beautiful hoapuh, around which she fastened a cotton cord, and on the fifth morning she placed Tiyo in it, with a maiden on each side. She then ascended through the hatch and disappeared, but soon a filament descended and attached itself to the cord, and the basket was drawn up to the white clouds, which sailed away to To-ko-na-bi, and there Spider Woman again spun out her filament and lowered the basket to the ground. Tiyo took the maidens to his mother's house, and no stranger saw them for four days, and the two brothers prepared the bridal presents.

Tiyo and his brother and the two Snake maidens thus became the progenitors of the Snake and Antelope Clans of the Hopi, who alone perform the thrilling ceremony which I have elsewhere fully described.*

FIG .26. POMA POUNDING ACORNS IN GRANITE
MORTAR WITH BASKET TOP.

The Havasupais of the Havasu Canyon have a legend that they are descended from a daughter of Tochopa, their good god, who, like Tiyo's father, fastened up his offspring in a hollowed-out tree. But in Tochopa's case it was because Hokomata, the bad god, was about to drown the world. After floating about for many days—so long, indeed, that she grew from a girl to a woman—the log settled at a point not far from the junction of the Little Colorado with the main river. Here, when she emerged from the tree, everything was dark and foggy. Soon she felt the desire for maternity, and, as the sun slowly rose for the first time upon the earth and dispelled the dark-

*Scientific American, June 24 and Sept. 9, 1899. Wide World Magazine, Jan. 1900. Outing, June, 1900.

ness and gloom, she determined that he should be the father of her child. The boy was born in due time. Then maternal longings again filling her breast she went and conceived of the waterfall, now known as Mooney Fall in Havasu Canyon. The offspring of this union was a daughter.

FIG. 26A. NAVAHO WATER CARRIERS.

As the children grew she sent the boy over the Kohonino basin to hunt, and taught her daughter to make baskets, she herself having been taught by Tochopa before the drowning of the world.

Thus it is that the Havasupais are good basket makers and excel so many other weavers in the exercise of the art.

FIG. 27.   SACRED BASKETS OF THE NAVAHOES,
PIMAS AND APACHES.   (Plimpton Collection.)

FIG. 28.   DANCE AND OTHER BASKETS OF THE
YOKUTS.   (Plimpton Collection.)

CHAPTER IV.

BASKETRY IN INDIAN CEREMONIAL.

In many Indian ceremonies baskets play a most important part. If all these were recorded a large volume would be the result. A few of the most important and best known are here briefly given.

In one of the great healing ceremonies and dances of the Navahoes the baskets shown in Figs. 27 and 29 have a distinct place. One or other of these baskets must be used.

To describe this wonderfully weird and singular series of ceremonies in full would take up three-score pages of this unpretentious work, so I must content myself with giving the briefest synopsis, merely showing where the baskets are ceremonially used. The whole series of dances, prayers, songs, etc., are called "Hasjelti Dailjis." They are conducted by one of the leading shamans of the tribe, and only the most wealthy can afford them, for the cost is great, even as high as hundreds, and often two or three thousands, of dollars. For nine days these ceremonies last, the first day being devoted to the building and dedication of a medicine hogan and a sweat house.

Around this sweat house wands of turkey feathers were placed, which were brought hither in one of these sacred baskets; and when the sweating process was over the wands were collected, placed in the basket and removed to the medicine hogan.

On the fourth day two of these baskets figured prominently in the ceremonies. A medicine basket containing amole root and water was placed in front of a circle made of sand and covered with pine boughs. A second basket contained water and a quantity of pine needles sufficiently thick to form a dry surface, and on the top of these needles a number of valuable necklaces of coral, turquoise and silver were placed. A square was formed on the edge of the basket with four of the turkey wands before mentioned. The song priest with rattle led several priests in singing. The invalid sat to the northeast of the circle, a breech cloth his only apparel. During the chanting an attendant made suds by macerating the amole and beating it up and down in the water. The basket remained in position; the man stooped over it, facing north; his position allowed the sunbeams which came through the fire opening to fall upon the suds. When the basket was a mass of white froth the attendant washed the suds from his hands by pouring water from a Paiuti basket water-bottle (Fig. 20) over them, after which the song priest came forward and with corn pollen drew a cross over the suds, which stood firm like the beaten whites of eggs, the arms of the cross pointing to the cardinal points. A circle of the pollen was then made around the edge of the suds." This crossing and circling of the basket of suds with the pollen is supposed to give them additional power in restoring the invalid to health. The invalid now knelt upon the pinion boughs in the center of the same circle. "A handful of the suds was placed on his head. The basket was now placed near to him, and he bathed his head thoroughly; the maker of the suds afterwards assisted him in bathing the entire body with the suds, and pieces of yucca were rubbed upon the body. The chant continued through the ceremony and closed just as the remainder of the suds was emptied by the attendant over the invalid's head. The song priest collected the four wands from the second basket, and an attendant gathered the necklaces; a second attendant placed the basket before the invalid, who was now sitting in the center of the circle, and the first attendant assisted him in bathing the entire body with this mixture; the body was quite covered with the pine needles, which had become very soft from soaking. The invalid then returned to his former position at the left of the song priest, and the pine needles of the yucca, or amole, together with the sands, were carried out and deposited at the foot of a pinion

FIG. 29. NAVAHO SACRED BASKET.

tree. The body of the invalid was dried by rubbing with meal." This taking out of the sands, pine needles, etc., used in the ceremony was supposed to take away so much of the disease that had been washed from the invalid.

Later in the day at another most elaborate ceremony baskets filled with food are placed in a circle around a fire in the medicine lodge. One of the priests takes a pinch of food from each basket, and places it in another basket. This is then prayed over, smoked over and thus made a powerful medicine by the song-priest. After the priest has gone through several performances with it, the invalid dips his three first fingers into the mixture, puts them in his mouth, and loudly sucks in the air. This is repeated four times. Then all the attendants do likewise, with a prayer for rain, good crops, health and riches. This food is afterwards dried by the chief medicine man, made into a powder, and is one of his most potent medicines.

On the sixth day a great sand painting is made in the medicine lodge, and the invalid, as he enters, is required to take the sacred medicine basket, which is now filled with sacred meal, and sprinkle the painting with it. The chief figures of the painting were the goddesses of the rainbow, whose favor it was desired he should gain. Again and again in the ceremonies these sacred baskets are used, and on the ninth day in the concluding dance the invalid takes it full of sacred meal and sprinkles all the dancers. The full description of this wonderful series of ceremonies is found in the Eighth Annual Report of the U. S. Bureau of Ethnology.

If the margin is worn through or torn, the basket is unfit for sacred use. The basket is one of the perquisites of the shaman when the rites are done; but he, in turn, must give it away, and must be careful never to eat out of it. Notwithstanding its sacred uses, food may be served in it by any other person than the shaman who has used it ceremonially.

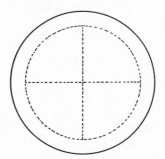

FIG 30.   CIRCLE OF MEAL
IN NAVAHO WEDDING BASKET.

Fig. 29 shows the other form of Navaho sacred basket. It is also made of aromatic sumac, and is used in the rites to hold sacred meal. The crosses are said to represent clouds, heavy with rain, and would indicate that this basketry design may have had its origin in its use during ceremonies intended to bring the rain.

Another important ceremony of the Navahoes in which this basket figures is that of marriage.

A. M. Stephen thus describes the wedding custom: "On the night set for the wedding both families and their friends meet at the hut of the bride's family. Here there are much feasting and singing, and the bride's family make return presents to the bridegroom's people, but not, of course, to the same amount. The women of the bride's family prepare corn meal porridge, which is poured into the basket. The bride's uncle then sprinkles the sacred blue pollen of the larkspur upon the porridge, forming a design as in Fig. 30.

The bride has hitherto been lying beside her mother, concealed under a blanket, on the woman's side of the hogan (hut). After calling to her to come to him, her uncle seats her on the west side of the hut, and the bridegroom sits down before her, with his face toward hers, and the basket of porridge set between them. A gourd

of water is then given to the bride, who pours some of it on the
bridegroom's hands while he washes them, and he then performs a
like office for her.　With the first two fingers of the right hand he
then takes a pinch of porridge, just where the line of pollen touches
the circle of the east side.　He eats this one pinch, and the bride dips
with her fingers from the same place.　He then takes in succession
a pinch from the other places where the lines touch the circle and a
final pinch from the center, the bride's fingers following his.　The
basket of porridge is then passed over to the younger guests, who
speedily devour it with merry clamor, a custom analagous to dividing
the bride's cake at a wedding.　The elder relatives of the couple now
give them much good and weighty advice, and the marriage is complete."

In Navaho ceremonies that I have witnessed the custom is somewhat different.　The pollen is sprinkled and a pinch taken from each
quarter and from the center by the shaman or medicine man and by
him breathed upon and thrown to the corresponding cardinal points,
N. W. S. E. and here, thus propitiating the powers of all the universe.
Then, handing the bowl to the bride and bridegroom, they, in the
presence of the assembled guests, begin at the point where the line
touches the east, and each take a pinch of the porridge and eat it,
the bride going one way and the bridegroom the other, until their
fingers meet on the opposite side of the bowl.　Then the marriage is
complete, and the rest of the porridge is handed to the guests.

Mr. G. H. Pepper, of the American Museum of Natural History,
New York, has seen a Navaho wedding ceremony conducted in a
different manner from either of these described.　On this occasion
he learned that a little Indian girl was at the point of death, having
been bitten by a rattlesnake while collecting pollen from growing
corn.　Pollen is the Navaho symbol of fertility, and its use in a
marriage ceremony is naturally obvious.　Although the child was
so dangerously ill, Mr. Pepper says the marriage ceremony went on,
regardless of her condition.　A small amount of corn meal was taken
and slightly moistened and then mixed together.　This half dry, half
wet meal was then sprinkled in four lines across the empty wedding
basket, dividing it into four equal parts.　At the end of each line a
small ball of the meal was placed, as well as one in the center.　This
done, all was ready for the ceremony.　The bridegroom, who up to
this time had been outside the hogan with his friends, now came in
and sat down.　Then the mother of the bride brought to the groom
a wicker or gourd bottle full of water, with which he advanced, and,
as the bride held out her hands, he poured the water over while she
washed them.　This done, the bride took the water bottle and poured
water over his hands.　Now the couple sat down on the west side
of the hogan, and in full view of all present.　The bridegroom then
took the wedding basket in his hands, holding it with the shipapu
opening turned towards the east.　Then, taking a small pinch of meal
from the end of the line which terminated towards the east, he put it in
the bride's mouth.　The bride then took a pinch and fed the groom
in like manner, after which groom and bride alternately took a pinch,
each feeding it to the other, from each of the lines in succession,
and finally from the center.　This done, the ceremony was completed.
In his preoccupation with the sick child Mr. Pepper does not remem-

ber whether the pinches of meal were taken from the lines beginning East and continuing North, West and South or the other way. It will be remembered that elsewhere I have called attention to the fact that as a rule the ceremonial circuit of the Indians of the Southwest is always East, North, West and South, which is describing a circle in the backward way from that generally followed by white men.

Another interesting thing about this Navaho wedding basket it is well to notice, and that is that the finishing off of the last coil of the basketry always comes directly opposite to the Shipapu opening. This is for the purpose of enabling those who use the basket at night to determine where the Shipapu opening is, so that they may hold the basket in the proper ceremonial way, which requires that the Shipapu opening shall always be turned towards the East. This finishing off place on the rim of the basket is called by the Navahoes the a-tha-at-lo.

According to Matthews, the sacred basket used in all these ceremonials has another important function to perform. It is used as a drum. He says: "In none of the ancient Navaho rites is a regular drum or tomtom employed. The inverted basket serves the purpose of one, and the way in which it is used for this simple object is rendered devious and difficult by ceremonious observances."

Then over a page of description is required to tell how the shamans proceed when they "turn down the basket" to make a drum of it at the beginning of the songs, and "turn up the basket" at the close. Everything is done with elaborate ceremony. "There are songs for turning up and turning down the basket, and there are certain words in these songs at which the shaman prepares to turn up the basket by putting his hand under its eastern rim, and other words at which he does the turning. For four nights, when the basket is turned down, the eastern part is laid on the outstretched blanket first, and it is inverted toward the west. On the fifth night it is inverted in the opposite direction. When it is turned up, it is always lifted first at the eastern edge. As it is raised an imaginary something is blown toward the east, in the direction of the smoke-hole of the lodge, and when it is completely turned up hands are waved in the same direction, to drive out the evil influences which the sacred songs have collected and imprisoned under the basket."

Even in the making of this sacred basket many ceremonial requirements must be heeded. In forming the helical coil, the fabricator must always put the butt end of the twig toward the center of the basket and the tip end toward the periphery, in accordance with the ceremonial laws governing the disposition of butts and tips.

This same basket is often called an Apache Medicine Basket. Its use by the Apaches seems somewhat singular, as they themselves are expert basket makers. The explanation of its use by their shamans was given to me by a medicine man as follows: On one occasion a great Navaho shaman was present and assisted his Apache brother in a healing ceremony of great importance. A noted and wealthy personage was very sick, and no expense was spared to restore him to health. The Apache medicine man sent for the Navaho, and among the paraphernalia of the latter was this basket. The ceremonies over, the patient recovered, and when the Apache thanked his Navaho coadjutor and asked for the secret of his power he was

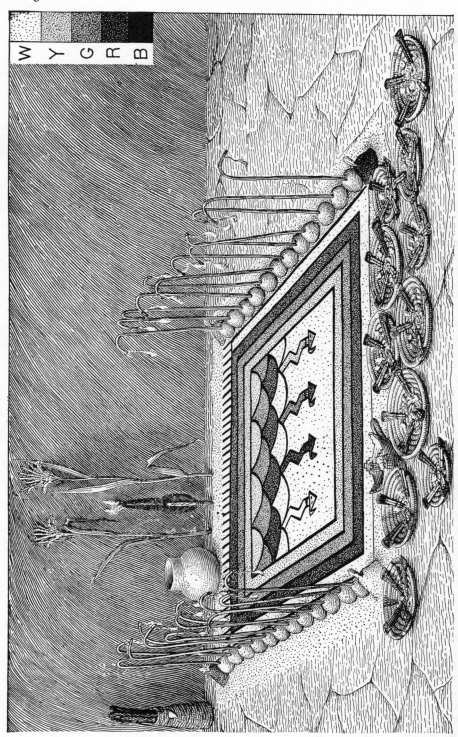

FIG. 31. ANTELOPE ALTAR AT SHIPAULUVI SHOWING LIGHTNING AND CLOUD SYMBOLS, AND COIL PLAQUES HOLDING BAHOS.

told, among other things, that the basket was "heap good medicine." From that day to this there are few Apache medicine men who do not count a Paiuti basket as one of the indispensable articles of their craft; for, as I have elsewhere explained, this celebrated basket is seldom made by any other than a Paiuti.

Among many tribes baskets are used for placing food at the graves of the dead. The Hopi believe that departed spirits linger around their own graves, and with a pathetic simplicity, that is as beautiful as it is useless, their mourning friends place offerings of bread and other foods in baskets and bowls, that the dead loved ones may not hunger while they still hover around their earthly remains. Around

FIG. 32. ANTELOPE ALTAR, SHOWING
KOHONINO BASKET IN WHICH
CHARM LIQUID IS MADE.

FIG. 33. PRAYING AT THE
SHRINE OF THE
SPIDER WOMAN.

the Hopi villages, graves are seen where the burials are in clefts of the rocks, which are then filled up with large stones. Upon these are the baskets and crockery bowls in which food is placed for the departed.

The accompanying engraving is of the Antelope Altar at Shipau-luvi and shows how the coiled plaques are used for holding the bahos or prayer sticks of the Hopis in their secret ceremonials of the Kiva. These ceremonials are connected with the observance of the Snake Dance, which, as I have elsewhere described, is a prayer for rain. Baskets have no unimportant part to play in various portions of this ceremony.

The Snake Charm Liquid is made in a Havasupai basket, shown in Fig. 32. This is placed in the center of a special altar, made for the purpose. In it are dropped some shells, charms, and a few pieces of crushed nuts and sticks. Then one of the priests, with considerable ritual, pours into the basket from north, west, south, east, up and down (the six cardinal points of the Hopi) liquid from a gourd vessel. By this time all the priests are squatted around the basket, chewing something that one of the older priests had given them. This chewed substance is then placed in the liquid of the basket. Water from gourds on the roof is also put in.

Now all is ready for the preparation of the charm. Each priest holds in his hand the snake whip (a stick to which eagle feathers are attached), while the ceremonial pipe-lighter, after lighting the sacred pipe, hands it to the chief priest, addressing him in terms of relationship. Smoking it in silence the chief puffs the smoke into the liquid and hands it to his neighbor, who does the like and passes it on. All thus participate in solemn silence.

FIG. 34.   HOPI BASKET, FROM ORAIBI, WITH
SPIDER WEB PATTERN.

Then the chief priest picks up his rattle and begins a prayer which is as fervent as one could desire. Shaking the rattle, all the priests commence to sing a weird song in rapid time, while one of them

FIG. 35. HOPI SACRED MEAL PLAQUE, MADE OF YUCCA.

holds upright in the middle of the basket a black stick, on the top of which is tied a feather. Moving their snake whips to and fro, they sing four songs, when one of the chiefs picks up all the objects on the altar and places them in the basket.

In a moment the kiva rings with the fierce yells of the Hopi war-cry, while the priest vigorously stirs the mixture in the basket. And the rapid song is sung while the priest stirs and kneads the contents of the basket with his hands. Sacred meal is cast into the mixture, while the song sinks to low tones, and gradually dies away altogether, though the quiet shaking of the rattles and gentle tremor of the snake whips continue for a short time.

A most painful silence follows. The hush is intense, the stillness perfect. It is broken by the prayer of the chief priest, who sprinkles more sacred meal into the mixture. Others do the same. The liquid is again stirred, and then sprinkled to all the cardinal points, and the same is done in the air outside, above the kiva.

Then the stirring priest takes some white earth, and mixing it with the charm liquid, makes white paint, which he rubs upon the breast,

FIG. 36. WOMEN WITH HOPI AND HAVASUPAI BASKETS
SPRINKLING SNAKES WITH SACRED MEAL.

back, cheeks, forearms, and legs of the chief priest. All the other priests are then likewise painted.

Now there is nothing whatever in this liquid that can either charm a snake or preserve an Indian from the deadly nature of its bite. Even the Hopis know that all its virtue is communicated in the ceremonies I have so imperfectly and inadequately described. I make this explanation lest my reader assume there is some subtle poison used in this mixture, which, if given to the snakes, stupefies them and renders them unable to do injury.

At a certain place in the nine days' ceremonies of the Snake-Antelope Kivas, which precede the open air Snake Dance, now so well known, another kind of basket is used as shown in Fig. 34. In this the color splints are so arranged in lines radiating from a common centre, and divided by cross lines, as rudely to imitate the spider's web. Among the Cahuillas of Southern California this is purely imitative, but with the Hopis it has a meaning of profound religious significance. Before rain can descend the clouds must exist.   These, according to Hopi mythology, are woven by the spider woman—Ko-kyan-wuh-ti— and, to propitiate her, offerings are ceremonially made at her shrine prior to the dance by the chief priest of the Antelope Fraternity. (See Fig. 33.)   Devout women of the tribe also seek to propitiate her by prayers, offerings and other things that will please her, and one of these ways is to weave the spider's web into the basket and present to her bahos—prayer sticks—upon this sacred and personal symbol. The so-called sacred meal trays of the Hopi, whether of willow or yucca, often bear this spider web design.

In the open air dance a score or more of married women and maidens may be seen—the former distinguishable by the hair rolls on each side of the face, and the latter by the big whorls over each ear—holding in their hands baskets or plaques of sacred meal.   This meal is reverently sprinkled on dancers and snakes as they pass by, and here and there an old woman may be seen wandering about on the edge of the dance circle ready to sprinkle any specially vicious reptile which might otherwise strike its poisonous fangs into the dancers.

But by far the most important place for the basket in Hopi ceremonial is in the Lalakonti Dance.

This is regularly performed in the five villages of Oraibi, Mashongnavi, Shipaluvi, Shimopavi and Walpi, generally in the month of October.   The open-air public dance, as in the case of the Snake Dance, is the concluding performance of nine days of secret ceremonials performed in the underground "kivas" of the organization or sisterhood.   The whole ceremony is known under the name of La-la-konti.   It is the harvest festival of the Rain Cloud clan, and the basket throwers personify the mythic ancestral mothers of the clan.   According to Hopi mythology much importance attaches to the primal maternal ancestors of each clan.   Their good gifts—such as the rain, the bountiful harvests, the increase of their flocks and herds—are largely attributed either to the beneficent powers of these maternal ancestors directly exercised on their behalf, or owing to the influence they exert over those who have the powers.

According to Dr. J. Walter Fewkes, the chief ethnologic authority on the Hopi, this ceremony was brought to its present home by various Rain Cloud clans that emigrated from the South.   "When their ancestors first came into the Walpi Valley the traditionists of the clan declare the priests who lived on the old site of Walpi knew only a few ceremonies to bring the rain.   Their chiefs, they declare, had much greater powers in this direction, for by their magic they could force the gods which control the rain and growth of corn to do their bidding.   The Rain Cloud clans, when they arrived at the Hopi mesas, practised a form of the rain cult which was much more highly developed than that of the people which they found living in this region. They were invited to exhibit their powers in this direction, for rain was sorely needed and a famine threatened them.   The priests of the Rain Cloud clans accepted the invitation, and, it is said, erected their altars not far from a spring now called Tawapa.   After they had sung their songs for some time mist began to form, then violent rains fell and frightful lightning, which alarmed the women of Walpi.   The legends state that after this show of power the Rain Cloud clans were

THE BASKET THROWERS, OR LAKONE MANAS

PRIEST HANDING OFFERINGS TO BASKET THROWERS

invited to join the Hopi pueblo, assimilated with the original Hopi, and from that time to the present have always lived with them."

Excavations made by Dr. Fewkes at Homolobi and at the Chevelon ruins (Cakwabaiyaki), about fifteen miles east of Winslow, Arizona, near the main line of the Santa Fe Railway, support the idea above advanced, for large quantities of basketry similar to that still made at Oraibi and on the middle mesa were found, demonstrating that the inhabitants of these villages were expert basket makers. As before noted, no Hopi baskets are made on the first mesa, the chief town of which is Walpi, and yet nowhere is this basket dance celebrated with greater elaboration than at that city, where not a single known woman is a basket maker.

Now to a brief description of the dance.* It is a women's ceremony and the participants may be divided into two groups, the basket bearers (or chorus and dancers) and the basket throwers (lakone manas). The only man participant is a priest called lakone taka. The illustrations, made by Mr. G. L. Rose, of Pasadena, Cal., are of the dance at Oraibi in 1898.

There were about forty basket bearers, consisting of women of all ages—married women, maids and young girls. Each wore an elaborate headdress that has a distinct significance. The chief priestesses led the procession, the girls closing the line as it entered the dance plaza. Each woman carried a flat basket, which she held vertically in both hands by the rim, so that the concave side was outermost. After marching into the plaza, a circle was formed by the women, and all sang in chorus a song, parts of which were not audible. As the song continued the baskets were slowly raised, first to one breast, then to the other, and then brought slowly downward to the level of the hips, in cadence with the songs. At the same time the body was slightly inclined forward, but the feet were not raised from the ground.

In the meantime the basket throwers were going through a separate religious ceremony with the priest, as pictured in the accompanying engravings.

Now the throwers, led by the priest, approached the circle, and soon untied the bundles which they bore on their backs, and took positions within the ring of basket throwers diametrically opposite each other. Each held a basket aloft, making a movement as if to hurl it in the air. She did not cast it, however, but crossed to the opposite side of the ring, exchanging position with the woman facing her. Groups of men outside the ring of basket bearers among the spectators shouted to the basket throwers for the baskets. Finally they threw them, one after another, until none were left, and with wild shouts the lads and men struggled for them, as seen in the engraving.

In these good natured scuffles the basket was often torn to pieces and the clothing of the young men almost torn from their backs.

The women leave the plaza after the baskets are thrown, but the struggle for them often continues for a long time.

The Hopi have two other basket dances, one of which, the Owakulti, is a worn down fragment of the Lalakonti, and the other, the Kohonino Basket Dance, is slightly different. The Kohonino, or

---

* For fuller description see Dr. Fewkes's interesting accounts in the American Anthropologist, April 1892, p. 105, and The Journal of American Folk Lore, April-June, 1899, p. 81.

DANCE OF BASKET BEARERS

STRUGGLE FOR BASKETS

Havasupais, of Cataract Canyon, trade largely with the Hopi, and in this dance Havasupai (Kohonino) baskets alone are used. Six maids with elaborate headdresses and five others with simple fillets of yucca on their heads participated in the dance, when it was given as a part of the Mamzrauti ceremony at Walpi, in 1893. The eleven maids, to the beating of the drum, danced before a group of women of the Mamzrau Society, moving the basket in time, but there was no throwing of the baskets as in the Lalakonti.

Allen Seymour, in The Traveler for September, 1900, relates how he purchased a fine basket of a Yolo Indian (Northern California). From the photograph (Fig. 41) it can be seen that the stitches are fine and the decoration exquisite. It is small; only eight inches across. About the upper edge are sixty pieces of shell money and the pendants are of abalone. The upper, middle and lowest bands are of the brightest

FIG. 41. YOLO INDIAN CEREMONIAL BASKET.

red from the small spot on the male blackbird's wing, and the two intermediate stripes are of bright bronze green from the breast of a small local bird. After he had arranged for its purchase Mr. Seymour thus relates the ceremony of transfer to him: "Soon three or four of the old men of the camp came in and ranged themselves silently around the walls. Then the chief followed. In his left hand was a small, wooden whistle, or 'tolkah,' with a long, red cord attached. In his right hand he held what looked like a broomstick eighteen inches long. This was a rattle, or 'sak-ka-tah,' beautifully made of elder, with the pith removed, and the sides split down to the handle. By a slight, rapid movement of the wrist it produces a sound resembling the warning of a rattlesnake.

"Facing me, in the center of the room, he placed the whistle to his mouth and for several minutes blew a succession of soft, varying notes, accompanied by a continuous rattle. Then, dropping the whistle, he spent some ten minutes in chanting or intoning, always keeping up the rattle. All of this time his face and eyes were cast upward.

with a look of rapt devotion, and an occasional break in his voice almost changing to a sob. I am not able to express the gravity of everyone present. Then he said: 'Two times I give you basket; you no take it. Then you take it.' Twice, with a long, mournful chant and an extra rattle, he advanced the basket, only to withdraw it. The third time his chant and rattle were particularly long and supplicating, and the basket was placed in my hands, and the priest became a common Indian who said 'No more,' and the witnesses silently filed out, leaving me to settle the material part of the transfer with the chief who remained."

A young lady, at the ranch where he stopped, informed him that some time previously she had seen this basket used in one of their ceremonies. "Silently approaching the circle, in which stood the chief and medicine man, she found they were, with much low-toned chanting, passing from hand to hand my basket, filled with some white, powdered substance, of which each partook in turn, after a short petition addressed to the sky. As soon as she was seen, the basket was hastily hidden, and no Indian moved or spoke until she had passed."

As one of the chief and most valuable of the earthly possessions of the women, the basket used to figure prominently in the Feasts of the Dead so common among the Indians of Southern California. These feasts are not always conducted in the same manner, and they are far less frequent now than formerly, yet they generally include a period of general wailing for the dead. Images, representing the dead, are made, and these are placed in positions around a large oval shallow pit, in which a fierce fire is kept burning. Baskets and other valuable or useless property of the deceased are placed near her image. In their frenzy of grief the wailers jump to and fro over the pit, emitting the most horrible yells, and then, when all is ready, the images are thrown into the fire, to be shortly followed by the baskets.

In this way many most valuable and priceless specimens of the weaver's art have been destroyed, and it is doubtless owing to an appeal having been made to the cupidity of the mourners, as well as to their intelligence, that the practice is now so nearly discontinued.

Thomas Hill, the veteran artist of the Yosemite Valley, recently made a sketch of a funeral ceremony in which baskets largely figured. The story he told me, as near as I can recall it, is as follows: "A certain medicine man, who lived not far from Wawona, across the South Fork, was shot and killed by several Indians, because he failed to cure their relatives of grippe. One of the murderers was caught and sentenced to death. He was hung at San Quentin, the California State penitentiary. His widow, who was well off, determined to give him a good entrance to the land of the departed, so she engaged two professional dancers and wailers, or mourners, and a master of ceremonies, and then sent out invitations to all her friends and neighbors to take part in the ceremony.

As they were old friends, Mr. Hill and his daughter were allowed to be present. The usual feasting and wailing were indulged in, but the most interesting and picturesque feature of the affair was a death dance, led by the master of ceremonies, and in which the two professionals outdid themselves. There was a large bonfire, and around this the dancers ranged themselves in a circle. Each dancer had a basket, some of them being exceedingly fine ones—heirlooms that had been kept hidden from all vulgar eyes for just such an important event. To the low singing of the medicine man—there being no drum—the dance began. Gradually the song increased in power, and as it did so the dance increased in speed, fury and frenzy. The baskets were used in rhythmic movement with the motions of the dancers. Down to the feet, across the hips, before each breast in turn, then

FIG. 27A.   THE AUTHOR DESCRIBING THE NAVAHO SACRED BASKET.

above the head. All this time the wailing was kept up, and tears rolled down the cheeks of the "best" mourners. At the height of the dance, at a signal from the leader, all the baskets were thrown into the fire, and, as the last flame from them expired, the dance was brought to a conclusion."

FIG. 42. A SABOBA INDIAN BASKET MAKER, SOUTHERN CALIFORNIA.

CHAPTER V.

BASKET MAKING PEOPLE.

As elsewhere stated, the scope of this book is limited to the basketry of the Southwest, the Pacific Coast and Alaska. It is within these boundaries that the art attained its highest perfection (as far as what is now American territory is concerned) and where it is now most practised in its primitive simplicity.

The following accounts of the basket-making peoples necessarily are brief. They purpose merely to give an idea as to their location, so that the collector may have better clues to work upon for the identification of specimens than the guess-work statements of some dealers. In any good library further information may be gained about the people named.

To visit the Navahoes, Hopi, Havasupais, Wallapais and Chemehuevis, or the Mission Indians, west of Mt. San Jacinto, in California, the collector should consult the Santa Fe Railway officials as their line runs through the territory occupied by these people. The Mescalero, White Mountain and other Apaches, the Pimas, Papagoes, Maricopas and Mission Indians east of Mt. San Jacinto, are reached by the Sunset Route of the Southern Pacific Railway. The Mid-California Indians, such as Monos, Yokuts, Tulares, etc., are reached by both lines. The Inyos can be found near the line of the Carson and Colorado River, which connects with the Central Route of the S. P. at Reno, Nevada. The Washoes and Paiutis are found around Reno, Carson and Wadsworth on the Central Route of the S. P. Co. The S. P. officials in San Francisco will gladly give information to those interested how they may best reach the Basket Makers of the Northern Pacific States, and the Pacific Coast Steamship Co., in the same city, will give like information about Alaska.

Perhaps the finest and most delicate weaving of the North American Indians is done by the Aleuts of Attu Island, the most westerly point of Alaska. This tiny island is the remotest and most isolated of the possessions of the United States. The homes, or "barabas," of the Aleuts are built of sod, and in these dreary places, which the long winter makes inconceivably dark and desolate they work at their interesting basketry, singing or crooning to themselves to help the weary days pass along. Some of their weaving is shown in Fig. 45.

In Alaska the chief basket-makers are the Tlinkits and Haidas. The former are located on the coast and islands of Southern Alaska, and are regarded as one of the most interesting of the Alaskan tribes. They excel "in all manner of carving in wood, bone, or stone; they shape pipes, rattles and masks with all fantastical forms, from the hardest material. The women are equally skilfull in plaiting baskets. In former times they also made a practice of weaving the long hair of the mountain goat into cloaks and blankets in the most gorgeous colors and patterns."

The Haida people live on Dall and the Prince of Wales Islands, of Alaska, and the Queen Charlotte Islands, of British Columbia.

The Kauiags, who inhabit Kadiak and its surrounding islands, are also basket-makers, but are not so expert as the Thlinket and Haida women. They excel in embroidery.

The Thompson Indians live in the southern interior of British Columbia, mostly east of the Coast Range, though they penetrate far into the heart of that range. There are three rivers in this territory —the Fraser, the Thompson (which is its principal tributary), and a smaller tributary of the Thompson, the Nicola. In or near the valleys of these rivers the principal villages of the Thompson Indians may be

HAIDA WOMAN OF MASSET WEAVING A BASKET.
From Popular Science Monthly.

found. They hunt in the country on either side. They are of the Salishan stock. Basketry is an important industry among them.

Washington has several tribes who engage in basket-making on a small scale. These are the remnants of tribes which formerly used to occupy the whole territory. Among these, in Western Washington, are the Quinaielts. In the far north, on Cape Flattery, are the Makahs, belonging to the Nutka family. Still on the coast further south are the various branches of the great Salish family, often confused by local names that have no ethnological nor geographical significance. These extend south to the region of the Columbia River, where the Tsinuks, commonly known as the Chinooks, are found. Inland, south of Mt.

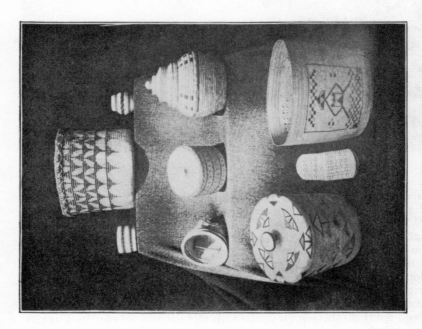

FIGS. 45 AND 46. VARIOUS ALEUTION
AND ALASKAN BASKETS.

St. Helen's, are the Klikatats, belonging to the Sahaptin family* and north are the Kowlitz, another tribe of the Salish family. Several tribes occupy the regions along the Puget Sound, mainly, however, belonging to the Salishes. These are the Miskuwallis, Puyullaps, Squaxin and Muckleshoots. The Snohomish and Skohomish peoples occupy the opposing sides of the upper portion of the Sound, and the Skagits and Lummis are to the extreme north. Inland there are the Yakimas, and, on the borders of British Columbia, the Tenaskots.

California has long been known as the home of particularly expert basket weavers. Possibly the finest baskets ever made, with but two or three exceptions, were the work of Gualalas, Yokuts or Pomas. The fertile well-wooded and well-watered western slopes of the majestic Sierra Nevada were long the home of an aboriginal people which, in early days, was so large as to command the astonishment of travelers familiar only with the populations of the cold forests of the Atlantic States or the vast sterile wastes of the interior of the Continent. Stephen Powers estimates that at the beginning of the century there must have been not less than 700,000 Indians in California alone. But, alas! civilization has swept most of them away. Regardless of what the 'carpet knights who wield compiling-pens' in comfortable Eastern or European libraries say, we, who have studied the Indian in his own home, have heard his traditions of the origin of his races and the stories of their decline; have seen the rapid diminution of population in recent years, know full well that it is sadly too true in most cases that "Civilization bestows all its vices and few, if any, of its virtues upon the American Indian."

The California Indian was very different from his warlike brother of the Atlantic Coast and Great Inland Basin. He was the type of quiet, contented, peaceful simplicity. Not that he never went to war, but he preferred to take life easy, enjoy his simple pleasures, engage in his religious dances, destroy his enemies by treacherous assassination rather than by open warfare, and run away with a good looking girl when he was too poor to purchase her. Of the vast and teeming populations of this ideal land but scattered remnants remain.

On the Klamath River are the Yuroks, Karoks and Modoks. The two former are generally called Klamaths. The Karoks (often spelled Cahrocs) are a fine, vigorous people, inhabiting the lower portion of Salmon River, and down the Klamath to a certain canyon a few miles above Waitspeh, where they merge into the Yuroks, who extend along the Klamath River from the mouth of Trinity River to the Pacific. The Indians and white settlers have intermarried so that there is little pure blood among them. About Crescent City a few of the Tolowas still live, a bold, warlike people, hated by the Klamath River Indians, with whom they used to be constantly at war.

On the lower Trinity River are the Hupas, the main reservation being in Hoopa Valley. Powers says of them: "Next after the Karok they are the finest race in all that region. They are the Romans of Northern California in their valor and their wide-reaching dominions;

---

*The Rev. W. C. Curtis, commenting upon the above statement, says: "I have been of the opinion that their habitat was north of the Columbia and east of the Cascade Mountains, centering in Klickitat and Yakima Counties, and that if there are any 'south of Mt. St. Helen's' they are out of place."

FIG. 47. A WASHINGTON WEAVER.

FIG. 48. A MONO WEAVER.

they are the French in the extended diffusion of their language." At one time their power was potent over many of the neighboring tribes except the Klamaths. Now they are a poor, peaceable and submissive race, whose women are expert basket makers and whose men earn their living whenever and wherever possible by farming, cattle raising, logging and giving general assistance to the whites.

Around Humboldt Bay and Arcata are a few of the Patawats, a black-skinned, pudgy, low-foreheaded race.

On Eel River are a few basket-makers. These are the Viards, or Wiyots, and are closely allied to the Patawats. On the Mattole Creek and Bear River and a part of the Eel River are the Mattoals, and these are the better basket-makers. On the South Fork of the Eel River are a few Flonhos, as the Lolonkuhs are improperly named.

FIG. 49. A WASHINGTON WEAVER

Under the control of the Round Valley United States Indian Agency are all that remain of the Wailakki, Yuki, and Tatu peoples, where among the women a few basket-makers are to be found.

Sixty years or so ago in Mendocino County, at the very source of the Russian River, in Potter Valley, lived a small tribe of Indians known as the Pomos. According to Dr. Hudson they should be called Pomas. "The Kulanapan term for certain of its tribes is Poma, not Pomo. Po, is red or rusty color, ma, earth," and the people say they sprung from a certain red knoll in Potter Valley; hence they are "the people of the red earth."

About thirty years ago they moved to the Ukiah Valley into the midst of civilization, where, however, they have retained their distinctive Indian character and individuality. Their basketry is most exquisite, delicate, rich and beautiful.

There are a few Indians still left of the Yokaia tribe, from which we get the corrupted Ukiah. Yo means "down below," and Kaia is a variation of the Poma Kai, valley." Hence these are the people who live in the valley below the Pomas.

FIG. 50.   ORNAMENTAL POMA SHI-BU BASKETS.
PLIMPTON COLLECTION.

FIG. 51.   FINE POMA BASKET OF GREAT AGE.
PLIMPTON COLLECTION.

The Gallinuomers are a branch of the Poma family, and a few of them may be found in the hills near Cloverdale and Healdsburg, and, closely related to them, but living on a small creek which empties into the ocean in the northwest corner of Sonoma County, are the Gualalas. The latter were among the best of the older basket-makers, and happy is that collector who can show a Gualala basket among his treasures.

The Ashochimi, commonly known as the Wappos, were once a powerful people inhabiting the region of the Geysers and Salistoga. Their name, Wappo, the unconquerable, was given to them by the Spaniards after a severe conflict in which the latter were defeated, though led by the redoubtable General M. G. Vallejo. But few are now to be found.

About Clear Lake are a few of the Kabiapeks and Makhelchels, and on the Sacramento a large family named the Patwin, from one branch of which we get the names Napa, Suisin, and (from one of the chiefs) Solano. On the upper Sacramento and upper Trinity still remain the Wintuns, many of which are known as Pitt River Indians. A pitiful few remain of the once fierce Shastika, who hover around the southern foothills of California's majestic giant, to whicn they have given a name.

Best known because of their sullen and desperate war in the seventies are the Modoks, who live east of Shasta and as far north as the Goose Lake Valley. Their baby and fancy baskets have always been greatly admired.

South of this region, even to the Tehachipi Mountains, are the remains of peoples who are rapidly passing away. They are mainly to be found in the foothills or slopes of the Sierra Nevada, and rejoice in the generic name "Diggers," as applied to them by the miners. cattle-men and ranchers, with whom they come in contact. Most of them dress in civilized costume, though few inhabit any other than the rude "wickiups" of their forefathers. Among them the basket-making habit is speedily dying out as the older women pass away. The proper names of these people are the Maidu, whose home was from the Sacramento to Honey Lake and from Big Chico Creek to Bear River; a little to the south are the Nishinam. But by far the largest nation of California was the Miwok, which occupied the territory from the snow line of the Sierra to the San Joaquin River, and from the Cosumnes to the Fresno, including all the fertile and well-watered valleys of the Mokelumne, the Stanislaus, the Tuolumne, the Merced and the Chowchilla. It is from the fact that they are a "river" people that they get their name.

Here and there small bands of Paiuti, who crossed the Sierras on predatory excursions and finally located, are to be found. They are expert basket-makers. Their chief location is midway between the original home of the Yokut nation, which used to extend from Fresno River to the Tehachipi. Many of the Indians now found in the region of the Tule River reservation, on Kern River, White River and Poso Creek and the Sierras near Walker Pass are Paiutis.

A few Yokuts are still to be found on the San Joaquin and Kings Rivers, the Kaweah and a portion of Tule River, and those at or near old Fort Tejon are the southern branch of this divided people. As basket-makers they excel, and most of the so-called Tulare baskets are either Yokut or Paiuti, generally the former, and none but those

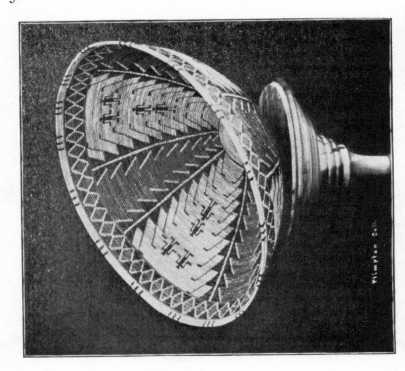

FIG. 52. YOKUT BASKET OF BEAUTIFUL WEAVE AND DESIGN. PLIMPTON COLLECTION.

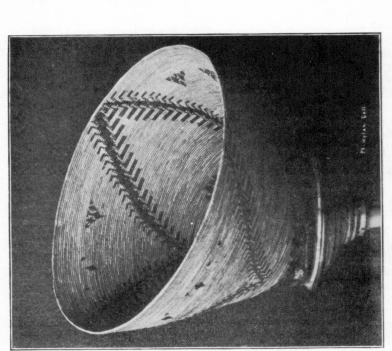

FIG. 53. POMA BASKET IN PLIMPTON COLLECTION.

who purchase on the ground can definitely state which they are. In the private collection of Mr. W. D. Campbell, of Los Angeles, are some fine specimens of Yokut work.

The Yokuts once occupied all the western slope of the Sierra Nevada and the great plains from the Fresno River to Fort Tejon, but owing to conditions it is somewhat interesting to review they were divided into two sections and their identity almost completely lost. The great Sierra Nevada range afforded a complete barrier between the pastoral California and the fierce and nomadic Athapascan tribes that roamed the trackless deserts of Arizona and Nevada. But as the struggle for existence became greater various tribes, as the Paiutis and Apaches, began to seek for and find the mountain passes, and soon succeeded in making incursions into California territory. The result was the wedging apart of the Yokut nation by Nevada Paiutis, who seized Kern River, White River, Poso Creek and Kern Lake. This fact (in addition to one stated on a later page) affords the explanation for the existence of so many Nevada Paiutis in this Southern California region.

Of the Yokuts there were originally many divisions, each having its own name. Of those named by Powers few now remain. The Chuc-chances and Wi-chum-na are still in existence and are basketmakers. I found, in a recent visit to the Tule River reservation, three sub-tribal names not mentioned by Powers, one of which, the Nu-cha-a-wai-i, is the branch of the Yokuts to which the major portion of the reservation Indians claim they belong. The others were the Yo-al-man-i and the Yo-er-kal-i. These are the Fort Tejon branches of the Yokuts. To the basket collector these people are most interesting, and it is a source of regret that more has not been done to gather reliable information in regard to their tribal life. It will be a matter of surprise to many to learn that the Yokuts used to have a rattle-snake dance, similar in hideousness (though far less ceremonially complex) to that of the Hopi Indians of Arizona, and this, in a measure, explains the universal prevalence of the rattlesnake design in their basketry.

Few dealers, when disposing of a Kern, Tule, Kaweah or Kings River Indian basket, or one of the celebrated so-called "Tulare" baskets, are aware of the fact that, most probably, they are selling the work of Yokuts or Paiutis. A Yokut basket is supposed to be entirely different from a Tulare, and yet, unless the Tulare happens to be a Paiuti (pardon the Irishism) there is no difference between the two, the Yokut being the tribal or national name, of which the Tulares are but a small section.

Below the Tehachipi, throughout Southern California and in the Coast Valleys between Santa Barbara and Monterey, are all that remain of the once numerous Mission Indians. These, as the name implies, were the tribes who were under the dominion of the Franciscan friars who controlled the Missions of California. The original names and locations of these people are now but a tradition, and they are generally known by some comparatively recently-given local name.

The most populous of these is the San Luis Rey tribe, known as Luisenos. These are found on the Mesa Grande, Potrero, Temecula, Rincon, Los Coyotes, Pauma, and Pala reservations, and at villages at Warner's Ranch, San Luis Rey and San Felipe.

FIG. 54. CAHUILLA BASKET MAKER.
Both photos copyright by George Wharton James.

FIG. 55. MERCED NOLASQUEZ OF AGUA CALIENTE,
MAKING BASKET WITH SPIDER-WEB DESIGN.

The Dieguinos occupy the Capitan Grande, Sycuan, Santa Ysabel, Campo, Cuyapipe, and Morongo reservations, and the Cahuillas, the Agua Caliente, Santa Rosa, Cabazon, Torres, Twenty-nine palms and Cahuilla reservations. At Saboba (near San Jacinto) is a small village where both Luisenos and Cahuillas are to be found, sadly mixed up and intermarried with degenerate Mexicans.

Among all the Mission Indians basket-making is carried on to a greater or lesser extent. The Cahuillas have some of the best basket-makers.

In Nevada there are two tribes who are noteworthy as basket-makers. These are the Paiutis and Washoes. The former is much the larger tribe. Its members are scattered over the greater part of Nevada, and isolated families or kindred tribes are to be found as far south as the northern "rim" of the Grand Canyon, and eastwards as far as the middle of Southern Utah. The town of Winnemucca, on the line of the Central Pacific Railway, is named after the last great chief of the Paiutis. During the early days of American occupancy of Nevada this people gave our government a great deal of trouble on account of their warlike spirit. A constant and annoying war was kept up, until a number of the leaders, with their families, were made prisoners and removed under military surveillance, to old Fort Tejon, in Southern California. Here they remained for awhile, then more than half of them were allowed to escape. They fled to the foot-hills of the Sierras, east of where Bakersfield and Porterville now are, and, being kindly received by the tribes of the Kern, Tule and Kahweah Rivers settled there, where they and their descendants are still to be found. Later they were joined by the remnant of the prisoners, who were released. As a result, the basketry of this Sierra foot-hill region varies. The pure Yokut and Paiuti types are to be found, and there is also a mixed product which shows the influence of both styles of weave.

The Washoes are a small remnant of a once powerful tribe that inhabited the eastern slopes of the Sierra Nevada in the region of Reno and Carson City. Washoe City and County, Nevada, take their names from this tribe.

In Arizona and New Mexico the chief basket makers are the Zunis, the Hopituh (commonly known as the Moki), the Mescalero, San Carlos and White Mountain Apaches, the Havasupais, the Pimas and the Maricopas.

Zuni is well known as the home for several years of Lieut. Frank H. Cushing, whose recent death was such a great blow to the science of practical ethnology. It is composed of seven small "cities," the chief one of which is on the banks of the Zuni River, where wonderful and marvelous ceremonials are performed each month. It was to Zuni that Coronado marched from Mexico, 350 years ago, and it was there that Spanish despotism first set down its foot in the heart of what afterwards became United States territory. The weavers here are few and far from expert.

The Hopi occupy seven villages on three Mesas about ten miles apart in Northern Arizona. Strange to say, no basket-makers are found in three of the villages, and of the other four three make one kind of basket and the fourth another kind. In the long, long ago the Hopituh migrated from southern and central Arizona to their present

FIG. 56.   DA-SO-LA-LE, WASHOE BASKET MAKER.

homes. They left, in the Red Rock country, several villages which have recently been excavated. In these, large numbers of basket fragments were discovered. Dr. J. Walter Fewkes, the chief authority on the Hopi, says that in his excavations at the Chevelon ruin, about fifteen miles east of Winslow, Arizona, he found much basketry in the graves that had the forms of the plaques still manufactured at Oraibi and on the middle Mesa.

The Mescalero Apaches occupy a reservation in the middle portion of Southern New Mexico. It is an elevated mountainous region of nearly 500,000 acres, with many and various trees, and yet water is so uncertain that little over 500 acres are available for practical farming purposes. Altogether there are about 500 Indians, men, women, and children. The nearest railway station is Las Cruces, on the main line of the Santa Fe, 110 miles away, hence they see very few whites, though the town of Tularosa with several hundred Mexicans, is only 18 miles away. The women of this tribe make a rude basket which will be described later.

The San Carlos and White Mountain Apaches live in Southeastern Arizona. There are in the neighborhood of 4000 to 5000 of them, but the number of basket-makers is comparatively small. These are the people whose very name strikes terror to many hearts, and yet, when reasonably treated, no more intelligent and appreciative Indians are to be found in the country. The basketry of these weavers is remarkably interesting, both for form and design, as all who have seen the beautiful collection in the American Museum of Natural History in New York City will acknowledge.

The Havasupais are a small tribe of not more than 200 men, women, and children, inhabiting one of the side canyons tributary on the South to the Grand Canyon of the Colorado River in Northern Arizona. Their name is poetic and is gained from the chief characteristic of their rocky canyon home. Just above where their village begins a thousand springs of varying sizes burst forth from under the rocks and form a singularly beautiful stream, which they term the "Ha-ha-va-su," "water blue." They are the pai, people, of this blue water. They were named by the Spaniards the Kohonino, and their basketry is occasionally found among other tribes bearing this name. They trade largely with the Hopis and Navahoes and exchange baskets for blankets, ponies, etc. Though their basketry is not of fine weave, the designs are often striking, and a good specimen is eagerly sought after and highly prized.

The Pimas and Maricopas inhabit their reservation in Southern Arizona, not far from Phoenix. These Indians have always been noted for their quiet, peaceful and pastoral character, and they are great basket makers. They live a semi-nomadic life. Their basketry contains some wonderful specimens of Greek and Oriental figures, and in the variations of the Swastika alone they have given the student enough splendid examples to illustrate several volumes.

For a long time it was doubted whether the Navahoes made baskets. This nomadic and interesting tribe occupies a large reservation in the Northeastern part of Arizona, lapping over a little into both New Mexico and Utah. But, as I have shown in the chapter devoted to legendary lore connected with basketry, there is little doubt that they are properly a basket-making people, though the art

FIG. 57. BASKETS IN THE BURNELL COLLECTION.

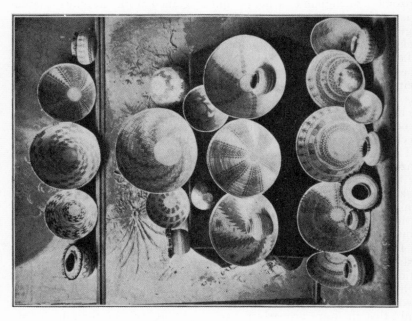

FIG. 58. YOKUT BASKETS IN THE McLEOD COLLECTION

FIG. 59. ORAIBI BASKET MAKER.

FIG. 60. HOPI YUCCA BASKET.

FIG. 61. HOPI SACRED PLAQUE

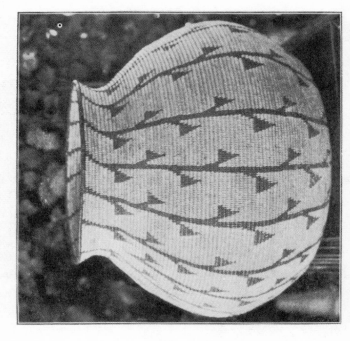

FIG. 63. CHEMEHUEVI BASKET WITH TREE AND
LEAF DESIGN.

Both photographs copyright by George Wharton James.

FIG. 62. WALLAPAI BASKET MAKER

has largely declined amongst them. The reasons for this decline are obvious. Their women find pleasanter, more congenial and more profitable employment in the art of blanket weaving, in which they excel, their work comparing favorably with the highest art productions of the world. They have large flocks of sheep, and it is more to their interest to wash, dye, card, spin and weave the wool, which the sheep bring to their very doors, than spend long and weary days in

FIG. 69. A FINISHED MENOMINI

FIG. 65.   FIG. 66.   BASKET.

making the long and weary journeys to gather the various materials needed for basket-making.

Still, there are a few Navaho basket weavers, and genuine specimens purchased from the weavers themselves or satisfactorily authenticated are valuable acquisitions to a collection.

It has also been stated that the Chemehuevis and Wallapais do not make baskets. This is an error. Both tribes make a few baskets, the former being excellent weavers as will be seen from the specimen here shown (Fig. 63).

The Chemehuevis live on a reservation on the California side of the Colorado River not far from the town of Needles, and the Wallapais occupy their reservation adjoining that of the Havasupai on the west.

The Wallapais had almost lost the art when, fortunately for them, Miss Frances S. Calfee was sent among them as a field matron. For over seven years she has worked with them, and from their very name being a reproach and a synonym of debauchery and degradation

FIG. 64. MENOMINI INDIANS WEAVING A MAT.

they have reached a degree of self-respect that is highly commendable. In her endeavors for their betterment Miss Calfee has reintroduced the art of basket-making, and, recently I secured five specimens of their work that show considerable ability and make it certain that, if the art is cultivated, the Wallapais may soon rank as a great basket-making people.

Located in the Northeastern interior of the State of Wisconsin, on a 360 square mile reservation, are the Menomini Indians. They are mat

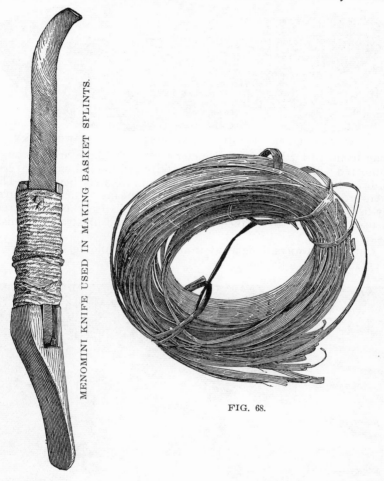

MENOMINI KNIFE USED IN MAKING BASKET SPLINTS.

FIG. 68.

FIG. 67.

weavers and basket makers, and a brief reference to their work and methods is here introduced for comparison with the work of the Indians of the West and Southwest.

Their bark mats are woven as is shown in the accompanying full page engraving from Mary Irvin Wright's painting. They are made from the inner bark of the cedar, cut in strips averaging half an inch in width. Some of the mats are nearly white, others are colored dark red and sometimes black with native vegetal dyes. The decoration is effectively produced in diamond and lozenge patterns, as well as in zigzag lines, both by color and by the weaving of the weft strips, the latter being accomplished by taking up and dropping certain members of the warp strips.

Baskets are made on the same principle of plaiting as is employed for bark mats. The strips are made from black elm, the necessary limbs

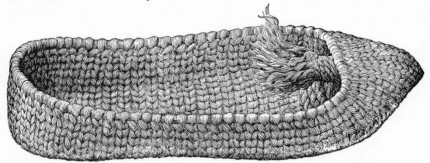

WOVEN SLIPPER FOUND IN SALTPETER CAVE IN KENTUCKY.

being from 3 to 4 inches in diameter (Fig. 65); these are thoroughly hammered with a wooden mallet (Fig. 66) until the individual layers of the branch are detached from the layers immediately beneath. These layers are then cut into thin narrow strips by means of the knife universally used (Fig. 67). The strips are kept in coils (Fig. 68) until ready for use, when they are soaked in water. Fig. 69 illustrates a finished basket.

Cutting is always done away from the hand holding the material to be cut, and toward the body.

FIG. 69a.—YOKUT GIRL WEAVERS.

The club or mallet employed in hammering the elm wood is about 20 inches long and has one end thinner than the other, so as to form a handle.

Cahuilla Indians Collecting Basket Material among the Palms of Palm Cañon.

CHAPTER VI.

MATERIALS USED IN INDIAN BASKETRY.

It would be a most interesting study, had one the time to devote to it, to see how change of environment has affected the basketry of any one tribe or race of people. Take the great Athapascan stock of central Alaska as an illustration. In this—possibly their original habitat—they wove with such materials as came to hand, birchbark, spruce roots, quills and the like. One migration brought some of the stock down into Oregon and Northern California. There they made their ware of hazel twigs, redbud, sweet grass, pine root, fern stalk, etc. Other migrations formed the Apache, the Wallapai and the Havasupai peoples, the first roaming the fierce deserts of Southern Arizona, and Northern Mexico; the second occupying the wastes of the Painted Desert, the depths of Peach Springs and Diamond Creek Canyons, and the pine clad summits and slopes of the Wallapai Mountains; while the third hides in the seclusion of the Canyon of the Havasu (Cataract Canyon), where willows and martynia abound.

Far away to the Northeast another migration brought the great Navaho family, and until recently it was not known whether they made baskets or not, but as I have elsewhere shown we now know that they are basket-makers.

Yet all these people are of one family and blood. Tinne in Alaska, Hupa in Northern California, Apache, Wallapai and Havasupai in Arizona, Navaho in New Mexico, each has a basketry, distinct and individual, and yet all follow somewhat the same family instincts and traits. A close student might possibly be able to determine from their basket work their family relationship, and it could not fail to be both instructive and interesting to trace the changes and modifications in their art compelled by the different environments*.

Dr. Franz Boas, in his concluding chapter of Teit's monograph on the Thompson Indians, makes some interesting observations upon this subject.

Hence it may be stated in general terms that the materials used for the basketry of any particular people is largely determined by that people's environment.

While, primarily, all basketry may be divided into two types, the woven and the sewed, there are a large number of species of each type. These subclasses or species were largely determined by the material the aboriginal weaver found at her hands when the time for weaving came, and the same law of environment shaping results is still seen in nearly all aboriginal work. One of the results of our modern and civilized methods of transportation is to largely do away with the limitations of our own surroundings, by placing in our hands whatever we need, no matter from how great a distance. But the Amerind has

---

* Since the above was in type Major J. W. Powell has convinced me that the Havasupais and Wallapais belong to the Yuman and not to the Athapascan stock.

not learned to utilize this modern force to any great extent, and where she has it has proven disastrous, as, for instance, where she purchases imported aniline dyes instead of using her own more reliable and beautiful native dyes.

In the chief material, however, the willows, grasses, etc., of which she makes the warp and woof of her basketry she is still subject to this law of environment. Hence, to the intelligent student of basketry, the ware itself becomes a book from which he may read many curious things—and read aright, too,—such as the geographic and physical conditions of the country in which the weaver lived and worked, the nature of the soil, the color of the rocks, the vegetable growths, etc.

This is the key to the diversity of material found in Indian basketry. It explains why the Hopi use yucca and fine grass; the Paiutis a coarse

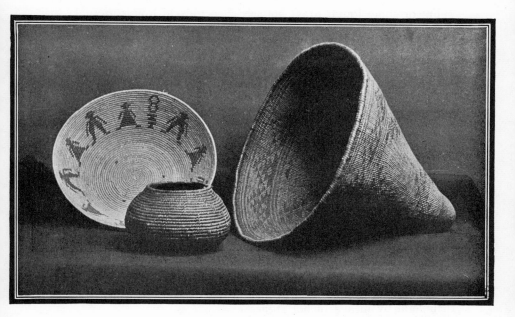

FIG. 72. CAHUILLA COILED BASKETS. McCLOUD RIVER CARRYING BASKET.

fibre; the Havasupais, willows; the Southern California Indians, tule root and squaw weed; the Monos other tender shoots, roots and fibres; the Pomas something different; and the tribes further north the bark of the cedar and the root of the spruce.

On this subject Dr. Mason well writes:—

"There is no work of woman's fingers that furnishes a better opportunity for the study of techno-geography, or the relationship existing between an industry and the region where it may have been developed, than the textile art. Suppose a certain kind of raw material to abound in any area or country; you may be sure that savage women search it out and develope it in their crude way. Furthermore, the peculiar qualities and idiosyncrasies of each substance suggest and demand a certain treatment. Women of the lowest grade of culture have not been slow in discovering this; so that between them and the natural product there has been a kind of understanding or co-operation leading to local styles."

"The most simple as well as the most beautiful types come from Siam and the other lands of the bamboo. The basket-maker provides herself with a number of small rods and a quantity of split bamboo of uniform thickness. The rods are coiled like a watch spring, and united firmly by wrapping a splint of bamboo around two rods continuously from the center of the bottom of the basket on to the last stitch on the border. As the work goes on the splint passes between two stitches of the preceding round and over the fundamental rod.

Ware quite as beautiful as that of the far east may be seen in the spruce country of North America, where the fine roots furnish a tough fiber when split.

Now, suppose that the woman in sewing her coil introduced a thin splint or some tough grass between her rods in going around; that would furnish a kind of packing or caulking, which would render the

FIG. 73. FINE CALIFORNIA BASKETS.

work water-tight. And that is the case with the Indians of British Columbia and Washington in making the baskets in which they boil their food by means of hot stones.

Going farther south, the fundamental rod becomes a bunch of coarse grass or the split stems of palm or other tropical plant. The sewing in such cases is done with stripped yucca or finely split and dressed splints of osier or rhus, of stems of grass, so nicely and homogeneously dressed as to enable the maker to produce a basket with hundreds of thousands of stitches over the surface which do not show the slightest variation in size.

Great variety is secured in this ware by the material, by the use of colored stitches, and by the introduction of birds' feathers, beads, and other decorative objects into the texture.

In the arctic regions spruce root is the material with which the coil is sewed. In California it is split osier and rhus. In the Hopi Pueblos it is extremely finely divided yucca fibre, while the stems serve for the body of the coil. The tropical regions of both hemispheres abound with palms of many varieties whose leaves when split supply the very best material for the coiled ware.

In Tierra del Fuego, as well as in Japan, the basket-maker produces an attractive variety in the coiled stitch by passing once around the standing part of the sewing splint, then between the coil rods, down, through, back, and over, to repeat the process for each stitch. Of all the varieties there are many subtypes too intricate to mention here. We have all the generic forms."

According to Jackson the Pacific Coast baskets were originally made for carrying and storing water, as well as for the uses already indicated; and hence the lightest, cleanest and most durable materials were selected. These are found in various species of willow, the "chippa" of the Southern Indians, while the fibers of the red bud (Cercis occidentalis) served the same purpose in the North, and are equal to those of the palm and bamboo in flexibility and strength. Among grasses used in the woof, the smooth, wiry culms of vilfa and sporobolus were preferred.

FIG. 74. A PORTION OF THE PLIMPTON COLLECTION, SAN DIEGO, CAL.

"In a country where the grasses are tough and pliable, like the sea-island grasses of the Aleutian archipelago, baskets have mostly been constructed from such fibre and are soft and pliable, partaking of the nature of bags. Where the lithe willow, or osier, abounds, both its branch and bark have been used, the larger stems forming the frame and the lighter twigs the filling; these baskets generally stand upright and take the shape of pots, jars and vases, acording to their purpose. The fibre of the yucca—the soap plant or Spanish bayonet—and many of the cacti have been used in this manufacture. The keen-sighted Indian women readily find in the mountain valleys and along the water courses the proper material to make into the plastic wands which they so deftly weave into these graceful vessels. They are very skillful at splitting the stems of the willow, the osier, the sauvis, the swamp ash, the vine-maple and other long-fibred quick growing plants, and preserving this material for use when needed. The proper season for gathering the material is when the stalk has just completed its growth and before the sap hardens into woody substance."

One can almost see and hear the squaw as she makes her way for miles through the sweet woods, before the sap has gone and the pliable fibre has hardened into wood, to the places where she finds the proper material for the plastic bands and grasses which she intends to weave into her baskets.   One can follow this woman of bronze as she trudges homeward, bending under her heavy load of pungent twigs and bark and grasses and leaves and roots.

"The long withes split from the rods are rolled up and protected from too much heat or moisture; just before using they are thoroughly soaked in water and woven while wet and soft.   This plastic woof is so firmly beaten down that a new basket, of the finer makes, will hold water for some time; to make them permanent water jars, either for

FIG. 75.   APACHE AND PIMA COILED BASKETS, SIFTER AND CARRYING BASKET
FROM OREGON.

household use or for transporting water on their journeys, the interstices are filled with pitch of fir trees."

In an article on "The Basket of the Klickitat," by Mrs. Velina P. Molson, she thus describes the material used in the manufacture of the baskets of this primitive and interesting people.

"To gather, prepare and manipulate the raw material meant time and arduous labor.   The foundation consists of the roots of young spruce and cedar trees; it was macerated and torn into threadlike shreds, and soaked for weeks and months in water to rid it of any superfluous vegetable matter and to render it strong and pliable.   The ornamentation is almost all made of Xerophyllum Tenax, which is commonly called "squaw's grass."   It grows on the east side of the Cascade Mountains, and can only be gathered during the late summer, when the snow has melted and the grass has matured.   This grass resembles the plant of garden cultivation, Yucca Filamentosa.

"The broad, swordlike leaves are split into the requisite width, and if they are to remain the natural color, an ivory white, they are soaked in water only; but if they are to be dyed they are soaked in mud and charcoal for black, for brown a dye made from the willow bark, and for yellow a longer time in the water.

"Sometimes the bast or inner bark of the cedar tree is dyed black instead of the grass, but it is not so durable owing to its short fibrous texture; or the willow bark itself is used instead of dyeing the grass brown; but the willow looks slightly shriveled, and neither presents the smooth surface as when made of squaw's grass, although only apparent to the practiced eye."

H. K. McArthur in a paper on the Basketry of the Northwest says: "The labor of gathering materials and preparing them, before the work of construction begins, occupies many months, and is most

FIG. 78.—KLAMATH TRAY; SKOKOMISH BASKET; IDAHO POUCH OF CEDAR-ROOT AND GRASS; ALASKAN SIDDED BASKETS AND BAG.*

arduous. The weary and toilsome climb to distant mountain tops, for rare and beautiful grasses that only adorn the face of nature in these lofty solitudes; the digging of certain tenacious roots and cutting of twigs, bark and fibre, all of which must be cured, made into proper lengths and macerated to a desired flexibility before being woven into the intricate and enduring beauty of baskets; coaxing from coy Nature her secrets of dyes, whether from peculiarly colored earth, charcoal, extracts of barks or immersion in water.

"Who of those who live in the Williamette valley has not seen some ancient dame trudging home, with dew-bedraggled skirts, with a bundle of hazel sticks on her bent shoulders, after an early expedition to the copse, or, it may be, grasses and roots from a neighboring swamp?

*The Idaho Pouch is undoubtedly of Skokomish make, the row of dogs around the top being one of their well-known designs.

FIGS. 76 AND 77. FINE POMA BASKETS IN THE PLIMPTON COLLECTION.

She is ancient, because in our day, the beautiful art is not taught to the young women; they do not desire to know it, and so the work is relegated to only the aged, who are skillful and learned.

"Summer is the season for this preliminary work. The kindly sun favors these children of Nature, the twigs and grasses are flexible, the barks are easily peeled and are rich in juices, and the store of materials is gathered in.

The baskets of the Cayuses, Umatillas Nez Perces and Wascos, and others living east of the Cascades, are not stiffly woven, but are made of split corn husks and the wild hemp of the Walla Walla valley.

The Shastas largely use sticks of hazel. The sticks are gathered in great quantities, the best ones from ground denuded by fire of its natural growth of fir and hemlock, where they spring up straight and strong from the rich soil. The teeth play no small part in peeling off the bark.

The fine white grass, used by the Shastas in the manufacture of their baskets is gained from great elevations in the mountains. It is almost like ivory in smoothness and tint. I have found the Indians up as high as the snow line of Mt. Shasta in summer time, gathering this exquisite grass.

The Mendocino county and Hoopa valley Indians make cradles for the infants from the peeled stems of tough young trees and shrubs."

The Tlinkits of Southern Alaska use spruce roots, split and soaked in water.

The Chilcotin, Lillooet, Lower Thompson Indians, and others that inhabit the Cascade Mountains in the State of Washington, make beautiful coiled basketry of cedar twigs. They use the small trailing roots of the cedar (Thuja Gigantea, Nutt). With a tool common with them, called a root digger, they dig up those portions of the root that are about the thickness of a finger, and of the required length, and bury them in the ground to keep them fresh. Before using they are peeled or scraped with a sharp stone or knife and hung up to dry. Then they are split with the bone awl. Those splints that are of equal width and thickness are used for stitching purposes, the others as material for forming the coil. In making the coil the stitch of the upper coil is made to pass through, and thus split, the splint of the lower coil. Work of this kind is practically water-tight. A less durable kind is made by substituting strips of cedar-sap for the cedar root strips of the inner coil.

The chief ornamentation of this basketry is made by hooking in strips of grass and bark with the stitches, so that they cover the latter on the outside only. Teit thus describes the process: "This is done by bringing the piece of grass over the inside of the last stitch, then doubling it back and catching the doubled end with the next stitch. The outsides of some baskets are completely covered in this manner. The grass used is that called nho' itlexin. It is long, very smooth, and of a glossy yellow-white color. To make it whiter, diatomaceous earth is spread over it and it is then beaten with a flat stick on a mat or skin. The grass is seldom dyed, as the colors are said to fade soon. The Upper Fraser and the Lytton band sometimes use Elymus triticoides, Nutt, instead of this grass. The bark used is that of Prunus demissa, Walpers, which is either left in its natural light reddish-brown color, or is dyed by burying it in damp earth. By thus keeping it

underground for a short time, it assumes a dark brown color, while
when kept longer it becomes quite black."

The Upper Fraser band of Thompson Indians occasionally make
baskets nowadays from corn leaves and stalks.

"The Indian women of the temperate belt were intimately
acquainted everywhere with the willow, rhus, cedar bark, Indian hemp,
bullrushes, cat-tail, vernal and other grasses, and many other kinds
of filament; with their colors, and the best way of dyeing them; and,
what is most noteworthy in this connection, these cunning savage
women knew so well what to do with each kind, and what each kind
could and could not do, that every effort to improve their methods
has failed."—Mason.

Dr. J. W. Hudson says of the Pomas:

"Collecting and preparing the materials that compose a basket is
almost as interesting as the weaving. The most necessary material

FIG. 79. YOKUT AND POMA BASKETS FROM THE PRIVATE COLLECTION
OF W. D. CAMPBELL, LOS ANGELES, CAL.

used is "kah hoom" (water gift), and "kah lall (water son) or willow
shoots. Both are in baskets of nearly all sizes or uses. Kah lall gives
strength and shape, while the kah hoom knits together the ribs and
preserves smoothness in outline. These two plants as their names
imply, grow beside or in the shallow edges of nearly all water courses
in Mendocino.

The kah hoom is taken from the roots of a California variety of the
well known slough grass, "carex Mendocinoensis," so abominable to
orchardists, and so defiant of his plough and hoe in efforts towards its
eradication. The finest kah hoom, because the toughest and most
capable of being evenly split, grows in low, sandy bottom land, and
necessarily near a running stream.

The Russian River near the small town of Hopland, annually overflows several hundred adjacent acres, and before the thrifty rancher
found the true value of this rich alluvium in hop culture the digger from
rancherias far and near would come and gather these preferred roots

During the summer months and even far into the fall, as long as the rising waters would permit, temporary shahs of woven willow and alder shoots were always occupied by transient bands of Indians. Men and women here worked alike; for this occasion the dignity and indolence of the hombre were laid aside. Whether he really liked the work, or whether envy of his neighbor's success induces him to assist his wife, it is difficult to say. Armed with a clam shell in one hand and a short stick in the other, he takes a bunch of this grass as a starting point, and lays bare its radiating roots. Selecting the best of these, he grasps the root between the first and second toe, and gently lifts it a little, to indicate its hidden course under the sand to the next bunch. This fact ascertained the clam shell scoops out, while the stick carefully loosens all stones or hardened earth in its path, till soon a little trench some three or four inches deep, uncovers the beginning of this kah hoom gem. The work is slow and careful, lest the sharp edge of a rock cut or bruise the tender fibre, whilst in the rear like a ship's rudder the guiding foot and protecting toe keep pace. Perhaps in half an hour, according to the condition of the soil and disposition of the digger, the entire length (four or five feet) of a cream-colored scaly cord about half the size of a pencil is uncovered. This is cut out as long as possible, taken immediately to the river's edge, and stretched out in shallow water. If exposed too long in this state to the warm air it becomes dry and brittle beside increasing the difficulty of removing the outer rough bark. A good day's work for a man is ten kah hoom, but a majella will often double this amount, not because she is quicker, but because she abjures those little necessities of her liege's noonday hours, the pipe and siesta.

During the night the gem becomes thoroughly soaked, and daybreak finds the old people of the party hard at work literally and actually with tooth and toe nail, stripping off the bark. This process is facinating, yet often repulsive, to one seeing it for the first time. She will put one end of the root in her mouth, mumble it around between her gums, till finally the warmth and saliva break up the adhesion and fray the bark loose. This fray is then held with perhaps the only remaining fang in her jaw, and assisted with hands and toes in holding the cord taut, she scrapes it clean. A satisfaction as to the thoroughness of the job is manifested by a grunt, and the ejectment from her mouth of accumulated debris. For hours this ancient but willing creature will squat in the broiling sun, for all the world as one pictures an anthropoid ape or other quadrumana; either or both feet are in use constantly, as essential to her task as teeth or hands. The kah hoom has now reached its second stage in preparing, and is only half of its original size, closely resembling a long, creamy-tinted tendon fresh from the leg or neck of the deer.

When a family starts for home these roots are made into coils and packed in baskets to be carried on the majella's backs, be the distance five or twenty-five miles. The procession files out, the hombres in front, burdened only with what the females cannot carry; the children follow, close in front of their mothers, while the old ones waddle behind, occasionally reminded of the dangers from a panther to anyone who lags.

A few days later the kah hoom is split into flat strings, varying in width from a tenth to a twentieth of an inch, and oftimes as thin as an apple peeling. This was formerly accomplished by aid of a bit of sharp obsidian found in the mountains, but now the American case knife is universally known and used. The fibre of this root is very tough, and the grain so even that a tyro can split it from end to end without a knife and cause no flaw. Splittings from two roots make a coil convenient to handle, and this is hung up in the shah ready for the basket maker.

The next important thread is called mil-lay, which is the generic digger term for any dark red bark. Its chief requisites other than color are strength and thinness. The red bud, sumach, and rhus all produce good mil-lay; but the best and rarest specimen is the thin skin of a small deciduous shrub growing high up the mountain side. To learn its habitat, botanical classification, or common English name, if any, has thus far proven an impossibility. Cajolery and patient search have been fruitless; we only know that the shoots or

FIG. 80. FINE YOKUT DANCE AND OTHER BASKETS.

twigs are straight, leafless, and never larger than a quarter of an inch in diameter.

Steeped for an hour in hot water, the skin loosens so that a simple incision down its length with the thumb nail is ample to complete what the confined steam underneath had commenced. These woody cylinders being split into desired widths are coiled and hung with the kah hoom.

We have now the two threads necessary in weaving baskets of utility, but there is a third one, called tsu wish, or triplets, because its handsome variety is taken from the trifoliate stems of the maiden hair fern (Adiantum). The root of the tule (scirpus) furnishes a long tsu wish, but is less esteemed than the fern, being coarser, and the color not quite so black or permanent.

As it is an aquatic plant the hombre must wade after it, his educated toes performing almost the entire process of digging, select- ing, and loosening up the root. Its color when first taken out is a dirty brown, but when denuded of its useless bark it is similar in appearance to the kah hoom, differing in being shorter, and studded with minute lateral rootlets.

Slitting into strings requires its quota of caution, for tsu wish is rather cross-grained and will allow no carelessness. Like the mil-lay and kah hoom, these strings are also coiled and hung up for the basket maker.

Tsu wish, however, is valued more than either of the others, ranking next to the kiah, or wampum.

"One hundred kiah will purchase a small bunch of tsu wish, while this amount is equivalent to five bunches of kah hoom, or six of mil-lay. It is very rarely seen in any but ornamental baskets, or those pertaining to political or religious uses."

Among the Snohomish Indians the white work is made of grasses that, when dry, are white naturally. "The most common grass used

FIG. 81. THREE TYPES OF HOPI BASKETRY. THE CENTER BASKET IN FRONT IS A HADRUYA OF HAVASUPAI WEAVE.

for this purpose is the so-called 'Mountain Grass,' found in the neighborhood of the Cascade Mountains; it dries to a creamy white with a sort of a half-gloss upon its surface. For the black shade, succulent roots or grasses are chosen which naturally dye to a black. Sometimes the purplish-black stem of the maiden-hair fern is used in the texture of the work of finer texture. As a rule the simpler the color scheme the more likely it is to be permanent and durable—and, indeed, even beautified by the mellowing of time.

"Further chromatic complexity is secured by the use of juices of various berries and the coloring principles of the commoner indigenous plants."

Most of the California Indians use the willow—chippa—the long twigs of which are in favor the world over for this purpose. For the woof the wood of the redbud (cercis occidentalis; Indian name, pad-dit), which is split up with flints or the finger-nails into fine strings, used substantially as thread. The willow twig is passed round and round the basket, the butt of one lapping the tip of the other, while the red-bud strings are sewn over the upper and under the lower.

The Yuroks use willow twigs and pine roots, and, for ornamentation, black rootlets or strips of bark.

On Tule River the Yokuts use for the frame work or warp, not willows, but long stalks of grass (Sporobolus); and for the threads on the woof various barks or roots split fine—pine roots for a white color, willow bark for a brown, and some unknown bark for a black.

In Southern California, according to Professor C. F. Holder, "the material differs according to locality. The tule grass (Juncus robustus) is commonly employed. This grass is collected and dried,

FIG. 82. APACHE AND PIMA BOWLS, ANCIENT BASKET FROM SIA, PAPAGO MEAL BOWL, UTE WINNOWER, HAVASUPAI WATER BOTTLE.

and what are often thought to be brushes by strangers are merely bunches of this tule prepared for the weavers' use. A tall, thin grass (Vilfa rigens) is used as the body of the coil, about which pieces of the juncus are wound. Such of the latter as are intended for ornamentation are dyed black by steeping in water portions of Sueda diffusa, and a rich yellowish brown is produced in a like manner from the plants Dalea Emoryi and Dalea Polyadenia. The bottoms of large baskets are often strengthened by introducing twigs of Rhus aromatica or aromatic oak."

Among the Cahuillas the inner grass of the coil is called "su-lim," and is akin to our broom corn in appearance. The coil is made by wrapping with the outer husk of the stalk of the squaw weed and the tule, the former being termed "se-e-let" and the latter "se eel."

The Hopi makes two kinds of plaques and baskets, viz.: The willow and the Yucca or Amole. The former kind is made in the village of Oraibi only, and the latter in the three villages of the middle mesa of Tusayan. The filling for the coil of the latter style is a grass, which looks somewhat similar to our broom corn, but which bears the name "wu-u-shi." The outer wrapping of the coil is shredded from the Amole—one of the Yucca family—and termed by the Hopi "mo-bi."

Mr. F. V. Coville says that the Panamint Indian women of Death Valley, California, make their baskets of the year-old shoots of tough willow (Salix lasiandra), the year-old shoots of aromatic sumac (Rhus trilobata), the long black horns on the pods of the unicorn plant (Martynia proboscidea), and the long red roots of the tree yucca (Yucca brevifolia). The first two named give the light wood colors, the third the black color and the fourth the red. The women prepare the willow and the sumac in the same way. The bark is removed from the fresh shoots by biting it loose at the end and tearing it off. The woody portion is scraped to remove bud protuberances and allowed to dry. As these Indians make coiled basketry, the rods just described form the basis of the work. The splints for sewing are prepared as follows: A squaw selects a fresh shoot, breaks off the too slender upper portion, and bites one end so that it starts to split into three nearly equal parts. Holding one of these parts in her teeth and one in either hand, she pulls them apart, guiding the splits with her hand so dexterously that the whole root is divided into three nearly even portions. Taking one of these, by a similar process she splits off the pith and the adjacent less flexible tissue from the inner face and the bark from the outer, leaving a pliant, strong, flat strip of young willow or sumac wood. This serves as a fillet in sewing or whipping the coils of the basket together, or in twined basketry two of them become the weft or filling. The coiled basketry is most carefully made. In the olden times a stout, horny cactus spine from the devil's pincushion (Echinocactus polycephalus), set in a head of hard pitch, furnished the needle. When grass stems are carried around inside the coil with the shoot of willow or rhus they form a water-tight packing for the pot baskets. Patterns in red and black are wrought in by means of fillets from the martynia or fern root.

The Pimas and Maricopas use the sisal willow, the squaw weed, the skunk weed, the root of the tule and the martynia or cat's claw, as do also the Paiutis and Havasupais. The shredded leaves of the yucca and amole are often used as the filling material for the inner coils.

"The tools of the basket-maker are of the simplest character—those necessary to the harvesting of the material and those used in manufacture. As baskets are made of wood in one place, of bark in another, and of grass, bast, skins, roots, and so forth, according to locality, the tools for harvesting and preparing the material must vary from tribe to tribe. But the one tool that is never absent is the bone awl or stiletto, which is useful with every type of manufacture, and is ever present in the graves of primitive women."—O. T. Mason.

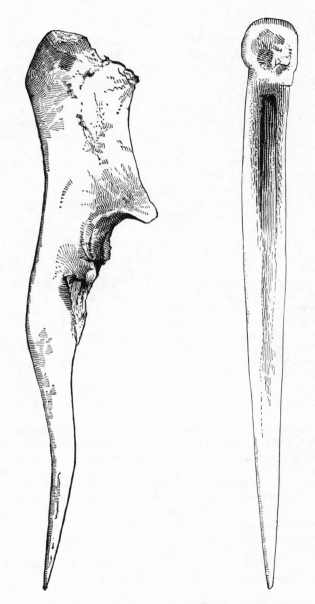

FIGS. 83 AND 84. BONE AWLS USED IN BASKET MAKING.

FIG. 85.   ORAIBI WEAVER MAKING YUCCA BASKET.

CHAPTER VII.

COLORS IN INDIAN BASKETRY.

Some of the oldest known specimens of Indian basketry are the finest weave but without decoration. Hence, as Mrs. Carr writes, We conclude that, having attained perfection in these respects, the native genius reached out toward surface embellishment for its more adequate expression. What they found to be the only mode of ornamentation which would not interfere with the smoothness and flatness of the surfaces, and hence with the durability of their work, was color. It is precisely at this point that the fine art of basketry has its beginning.

"As the woof or willow coils always covered the more perishable warps of grass stems, the artist was necessarily limited to changes in the woof, and to purely geometric patterns. Every kindergartner knows how infinitely varied these may be, and how every new combination stimulates invention. How far back in the ages the discovery was made that simply by breaking off the plain fillet and introducing a colored piece in its place pictures might be made in basketry we never shall know, but this is certain—the result has proved the capacity of our patient Indian drudge for development along the lines which have made the Japanese so wonderful a people.

"The Indian women were very skillful in the preparation of dyes and mordants, and of the colors used, black, red, and various shades of brown, were permanent. The basket hats in common use were of plain colors, and left to steep in the dyes for months, a quantity of pigeon's dung being used as a fixture."

"Changes of color on the surface are produced by varieties of the fundamental monotonies. The geometric decorations on basketry are variations simply in number and color, the size of the mesh remaining uniform. This part of art evolution was almost exhausted by savage women. Hence one sees on basketry and on soft textiles alike patterns which the modern weaver and the jeweler are never tired of copying, which have become classic, and entered the great world-encompassing stream of art forms, pleasing to the whole species."—Mason.

"Colors in textiles are produced first by the happy mixture of natural materials of different tints. Often the two sides of the leaf will give distinct colors, as in the case of the yuccas (out of which the Hopi women of Arizona make the pretty and substantial meal trays), or the palm leaves abounding in the tropics. The Californian women get a black effect with martynia pods, a deep brown with the stem of the maidenhair fern, a bright red in the use of the roots of a yucca. These added to the wood color of different plants produce a pleasing variety. The women of our Pacific coast have found out that burying spruce root and other woody fibres in certain springs or muds produces a chocolate color, and natural dyeing may be found elsewhere. But our primitive folk also know how to make dyes from mineral and vegetable substances and how to fix colors by means of mordants. Until the discovery of the coal-tar dyes—a plague upon them!—the most commonly used colors were those borrowed from the hands of savage women."
—Mason.

Of the colors used by the Potawatomies in their basketry Simon Pokagon says: "They are proficient in the production of natural colors that please the eye. Those best skilled in the art educate themselves in this branch of their work by watching the rainbow in the storm and the golden clouds of sunset. In fact no true admirer of the beautiful can look through a well-arranged bazaar of these goods without feeling in his heart that they must have been dipped in the rainbow and washed in the sunshine."

The squaw grass—Xerophyllum tenax—of the Klickitats' basketry in its natural color is white. By soaking in water for a certain length of time it becomes yellow, and one of the rich browns is created by soaking in hot water. An extract of willow bark also gives a dark brown, and charcoal, black. Urine as a mordaunt was almost universal with all Indian peoples, though, as elsewhere stated, pigeon's dung was used by the Southern California Indians for the same purpose. Among the Hopi, Zunis, Acomas and other pueblo Indians of Arizona and New Mexico at the present time the urine is often preserved for this purpose, and many times I have seen it thus used.

The Shastas dye their white grass brown with an extract of alder-bark, and they use their maidenhair fern stem, which is unfading, and of perfect beauty for the blacks of their basketry.

In similar fashion the Havasupais, or Kohoninos, do not dye their willows black, but use, instead of willows, the peeled pod of the martynia, which is jet black and, as far as I have seen, fadeless.

The Hopi use plants, blossoms and roots from which they largely distill dyes even to the present day, though most of their modern baskets are degraded by aniline dyes.

Dr. Hudson thus writes of the dyeing processes of the Pomas: "The gem (either the kah hoom or mil lay) is evenly painted with charcoal paste, placed in the bottom of a pit, much resembling a grave in proportions. Willow ashes are sprinkled over it to a depth of two inches, and the pit finally filled with loose, damp earth. It takes nearly eighty hours for the charcoal, potash, and tannin to complete their chemical action in producing a perfect dye. If taken out too soon the color will be a dark brown, or if allowed to remain several hours too long, the gem will be eaten into and rendered worthless. Successfully done, a glossy black permeates the fibre which is unimpaired by the burial."

With some of the Southern California tribes a wild-bird guano, found in quantities where native roots existed, was and is used. A small pool by the side of a brook is filled with the prepared splints and then covered over with this guano in a moistened condition. A month of soaking produces a light chestnut, and a longer period the darker chestnuts. Wild berries often give a good red.

Among the Cahuillas the only colors used are black, brown, yellow and white. The white, yellow and brown are colors natural to the growth and are neither bleached nor dyed. The black is made by taking a pot full of mud from the sulphur springs that abound on the reservation and boiling it, stirring the mud and water together. As the mud settles the liquid is poured off, and, while hot, is used to color the splints. Two or three "soakings" are necessary to give a fast and perfect color. The brown is the natural color of the tule root. The outer coating is peeled off into splints never longer than ten inches. but generally nearer six or seven. It is a common sight to find "skeins" of this basket-making material in the four different colors, and now and again one may see the patient woman peeling off the cuticle of the tule root, stripping the skunk weed, boiling the black mud or soaking the skunk weed strips in the black dye.

Native Indian dyes are permanent, and the softening touch of time gives to them a richness, an exquisite harmony in gentle, subtle tone that is delightful to the artistic soul. Some one has well written:

"It is true that the native pigments may be duller and that they do not run through such a lengthy, diverse, and brilliant chromatic gamut as the white man's dyes. But the Indian dyes are permanent, and they are so softened by the mellowing touch of time as to gain with age an exquisite combination of color values altogether inimitable. Who that desires Indian basketry cares for mongrel work? What of a piece of Indian work masquerading in gaudy garments that are not really its own? In the process of crossing, the individuality and the distinctiveness are almost invariably lost and the decorative scheme has degenerated to a degree such as fits it only for the commercial collector of hodge-podge. Most of the Indian basket work that reaches the East is a degenerate product born of the modern commercial spirit, and can never hope to match the purer form of aboriginal days, or even some types yet to be found in the far west—particularly where civilization has touched the red man with a lightsome touch indeed."

The introduction of extraneous substances, such as beads and feathers, belongs to a comparatively late period in the history of the art. In the feather work of the interior tribes we find proof of the delicacy of the native taste; no inharmonious colors are used; and while the splendor of the color seems to have answered every demand, this was often enhanced by contrast. The earlier explorers and discoverers of the Pacific Coast reported the beauty and perfection of this work of the Indian woman. Mr. Stephen Powers describes a fancy work basket "covered entirely with the down of woodpeckers' scalps, among which were a great number of hanging loops of strung beads; and around the rim an upright row of little black quails' plumes gaily nodding." There were eighty plumes, which required the sacrifice of as many quails; and at least a hundred and fifty woodpeckers had been robbed to furnish that royal scarlet nap for the outside.

The bits of shell found on the Poma baskets are of wampum, or ka yah. These are made from the clam shells, Saxidormis gracilis and Cardium corbis. The shell is divided into roughly rounded disks, approximately the size desired, and then, with rude hand drill, or ka win, bored on one side and then on the other. A string of these is made on a willow shoot and rolled over and over on a sandstone slab, on which marble dust and water are placed. This, to the Poma, has its distinct monetary value, hence to find it on a basket is to see work that a majella has decorated with her wealth.

From the earliest ages color has had definite significance. Mallery says: "The Babylonians represented the Sun and its sphere of motion by gold, the Moon by silver, Saturn by black, Jupiter by orange, Mars by red, Venus by pale yellow, and Mercury by deep blue. Red was anciently and generally connected with divinity and power both priestly and royal. The tabernacle of the Israelites was covered with skins dyed red, and the gods and images of Egypt and Chaldea were of that color, which to this day is the one distinguishing the Roman Pontiff and the cardinals.

"In ancient art each color had a mystic sense or symbolism, and its proper use was an essential consideration. With regard to early Christian art Mrs. Clement furnishes the following account:

"White is worn by the Saviour after his resurrection; by the Virgin in representations of the Assumption; by women as the emblem of chastity; by rich men to indicate humility; and by the judge as the symbol of integrity. It is represented sometimes by silver or the diamond, and its sentiment is purity, virginity, innocence, faith, joy, and light.

"Red, the color of the ruby, speaks of royalty, fire, divine love, the holy spirit, creative power, and heat. In an opposite sense it symbolized blood, war, and hatred. Red and black combined were the colors of Satan, purgatory, and evil spirits. Red and white roses are emblems of love and innocence or love and wisdom, as in the garland of St. Cecilia.

"Blue, that of the sapphire, signified heaven, heavenly love and truth, constancy and fidelity. Christ and the Virgin Mary wear the blue mantle; St. John a blue tunic.

"Green, the emerald, the color of spring, expressed hope and victory.

"Yellow or gold was the emblem of the sun, the goodness of God, marriage and fruitfulness. St. Joseph and St. Peter wear yellow. Yellow has also a bad signification when it has a dirty, dingy hue, such as the usual dress of Judas, and then signifies jealousy, inconstancy and deceit.

"Violet or amethyst signified passion and suffering or love and truth. Penitents, as the Magdalene, wear it. The Madonna wears it after the crucifixion, and Christ after the resurrection.

"Gray is the color of penance, mourning, humility or accused innocence.

"Black with white signified humility, mourning, and purity of life. Alone, it spoke of darkness, wickedness, and death, and belonged to Satan. In pictures of the Temptation Jesus sometimes wears black."

A note in the American Journal of Psychology, Vol. 1, November, 1887, p. 190, gives another list substantially as follows: "Yellow, the color of gold and fire, symbolizes reason. Green, the color of vegetable life, symbolizes utility and labor. Red, the color of blood, symbolizes war and love. Blue, the color of the sky, symbolizes spiritual life, duty, religion."

The ceremonial scheme of the Navaho colors symbolic of the cardinal points is as follows: "The eagle plumes were laid to the east, and near by them white corn and white shell; the blue feathers were laid to the south, with blue corn and turquoise; the hawk feathers were laid to the west, with yellow corn and abalone shell; and to the north were laid the whippoorwill feathers, with black beads and corn of all the several colors."

Mooney says that the symbolic color system of the Cherokees is: East—red—success; triumph. North—blue—defeat; trouble. West—black—death. South—white—peace; happiness."

Black is pretty generally the color of death and mourning among the Amerinds, as it is with many civilized races to-day. Red is a sacred color with almost all Indians. It generally symbolizes the blood, the

FIG. 87. YOKUT BASKET IN PLIMPTON COLLECTION.

FIG. 86. YOKUT BASKET, WITH BEAUTIFUL COLOR

life, the strength of man, and, therefore, success. This explains its common use on body, face, lance, war-pony, shield, etc., in the dance, and when going on the war-path.

Among the Mayas the four cardinal points are supposed to have been represented by the colors blue, yellow, black and red. Yellow also suggested to them the ripening of fruit, especially their chief product, maize, and was, therefore, a propitious, a good, a sacred color.

Among the Cheyennes the rivers that are supposed to exist in the spirit world are symbolized by colors, as blue and green, etc.

During the Ghost Dance those who were about to perform were always painted in elaborate designs in red, yellow, green and blue. The sacred colors were supposed to sharpen the spiritual vision.

Formerly, among the Menomini Indians colors were made from earth pigments and represented certain degrees of initiation into the Grand Medicine Society. Those who had received but one degree "were allowed and expected to adorn their faces by making a white stripe horizontally across the forehead, and band of white clay of a finger's width, and extending outward as far as the outer angle of each eye. In addition, a spot of green about an inch in diameter was placed upon the middle of the breast." The decorations of the second degree consisted of a fanciful application to the face of red ochre, or vermillion, and one spot of green beneath each eye. The third degree initiate placed a stripe of green so as to extend horizontally outward from the corners of the mouth. The fourth degree was distinguished by its associates painting the chin with green paint.

During the Ghost Dance excitement Major MacMurray visited Smohalla, the leader of a tribe that bears his name. They are of Shahaptian stock and closely akin to the Yakima and Nez Perces. Smohalla's flag illustrates the Indian's ideas in regard to color, and also the symbolism of signs. The flag was rectangular, suggesting a target. In the center of the flag was a round red patch. The field was yellow, representing grass, which is there of a yellow hue in summer. A green border indicated the boundary of the world, the hills being moist and green near their tops. At the top of the flag was a small extension of blue color, with a white star in the center. Smohalla explained: "This is my flag, and it represents the world. God told me to look after my people—all are my people. There are four ways in the world—north and south and east and west. I have been all those ways. This is the center. I live here. The red spot is my heart—everybody can see it. The yellow grass grows everywhere around this place. The green mountains are far away all around the world. There is only water beyond, salt water. The blue (referring to the blue cloth strip) is the sky, and the star is the north star. That star never changes; it is always in the same place. I keep my heart on that star. I never change." The venerated garments used in this dance were of white, red and blue, old and sacred colors.

Among the Yakimas of Washington yellow, white and blue represent the colors of the celestial world; hence these are favorite colors with them. Yellow is also symbolic of the celestial glory; white of the terrestrial light which comes from "Those Above," while blue is the color of the sky, the abode of the gods.

Among the Zunis color has its distinct significance. "Thus the north is designated as yellow, because the light at morning and evening in winter time is yellow, as also is the auroral light. The west is known as the blue world, not only because of the blue or gray twilight at evening, but also because westward from Zuniland lies the blue Pacific. The south is designated as red, it being the region of summer and of fire, which is red; and for an obvious reason the east is designated white (like dawn light); while the upper region is many-colored, like the sunlight on the clouds, and the lower region black, like the caves and deep springs of the world. Finally, the midmost, so often mentioned in the following outline, is colored of all these colors, because, being representative of this (which is the central world and of which in turn Zuni is the very middle or navel), it contains all the other quarters or regions, or is at least divisible into them. In Zuni, the above—the region of the sky—is symbolized by any and all colors, the below is black. Among the Hopi (Moki) the reverse is the case. With the Hopi the sacred colors of the cardinal points are yellow, green red and white. On the Antelope altar at Shipauluvi the border like that of the Walpi altar, was composed of four bands of sand, colored yellow, green, red, and white, respectively, separated by black lines, as in the Antelope sand picture at Walpi. This border inclosed a rectangular field on which were depicted, in different colored sands, the semicircular rainclouds; four yellow, adjacent to the border; three whole and two half semicircles of green; four red, and three whole and two half semicircles in white. All of these were outlined with black

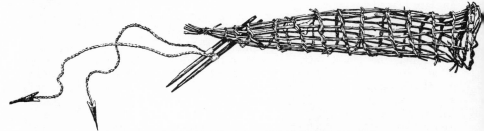

FIG. 88. PSHU-KAN, OR FISH-NET OF POMAS

lines. On the remaining part of the inclosed rectangle, which was covered with white sand, there were four zigzag figures with triangular heads, one yellow, one green, one red, and one white, beginning at the left of the sand picture as one approached it from the ladder. Each of these figures had a single black mark on the neck representing a necklace, and a curved horn on the left side of the head, and was outlined in black.

In order that different colored corn may grow in their fields the priests often take pinches of these different colored sands from their altars and sprinkle them in their corn fields.

The Navahoes, when laying down their sacred corn, follow a certain prescribed order, according to color. The white, being the color of the east, has precedence of all and is laid down first. The blue, the color of the south, comes next, for when we move sunwise (the sacred ceremonial circuit of the Navahoes) south follows immediately after east. Yellow, the color of the west, on the same principle, comes third, and black (in this case mixed) comes fourth. Mixed is properly the coloring of the upper region, and usually follows after black, but it sometimes takes the place of black. These apparently superfluous particulars of laying down the corn have a ceremonial or religious significance.

In placing sacred objects ceremonially in a straight row, the operator proceeds southward from his starting-point, for this approximates the sunwise circuit, and he makes the tip ends point east.

I have not attempted an exhaustive presentation of this interesting subject, but I have sufficiently shown that it is a complex and fascinating one when reasonably understood. One of the difficulties in the way of writing upon such matters is to clear away the rubbish. It is an ungracious task for which enmity and abuse are often the chief returns. Not only must the author satisfy himself of the weight that should be given to that which he reads, and sift out all that seems unreliable, but he must now and again take it upon himself to warn his

FIG. 89. POMA BAM-TUSH WEAVE

readers against the grossly erroneous statements made by those who pose as experts and authorities. For instance, one author asserts that the "real" Indian hues are "red, white and blue," and that the other colors are accursed. That this statement is an utterly foolish and false one I think I have satisfactorily shown by my quotations from acknowledged authorities, and those who desire to pursue the subject further will find it well discussed in the Tenth Annual Report of the U. S. Bureau of Ethnology.

CHAPTER VIII.

WEAVES OR STITCHES OF INDIAN BASKETRY.

To the casual observer there are but slight differences to be noted in the stitches or methods of weaving followed by different tribes in their basketry. The subject is presented in various phases in preceding or succeeding chapters, but I deem it of sufficient interest and importance to devote a special chapter to its immediate consideration.

How a hasty and ignorant generalizer may draw false conclusions and thus mislead others, when those conclusions are presented in a magazine that is edited by a loudly boastful "expert," is evidenced by the following extract: "With infinite care and patience the Indian woman weaves the flexible twigs of trees, or the stems of reeds and the long grass stalks into a shape so perfect that you wonder at the beauty of it; counting her stitches so carefully that seldom does the decorative pattern fail to join properly. There are, practically, but two kinds of weaving, the horizontal and the upright."

Now compare the latter part of this "expert" statement with the modest declaration of an "amateur," Dr. J. W. Hudson, who has made, according to Dr. Otis T. Mason, "the best scientific collection of basketry known to the writer from any people on the earth." Dr. Hudson states that the Poma of to-day uses nine distinct weaves, and that in old baskets are found five others that are now extinct. Of these latter five he exclaims: "Happy the collector that possesses one of such."

The following descriptions of Poma weaves are written by Dr. Hudson or Dr. Mason:

Pshu-kan. "In this type a number of upright work-rods are held together by pairs of hazel or willow shoots passing around horizontally, as in a winding stairway, and making a half twist in each space as in a wattle hedge or fence, enclosing also a horizontal stem as in the fine "ti" style. In the fish weirs and coarser articles the rough material is used, but in household utensils the willow may be decorticated and even polished. The original material for articles of this kind was hazel, (shu-ba)."—Mason.

"Pshu-kan means fish net, and the weave known by this name was undoubtedly the Pomas' first crude effort toward basketry. The idea was suggested probably to the savage mind in noting the salmon's difficulty in passing through submerged interlacing limbs of some fallen tree. Artificial dams followed, then wiers, then vehicles to facilitate the handling and carrying home of their slippery game, then domestic utensils and houses. To strength, further improvement has added lightness and symmetry, till we find in the present Pshu-kan much to admire. In all but the strongest packing baskets, willow shoots have since superceded alder limbs, and each rib is bound with kah hoom."—Hudson.

2. Pshu-tsin. "This is an obsolete method of binding house rafters, stationary granaries, game fences, etc., with split grape-vine weft by starting at the periphery at intervals and spirally looping each second rib, on and up to the common centre."—Hudson.

3. Bam-tush. "A style of twined weaving called, in the Poma lan-

guage, bam-tush, from bam-tu, a grape-vine, the original material; but this has been discarded for stronger and more polished substances. In the splints used for this style of basketry, the brown bark and the pale yellow interior of the stem afford the basket maker an opportunity for ornamentation. By the term bam-tush is evidently meant the plain twined weaving in which only one warp stem is included in each half-turn of the weft."—Mason.

This style of weave is illustrated in Figs. 89 and 90.

Dr. Hudson thus describes the bam-tush: "Three boms are laid side by side across the centers of a similar bunch at right angles, and the six bound together at their intersection with kah hoom. This done, the two ends of thread select a rib and bind it from above and below, twisting on themselves before grasping the next radiating bom. The process con-

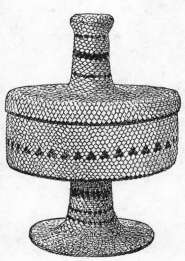

FIG. 90. POMA "BAM-TUSH" GRANARY AND "SHI-PU" TOY.

FIG. 91. NORTH COAST BASKET OF VICIOUS FORM.

tinues around in a gradually increasing spiral until spaces require extra ribs. These, sharpened at the end, fit snugly into openings between stitches made with a bone awl. According to the shape desired, boms are inserted or taken out, all ends being carefully covered.

Patterns make their first appearance in this weave, and to accomplish this a change of thread is required, mil-lay being substituted, its smooth side presenting a burnt sienna hue in contrast to the pale lemon of the kah-hoom. We often find rings of shi-tsin, or "ti" stitch, worked in at intervals, increasing in stability and artistic effect, for during and after this period neither of these two qualities are allowed preponderance. In smaller pieces of work, like the pinole mush basket or those designed for cooking utensils, the rim is left raw, but the big cone shapes require a hoop of alder lashed over with fir fibre.

A bam-tush basket is readily recognised by the vertical ribs, each of which is plainly indicated from bottom to top. Closer inspection finds weight, durability, and a mesh sufficient to retain any seed larger than mustard.

Fig. 91 is here introduced as a striking contrast to the simple and natural forms of the Pomas. This is a Northern Pacific coast basket, and construction and use are sacrificed to a false idea of beauty.

Shu-set. "Among the Poma the shu-set is the most highly decorated of this type of weaving. Upon the pieces marked as belonging to this type there are two styles of manipulation. In all cases, however, the twine stitch or mesh passes over two warp strands instead of one, so that the ribbed appearance on the outside has a diagonal effect. This

FIG. 92. POMA "SHU-SET" AND "TI" WEAVES.

method is always employed in the Ute basketry and as far south as the Pueblo country." See Fig. 92.

Dr. Hudson thus writes of shu-set: "Beauty seems to have been the incentive in its conception, though baskets of this kind possess no unusual shapes or uses. Their pretentions to the eye lie in a smoothness, a perfection in outline and color, that somehow remind you of a delicately rounded, warm cheek. Not a flaw, discoloration or projection can be found on its surface, for this weave is capable of great possibilities in effective displays. In all other textiles the pattern is woven through, that is, the mil-lay or tsu wish threads invariably keep their colored side away from the rib they cover. The shu set is the only exception of this rule, its interior exhibiting only slight indications of the external color. The reason for this becomes obvious, on seeing the weaver carry the stitch through without twisting. Shu-sets were not intended for hard usage—in some degree utility has been sacrificed to grace. It is the lightest and most fragile textile made by the Pomas. Preparation consumes much time, for only the toughest, smallest, and most flexible boms are selected,—also unusually thin, even thread. Begun in the same manner as bam tush the change occurs several inches from the center. Instead of wrapping a single bom from each side, the threads cross each other, untwisted in every other space, thus binding two boms in one loop. (Fig. 93 S.) A shu set foundation called sil lick (spider), from its appearance, illustrates the point.

As may be supposed, this weave requires more ribs than the bam tushs, in fact, about twice as many. The mesh is comparatively open, but is serviceable in carrying seeds of clover, tar weed, or wild millet. Ovoid shapes answer as receptacles for sugar, coffee, trinkets, clothing, etc.

As indicated by its shape, the conical is the basket of transpor-

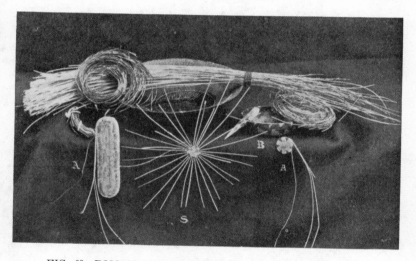

FIG. 93. POMA BASKET MATERIAL AND FOUNDATION.

tation, being held on the back in a net whose head band passes over the carrier's brows. They supply the place in an Indian's needs that a wheelbarrow does in ours, the capacities of each being equal, and if any discrepancy exists, it is not in favor of the wheelbarrow."—Hudson.

Lit. An accessory weave to the shu-set is the Lit, which is "employed to preserve symmetry of outline and harmony of pattern when the pattern requires change of color. It is a distinct method of weave, however, and specimens can be woven entirely by it, though it is rather too delicate and unstable for practical purposes."—Hudson.

Ti. "This is the Poma name for a style of twined weaving in which four elements are employed, namely (a) a set of perpendicular warp-stems, usually of willow (Salix hindsiana); (b) a stem of the same material carried around, in the form of a coil, horizontally on the outside of the upright warp-stems; (c) a regular course of twined weaving, with two splints, which at each half turn encloses the upright and horizontal warp-stem. This makes a very solid double basket for domestic

FIG. 94. THOMPSON, KLICKITAT, KAHROC AND YUROCK, MODOC, POMAN AND ARIZONA BASKETS IN THE WILCOMB COLLECTION SAN FRANCISCO CAL.

FIG. 95. ORNAMENTED POMA "SHLBU" WEAVES.

purposes. (See Fig. 92 the large basket to the right). On the outside the appearance is that of the shu-set basketry, but the ridges are diagonal; on the inside the appearance is that of the bam-tush or plain twined weaving."—Mason.

The interior of a timpekah is identical in appearance to the ribbed bam tush, but, viewed externally, the intricacies of this most difficult and tedious of useful weaves is made manifest.

The fact is, that a ti is a double basket, consisting of an inner bam tush supplemented with an extra rib externally, which, commencing below at the common center, accompanies and participates in each stitch in ever-increasing spirals to the rim. In making, a ti consumes nearly twice the time and material of any basket yet mentioned, and is esteemed as highly as any in the catalogue. Its qualities are, exceeding durability, with lightness; its uses, cooking mush and pinole, boiling

FIG. 96. POMA "SHI-BU."

water, storing fluids, parching wheat or other grains, and as mortars for pounding out flour. The largest ti in Fig. 92 was over twelve months in constructing, while the larger bam-tush Fig. 90 took less time and care. The spiral rib in a ti necessitates its wrapping being put on a slant, thus giving the pattern an indistinctness to be seen in no other weave.

The Poma meaning of the word "ti" is ponderous, stable, unyielding, and it well describes the strong double-weave of the Pomas where durability is required.

Dah-lah is the Poma word for plate; hence ti dah-lah is a platter of the ti make. It is exhilarating to watch an old crone toast wheat. With bended shoulders and pursed-out lips, she frantically waves a dah-lah at arm's length; the grains and glowing coals dance in unison to her puffs, while, "black in the face," she is "never out of breath till the task is done."—Hudson.

"In addition to these species of twined weaving the following are employed by the Pomas in bottoms or bands of ornamentation and occasionally in the strands of the basket:

(a) "Three-ply twine, by which is meant the employment of three members or filaments instead of two in the twining. In the process of twisting, when the third of a turn is made, one of the filaments is caught over a warp-stem, at the next third another filament, and at the end of the whole turn the third is caught over, and so on, the process being repeated from round to round. A moment's thought will show that upon the outside two of the strands will always be shown, while on the inside, therefore, will be that of plain twined weaving; but on the outside it will be diagonal, in which each of the stitches passes over two warp-stems and, under the circumstances, are imbricated or overlapping.

FIG. 97. POMA "TSI" AND "BAM-TSU-WU."

(b) Three-ply braid (shi-tsin), used on bottoms and resembling the last-named, save that the filaments are plaited instead of twisted, but alternately they pass one at a time over warp-stems on the inside, and on the outside this is distinguishable from a."—Mason.

Dr. Hudson writes of shi-tsin: "Gathering of acorns necessitated a closer mesh; small seed, still finer, and lastly, the water-tight basket was evolved. In this order the shi-tsin weave followed the pshu kan. But two specimens of this second stage in textile improvement have been discovered during the past four years, both of them so battered out of shape and black with age as to obliterate all vestiges of pattern, if any ever existed. However, their manner of construction yet remains to supply an important link in the evolution of the basket. Willow limbs the size of a pencil form ribs or bones running from rim down across the bottom and back to the rim again on the opposite side, thus multiplying the bottom's strength while giving it a rough, clumsy appearance.   Deer tendon is probably the binding thread used, three ribs being taken in at one wrap.

Such vessels must have answered a variety of uses, from the gathering of nuts and storing the same, or other mah-ha for food, to packing of fuel. This weave has long since been abandoned, except in cases where its use adds extra strength and variety to baskets of different constructions." Later he writes of this weave: "This weave or weft is identical with our three ply braid or plait. It is too cumbersome to be employed alone, but is often found in rings in specimens of other weaves ti (bamtush) as a reinforcement or stiffener of particular parts of the basket, especially on the bottoms or convexities."

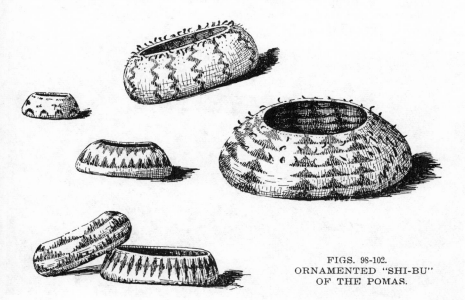

FIGS. 98-102.
ORNAMENTED "SHI-BU"
OF THE POMAS.

He also describes tsa-wam: "This is to braid with a single filament. It is found only in the baby transport cradle, which is always made by men. It is a series of half stitches crossing back and forth, and is efficient for binding the warp firmly."

The coiled style of weave is called Shi-bu by the Pomas and of this there are three distinct types, viz., the Tsai or bam-tca (one rib), the bam-tsu-wu (three ribs) and the shi-lo.

Of these Dr. Hudson thus writes: "I have thus described the various modes of binding together a wooden fabric whose initial ribs, few in number, multiply in proportion to the magnitude of its outline; whose ribs also lie in vertical planes, while their two wrappings incline to a horizontal. Native ingenuity seems to have exhausted itself in this line, and experimenting with coil and spirals was begun. No doubt the outer half of the ti suggested the effort toward departure from orthodox methods. How complete has been the success of those ancient experiments a close study of Fig. 96, will reveal.

Shi bu baskets are made in three ways, each having a mode of procedure peculiar to itself. A specimen of the earliest demonstration of shi-bu practicability can be seen in No. 175, Fig. 96, an unsightly affair, void of all merit but stability and interest to antiquarians. Its composition is a single uninterrupted thread, binding a series of superimposed spirals by piercing the upper edge of the next spiral beneath, this spiral consisting of six fir fibres parallel and in juxtaposition. Pattern is an impossibility, because nearly half the coil is uncovered and the thread itself so coarse that color would provoke ridicule.

Tsai was an improvement. A single bom, uniform in size throughout is so bent on itself as to simulate the coil of a rattlesnake. After the first circle is completed, both boms are enclosed in one wrap, the third bom is bound to the second in the same manner, the stitches passing through and closing interstices between the first and second. Fig. 93 B illustrates stages, and Nos. 55, Fig. 96, 53 and 49, Fig. 97, the complete tsai.

FIG. 103   YOKUT, POMA AND EEL RIVER BASKETS.

Bam tsu wu (triplet boms) is our last; most tedious in construction, most capable of ornametation, and most prolific in aesthetic effects.

A, A, of Fig. 93, explain in detail the ground plan of the two ordinary shapes. Three boms here form the coil, which is held together and to the next lower coil by a thread envelope catching the loops on top of the adjacent lower coil. Nos. 278, 247, Fig. 96, are fine specimens of unornamented bam tsu wu, while Fig. 95 presents a few choice feathered ones. However, among the latter, No. 65, Fig. 95 is a ti. quite rare, with its quail plumes. The use of feathers is of comparatively recent date, though prevalent at the pioneer's advent. Its era may be safely located after the conception of bam tsu wu, which was doubtless created for this purpose.

As a work of art the shi bu basket deserves all the reputation it has received and more; for untold generations these people have concentrated their ingenuity and energy in perfecting a peculiar fibrous textile, and the result has been acknowledged by critics to be the peer among curios from all the barbaric nations of the earth. It is marvelous how one family, relegated from birth to one secluded spot, surrounded by rude, unsympathetic nomads, deprived of all resources but those nature created with them, should develop such an art and cherish it. It was not the demand of a necessity, but the pursuit of an ideal."—Hudson.

In 1892 my well informed friend, Mrs. Jeanne C. Carr, wrote: "The finest as well as the largest California baskets are of the coiled variety. The simplicity of their construction is well shown in the illustration

FIG. 104. PAUMA GRANARY, TRINKET BASKETS, WATER BOTTLES AND HAT.

(Fig. 104), which presents the bottom of a very old Indian basket from the Pauma reservation in San Diego County, California. The full size of this basket can be better understood by a glance at Fig. 231. Gregoria Majal, who made it, wove such a granary for each of her three daughters, who are venerable women; yet Gregoria's strength and skill are even now fully competent for work of this quality. This store-house is nine feet and nine inches in circumference, three feet deep, and has only four coils or stitches to the inch of weaving. Fifteen stitches is considered a fine weave, the finest ever seen by the writer had twenty-eight to the inch, and was truly a perfect work of art."

Yet Dr. Hudson says of the Poma weaves: "An ordinary shi bu contains eighteen stitches to the inch, as in Nos. 255 and 71, Fig. 97, but those on either side boast of forty-two to fifty-one within this measure-

FIG. 105. LARGE APACHE BASKET, IN THE PLIMPTON COLLECTION.

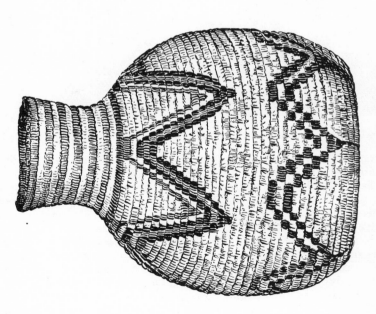

FIG. 106. APACHE WATER BOTTLE.

ment. Their equals will probably never be seen, for their makers are now on the eve of final departure."

Despite this statement, however, there is a California basket in the private collection of Mr. W. D. Campbell, of Los Angeles, which has fifty-three stitches to the inch, a most wonderful and exquisite piece of work.

In Fig. 57 I have marked a basket with the letter M. This is a typical Mescalero Apache coiled basket. In weave coarse and crude, in color neither striking nor harmonious, it represents a low stage of the art. Not until the commercial aspect of basketry presented itself to these pepole, did they attempt to do much at it, and the result is their efforts are neither skillful nor pleasing.

In the San Carlos and White Mountain Apaches, however, one has an entirely different class of weavers to deal with. Here are experts, proud of the fineness of their work, poetic in the designs they conceive and accomplished in weaving that which they imagine. Their basketry is of the coiled order and made generally of willow or twigs that are much similar. One or more willows serve for the inside of the coil and willow splints are wrapped around and caught into the coil below. Black and white are the main colors, the body of the basket, of course, always being white and the design worked out with black, which is generally the pod of the martynia. The more skillful weavers model their ware in a variety of shapes, so that one can have flat-bottomed bowls, conical bowls, saucers, jars of varied forms, bottles with wide necks, oval trinket baskets and the like. Fig. 105 was made by a White Mountain Apache and is possibly the largest in existence. It is over 40 inches in diameter and 42 inches high, and contains fully a quarter of a million stitches. It took Jattalouisa, its maker, two years to make, and its perfect shape attests her skill and patience. There is nothing distinctive about the design and the chief value of such a basket is in its size and perfect shape, it being a remarkable example of what can be accomplished in this regard. Such baskets were originally used as granaries and may still be found doing similar service. It is in the Plimpton collection, in San Diego, California.

Fig. 106 is a fine specimen of an Apache water bottle. This is much more beautifully and closely woven than the similar work of the Paiutis, care being taken to make the basket water tight without covering with gum. The design of this basket is fully explained in the chapter on Symbolism.

The Paiutis make three separate and distinct styles of baskets, as well as their "pa-bi-chi," or baby cradle. Their mush bowls are very similar to the work of the Apaches and Cahuillas, yet in weave are slightly different. Aromatic sumac (Rhus aromatica, Var. trilobata), split to the required width, and colored or white as desired, is used as the wrapping splint. The inner coil is composed of yucca, bast or fiber, two or three or more strips according to the fineness or coarseness desired. The larger the quantity of material inside the thicker and heavier the coil is. The sewing passes over the elements of the coil and through the upper element of the coil below, looping always under the subjacent stitches. The ornamentation is produced by working into the fabric various designs with strips of martynia or splints dyed to a dark brown or a reddish brown.

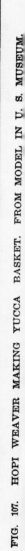

FIG. 107. HOPI WEAVER MAKING YUCCA BASKET. FROM MODEL IN U. S. MUSEUM.

The most noted work in mush bowls of the Paiutis, however, is not known by their name. These bowls are eagerly sought after and are known as "Navaho Wedding Baskets" and "Apache Medicine Baskets." This may be accepted as the highest type of Pauiti weaving found in their original habitat, for by contact with the Yokuts, the Pauitis of California have much improved in artist skill. Fig 29 and

FIG. 108.   KUCH-YE-AMP-SI, THE HOPI WEAVER.

the two baskets of the middle row of Fig. 27 represents these bowls. They are woven as above described, but finished on the border in a style peculiar to the Paiutis, Navahoes and Havasupais. No other weavers make this diagonal border whip stitch that I call the "herring bone" finish. It is both a beautiful and appropriate stitch, resembling somewhat the braiding on a whip, and is a distinguished mark of the weave of these three peoples.

This beautiful effect is produced by a single splint. The splint is passed under the sewing of the last coil and then drawn over it and backward. It is then passed under again, upward and forward, just in advance of the starting point. Thus by sewing backward and forward, as one coils a kite string, this braided effect is produced.

Matthews says the Navahoes claim this finishing stitch as peculiarly their own. "These Indians say that the Apaches and other neighboring tribes finish the margins of their baskets with simple circular turns of the investing fibre like that in the rest of the basket. The Navaho basket, they believe, may always be known by the peculiar finish described, and they say that if among other tribes a woman is found who makes the Navaho finish she is of Navaho descent or has learned her art of a Navaho. They account for this by a legend which is perhaps not wholly mythical. In the ancient days a Navaho woman was seated under a juniper tree finishing a basket in the style of the other tribes, as was then the Navaho custom, and while so engaged she was intently thinking if some stronger and more beautiful margin could not be devised. As she thus sat in thought the God Qastceyelci tore from the overhanging juniper tree a small spray and cast it into her basket.

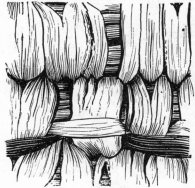

FIG. 109   SHOWING ONE INCH OF   FIG. 111   ONE SQUARE INCH OF
THE WEAVE OF HOPI SACRED   FIG. 110.
        TRAYS.

It immediately occurred to her to imitate in her work the peculiar fold of the juniper leaves and she soon devised a way of doing so. If this margin is worn through or torn in any way the basket is unfit for sacred use. The basket is given to the shaman when the rites are done. He must not keep it, but must give it away, and he must be careful never to eat out of it. Notwithstanding its sacred use, it is no desecration to serve food in it."

The colors are invariably white, black and reddish brown, and the design is interesting. Nearly twenty years ago the favorite wife of the last great chief of the Paiutis, Winnemucca, gave me one of these basket bowls, and told me the meaning of the design. The Paiuti believes in a lower, or underworld that corresponds in its hills and valleys to this upper world. These are represented in this design. It was from this underworld that all the Paiutis came, and from these have sprung all the races of the earth. The means of communication between the lower and upper worlds is called Shipapu, and is likewise represented in the opening. Now, strange to say, the simple-hearted Paiuti woman sincerely believes that if she closes this representation of shipapu she will render it impossible for any more Paiutis to be born into this upper world. This is the primal significance of the design, and the only one known to its maker. The hole is not made by her, as so many affirm, that the evil spirits (achindi) may be allowed to escape, but it is to her the representation of shipapu which she would not dare knowingly to close up.

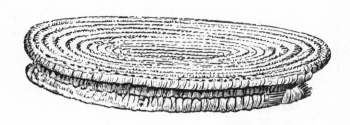

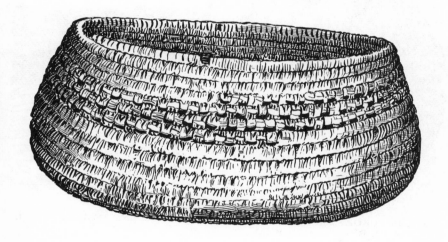

FIG. 110. COILED BASKET AND LID FROM UPPER EGYPT, NUBIA.

There may be, however, some color for the idea of this being an "escape hole" for evil spirits if one considers the remarks of the Navahoes, from whom most of these baskets are obtained. Believing that there are evil spirits in the underworld, and knowing the Paiuti idea represented in the basket, the Navahoes point to the opening and sententiously remark "Achindi! Achindi!" and from this the assumption referred to doubtless has grown.

The common Paiuti carrying baskets and seed roasting trays are coarsely woven. The warp twigs are made to open out and the new ones are added as the basket enlarges. The weft splints are carried around in pairs and twined around two of these warp twigs so as to produce a twilled effect, somewhat after the fashion of the work of the Haidas and Clallams.

Their basket water-bottles, or tus-jeh, as they are called by the Navahoes, are striking specimens of adaptability to environment. Wandering over trackless deserts, often miles away from water, a carrying vessel was needed for the precious element that would withstand more than ordinary risks of breakage. The white man's canteen of zinc is not so well adapted for desert uses as is the Paiuti tusjeh with two horse-hair lugs woven into the side. A thong of buckskin, passed through these and over the saddle fastens it so that it can safely be carried. Should it fall there is no danger of it being broken. Horses may run away, fall, kick and the tusjeh be in the heart of the difficulty and it will withstand all strains and resist all pressures. The shape is almost uniform; rounded at the bottom so that it can easily be rested in the sand, bellying out and retreating to the neck, which is wider at the lip than at the point of junction with the body. It is coated with pinion gum. The weave is very coarse and of the coiled order, with a neat wrap stitch on the rim.

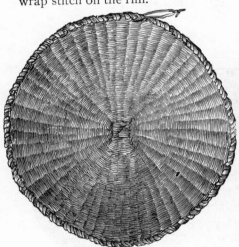

FIG. 112. UNORNAMENTED ORAIBI
PLAQUE OR SACRED MEAL
TRAY.

FIG. 113. ONE INCH OF FIG. 112.

The Hopituh, or Moki, are the makers of the sacred meal trays of striking design and coloring that find place in all collections. Of these there are three distinct types (see Fig. 81), the yucca or amole, made at the three villages of the middle mesa, Mashongnavi, Shipauluvi and Shimopavi, the willow, made at Oraibi on the western mesa, and the coarse yucca corn and peach baskets made at all the seven villages (see Figs. 107 and 85).

In Fig. 108 is represented Kuchyeampsi, the finest weaver of the former type among the Hopi, though she is here shown making baskets rather than plaques or trays. The weaving, however, is of exactly the same character. The material of the inner coil is a native grass, called wu-u-shi, something like our broom-corn. The coil is wrapped with splints stripped from the leaves of the amole, or soap-plant, one of the yucca family. (See Fig. 109). These splints are generally about a sixteenth of an inch in width, though for finer work they are made smaller. The wrapped coil varies from a quarter of an inch to an inch in diameter. As the coil progresses, each stitch or wrap is caught into a stitch of the coil beneath with such uniform exactness, that it has the appearance of a worm closely coiled up. The native colors of the designs were black, brown, yellow, red and the natural white of the yucca, but of late years the aniline dyes have been used with the Indian's fondness for glaring and incongrous results. The designs are

FIG. 114. ORAIBI SACRED MEAL TRAY. SPIDER WEB PATTERN.

multiform, every conceivable pattern being worked out as if from the suggestions of a kaleidescope.

These trays are used by the Hopi in their various ceremonials for the carrying of the "hoddentin" or sacred meal. Sprinkling of this meal constitutes an important part of all Hopi ritual for the propitiation of the evil powers of nature, for, as I have elsewhere shown the Hopi is the greatest ritualist of the world.

The singular and interesting symbolism of these trays I have elsewhere described.

For comparison with this style of Hopi basketry I have introduced Fig. 110 which represents a coiled basket of upper Egypt, made of bundles of palm-leaf veins, sewed with strips of palm leaf. The ornamentation is in red and black. A long red or black strip of leaf is laid on the outside of a coil and caught down by alternate stitches. The varying of the number of the stitches caught over or covered by these strips produces a multitude of effects. These baskets are frequently pitched for boats or "Moses' arks."

Fig. 111 represents one square inch of Fig. 110 showing the sewing and stripes of ornamentation.

It will also be noticed in the finishing off of the coil in the lower portion of the lid that the "open gate" of the Hopis is presented. Whether the Egyptians had the same symbolism in regard to this finishing off of the baskets, is an interesting subject of inquiry.

Fig. 112 is a plain unornamented willow-woven basket of the Oraibis. This latter, as far as I know, is the only example of aboriginal weaving similar to the ordinary willow ware basketry of civilization. It is made in exactly the same style, the warp twigs radiating from the center, and

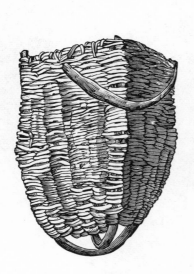
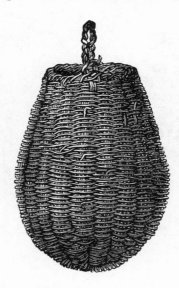

FIG. 115. COARSE WILLOW   FIG. 116. ZUNI CARRYING
HOPI CARRYING BASKET.   BASKET.

the woof twigs passing in and out in the simple weave. The designs found on these trays are often very striking. Though necessarily controlled by the weave stitch, the imaginative and poetic Hopi woman introduces the object she sees, the things she dreams of, the powers she worships and the elements of which she is afraid, by means of different colored twigs, and the results are both interesting and attractive.

Fig. 113 is one square inch, natural size, of Fig. 112, and shows the regular disposition of the weaving.

Fig. 114 is a similarly constructed Oraibi basket, but here a pattern is clearly made by the use of colored twigs. The ornamentation is the "spider-web" pattern elsewhere described.

The Hopis of all the villages weave a very coarse basket of which Fig. 115 is a type. Coarse willow twigs are woven around a warp, the four corners of which are composed of two strong sticks bent at the bottom as shown in Fig. 115. Between these, other upright twigs are placed, and the woof introduced according to the whim, or, more probably, lazy carelessness of the weaver. Sometimes the stitches are single, then double and even triple, and again, on a higher row of weave, just the reverse. The result is an irregular, uneven and slovenly-looking production, that has no other justification for its existence than its usefulness as a fruit or corn carrying basket.

Most of the Zuni basketry is of a coarse, rude character, with neither form nor ornament to make it attractive. Small round willows, and the stem of the yucca, which attains a long slender growth in this region, are used for this purpose, and most of the women can make baskets of this character. But I do not know a single weaver of the finer baskets in any of the villages of Zuni to-day.

Fig. 116 is a good example of the coarser kind of Zuni handicraft and is used for carrying peaches and such-like fruits, etc., and Fig 117 is a similar basket used for the same purpose, but of somewhat different shape.

FIG. 117. ZUNI CARRYING BASKET.

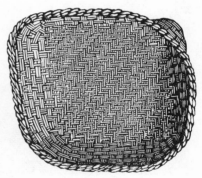

FIG. 118. EFFECTS PRODUCED BY VARYING THE ORDER OF INTERSECTION. SEMINOLE WORK.

The Washoes of Nevada make a basket similar in weave to the Paiutis, and which can be differentiated only in that the colors used are varied, the designs or symbols more diverse and generally the weave more varied, the designs or symbols more diverse and generally the weave is much finer. The "queen" of the Washoe weavers is Dat-so-la-lee, a full-blooded Indian, sixty years of age, whose work is wonderful in its shape, symbolization and weave. Fig. 56 shows her, surrounded by her work. Though heavy and plump, her delicacy of touch, artistic skill and poetical conception excite admiration. Her hand is symmetrically perfect, her fingers plump and tapering and her nails beautiful "filberts." She is fully conscious of the sensations and emotions her work arouses in the hearts of connoisseurs. During the past three years she has produced sixteen baskets with sixteen stitches to the inch, three baskets with twenty stitches to the inch; and four baskets with thirty stitches to the inch. Her white splints are made solely of willow. A willow shoot is split from twelve to twenty-four splints, with the teeth and finger nails. The finer the stitch desired the greater the number of splints from the shoot. Only those portions of the fibre immediately over the pith and under the bark are used. They are all then made of uniform size by scraping with a piece of glass. The warp, or inside of the coil, is generally composed of two thin willows stripped of the bark. For colors the red bark of the mountain birch, and the dark root of a large fern that grows in the foothills of the Sierra are used.

So exquisite is Dat-so-la-le's work that her baskets have brought fabulous prices ranging from $150 to $250. Three of her recent creations are valued even much higher. Fig. 119 is one of her masterpieces.

FIG. 119. HIGHLY DECORATED, BEAUTIFULLY WOVEN
WASHOE BASKET.

There is little that one can write about to differentiate the finer basketry of the White Mountain and San Carlos Apaches from that other branch of the great Apache family known as the Havasupais, and yet the expert can tell the difference in a moment. The finishing off border stitch of the Havasupais is the herring bone stitch before described as belonging to the basketry of the Paiutis, while that of the Southern Apaches is an ordinary wrapped stitch, a simple coiling around of the splint.

In the coarser work of the Havasupais two other distinct weaves are used, as will be seen later in illustration of their kathaks, or carrying-baskets, and their esuwas or pinion-gum-covered water ollas.

The Pimas and Maricopas make baskets similar to those of the Paiuti, Havasupai and Apache, and yet generally distinguishable. The work is coarser than that of the Havasupai or Apache, and the border stitch is generally of a backward and forward kind of weave peculiar to these people. Their designs are striking and varied, the Greek fret and circular forms of the Swastika being largely represented. Many illustrations of Pima work are found in these pages.

FIG. 121.—MONO COOKING BASKET IN THE PLIMPTON COLLECTION.

FIG. 120. PIMA BASKET, WITH CONVENTION-ALIZED DESIGN. PLIMPTON COLLECTION.

In later chapters, where individual specimens of many and varied baskets are shown, the weaves are explained and illustrated and to those chapters the student is referred for further information upon this interesting branch of the subject.

In a letter to the author Professor O. T. Mason suggests that:

FIG. 122. SOUTHERN CALIFORNIA BASKET, USED AS A DRUM.

"For my part, I believe that every type of basketry on the West Coast represents either a tribe or a linguistic family. That the various types get about from one tribe to another by intermarriage and by barter I do not doubt, but one tribe does not learn the art or finesse from the other."

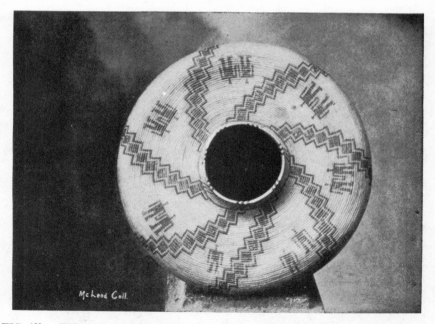

FIG. 122a.—TOP OF A BOTTLE-NECK BASKET IN THE McLEOD COLLECTION.

CHAPTER IX.

BASKET FORMS AND DESIGNS; THEIR ORIGIN AND RELATION TO ART.

UCH a large variety of basket forms is now found to exist that one is led by natural curiosity to inquire as to their origin. In preceding and succeeding chapters various forms are presented, and some of them discussed in connection with their origin. The great importance of this branch of the subject, however, demands that, even at the risk of repetition, a full chapter be devoted to a discussion as to the origin, uses, and relation to art of the various forms and decorations found thereupon, of the basketry of the regions under consideration. In the main the ideas and illustrations of this chapter are taken bodily from Professor William H. Holmes' admirable monograph entitled "Textile Art in its Relation to the Development of Form and Ornament."

While the advent of the Spaniards undoubtedly checked the free and spontaneous growth of American aboriginal art, there is still enough remains among the basket-making peoples to enable us distinctly to trace their mental methods and reach reasonably accurate conclusions as to the processes of their art development. The processes of manufacture and ornamentation of basketry are doubtless little, if any, changed, since precolumbian times, so that in studying its historic and every day manifestations, we are having the mystic veil drawn aside, in some measure, and taking glimpses of the native life of these people before the advent of the Spaniards became a disturbing element.

Indian basketry, though in a more circumscribed area than Indian pottery, presents two classes of phenomena of importance in the study of evolution of aesthetic culture. These relate, first, to form, and second, to ornament.

In form there are: 1. Useful shapes, which may or may not be ornamental. 2. Aesthetic shapes, which are ornamental and may be useful.

It is impossible to fix time boundaries and say when a certain form came into existence, or where and how it had its origin. Yet it is generally accepted that, the simpler the form the earlier its use and the more primitive the people who introduced it, while the more complex

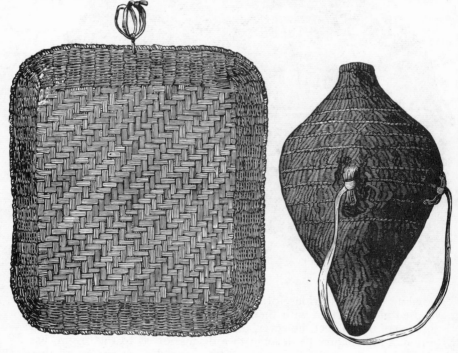

FIG. 124. PUEBLO INDIAN SLEEPING MAT.   Fig. 125. Havasupai Water Bottle.

and specialized forms are the product of the older peoples, more advanced in civilization.

That basketry antedates pottery has already been shown. The subject is ably presented by Lieut. Cushing in his "Pueblo Pottery and Zuni Culture Growth." Canes first and then gourds were used to carry water. Owing to the frangibility of the gourd, however, it was difficult of transportation, and, therefore, liable to be productive of great distress to those who relied upon it for carrying their water supply across the desert. To overcome this the gourd was encased in a rude net of fibrous yucca leaves or flexible willow or other splints. I have seen many such ancient water vessels used in Hopi, Navaho, Zuni and other ceremonials.

This was a crude beginning. The water-tight wicker-basket followed, which as Cushing shows, demonstrates by its nomenclature its origin from the gourd.

The strength, durability and consequent reliability in the carrying of water for long distances would soon make baskets common, even though difficult and tedious of manufacture. Pinion gum, mineral asphaltum, pitch or other glutinous substances, being at hand, were readily suggested for the repairing of any leakage.

As before shown baskets were used long before the advent of pottery for cooking purposes, and by the primitive Havasupais are still so used.

In studying basketry from its art side, the subject first presented naturally is that of form. As a piece of basketry, whether crude or artistic is considered, the question immediately arises, from whence did the maker obtain her idea of this form? Undoubtedly to the imitative

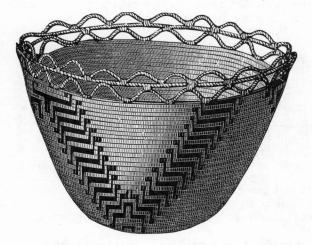

FIG. 126. YAKIMA BASKET, WITH ESTHETIC
CHARACTERISTICS OF FORM.

faculty all primitive forms owe their origin, and at the same time it is equally certain that the form must correspond to the function the basket is required to perform. The aesthetic features of form are a later development, brought about by general aesthetic growth and applied to this special industry.

Holmes well says: "In America there is a vast body of primitive, indigenous art having no parallel in the world. Uncontaminated by contact with the complex conditions of civilized art, it offers the best possible facilities for the study of the fundamental principles of aesthetic development."

Rigid objects in textile art (rigid, as opposed to pliable, compare water bottles and water-tight bowl baskets with nets, woven garments, etc.), depend largely for their form upon their adaptability to the usage required of them. This usage Holmes terms "function," and he states that, "while their shape still accords with their functional office, they exhibit attributes of form generally recognized as pleasing to the mind, which are expressed by the terms grace, elegance, symmetry, and the like. Such attributes are not separable from functional attributes, but originate and exist conjointly with them."

Basketry being one of the earliest of the textile industries manifests, as largely as all primary industries must, the imitative faculty in a high degree. Hence in natural objects are to be sought the form inspirations for primitive basketry.

"Woven mats, such as Fig. 124, in early use by many tribes of men and originating in the attempt to combine leaves, vines and branches for purposes of comfort, are flat because of function, the degree of flatness depending upon the size of filaments and mode of combination; and in outline they are irregular, square, round or oval, as a result of many causes and influences, embracing use, construction, material, models, etc."

In point of contour the plain food basket-bowls so common throughout the South-west, such as are shown in Figs. 12, 13, and many other pages, have somewhat more decided claims upon aesthetic attention than the preceding, as the curves exhibited mark a step of progress in

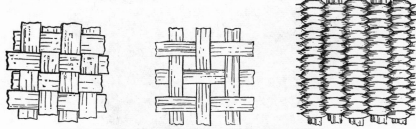

FIGS. 127, 128, 129. SIMPLE WEAVES IN ONE COLOR.

complexity and grace. How much of this is due to intention and how much to technical perfection must remain in doubt. In work so perfect we are wont, however unwarrantably, to recognize the influence of taste.

"A third example, presented in Fig. 125, illustrates an advanced stage in the art of basketry and exhibits a highly specialized shape. The forces and influences concerned in its evolution may be analyzed as follows: A primal origin in function and a final adaptation to a special function, the carrying and storing of water; a contour full to give result to a certain undetermined extent of the aesthetic tendencies of the capacity, narrow above for safety, and pointed below that it may be set in sand; curves kept within certain bounds by the limitations of construction; and a goodly share of variety, symmetry and grace, the result to a certain undetermined extent of the esthetic tendencies of the artist's mind. In regard to the last point there is generally in forms so simple an element of uncertainty; but many examples may be found in which there is positive evidence of the existence of a strong desire on the part of the primitive basket-maker to enhance beauty of form. It will be observed that the textile materials and construction do not lend themselves freely to minuteness in detail or to complexity of outline, especially in those small ways in which beauty is most readily expressed

"Modifications of a decidedly aesthetic character are generally suggested to the primitive mind by some functional, constructive or accidental feature which may with ease be turned in the new direction. In the vessel presented in Fig. 126, the work of Alaskan Indians, the margin is varied by altering the relations of the three marginal turns of the coil, producing a scalloped effect. This is without reference to use, is uncalled for in construction, and hence is, in all probability, the direct result of aesthetic tendencies."

"In the pursuit of this class of enrichment there is occasionally noticeable a tendency to overload the subject with extraneous details. This is not apt to occur, however, in the indigenous practice of an art, but comes more frequently from a loss of equilibrium or balance in motives or desires, caused by untoward exotic influence.

"When, through suggestions derived from contact with civilized art, the savage undertakes to secure all the grace and complexity observed in the works of more cultured peoples, he does so at the expense of construction and adaptability to use. An example of such work is presented in Fig. 91, a weak, useless, and wholly vicious piece of basketry. Other equally meretricious pieces represent goblets,

FIG. 130. DIAGONAL COMBINATION, GIVING HERRING BONE EFFECT.

FIG. 131. ELABORATION OF DIAGONAL COMBINATION, GIVING TRIANGULAR FIGURES.

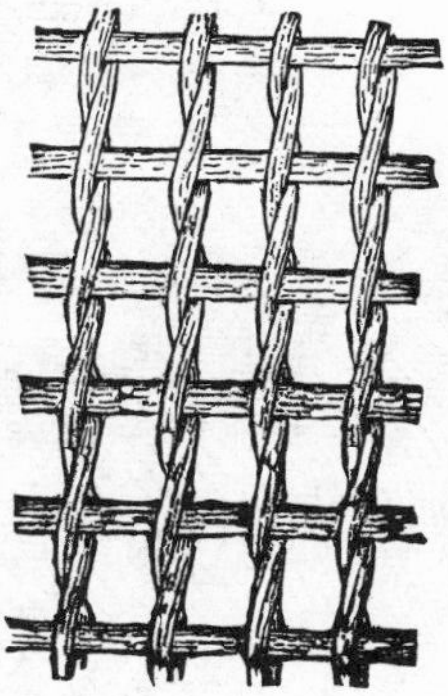

FIG. 133. SIMPLE TWINED WEAVE.

bottles and teapots. They are the work of the Indians of the northwest coast and are executed in the neatest possible manner, bearing evidence of the existence of cultivated taste.

"If, in the making of a vessel, the demands of use are fully satisfied, if construction is perfect of its kind, if materials are uniformly suitable, and if models are not absolutely bad, it follows that the result must necessarily possess in a high degree those very attributes that all agree are pleasing to the eye.

"Form has its relation to ornament in that the contour of the vessel controls its ornament to a large extent, dictating the positions of design and setting its limits; figures are in stripes, zones, rays, circles, ovals or rectangles—according, in no slight measure, to the character of the spaces afforded by details of contour."

Having dealt clearly with the main subject of form as related to art, Professor Holmes thus expatiates upon color and design modifying form and their joint and combined relations to the development of art.

"Color is one of the most constant factors in man's environment, and it is so strongly and persistently forced upon his attention, so useful as a means of identification and distinction, that it necessarily receives a large share of consideration. It is probably one of the foremost objective agencies in the formation and development of the aesthetic sense.

"Color employed in the art is not related to use, excepting, perhaps, in symbolic and superstitious matters; nor is it of consequence in construction, although it derives importance from the manner in which construction causes it to be manifested to the eye. It finds its chief use in the field of design, in making evident to the eye the figures with which objects of art are embellished."

In enhancing beauty there are phenomena present in the art without man's volition that tend to suggest decorative conceptions and give shape to them. "The latter class of features arise as a necessity of the art, they gradually come into notice and are seized upon by the aesthetic faculty, and under its guidance they assist in the development of a system of ornament of world-wide application."

Figures or patterns of a relievo nature arise during construction

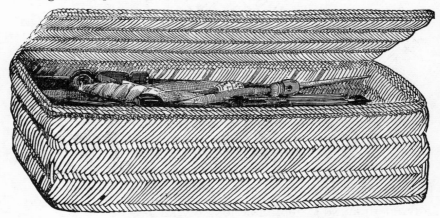

FIG. 132. PERUVIAN WORK BASKET OF REEDS,
WITH STRONGLY RELIEVED RIDGES.

as a result of the intersections and other more complex relations, the bindings, of the warp and woof or of inserted or applied elements. And when color was applied to either warp or woof new conceptions of design would arise entirely independent of the will of the artisan. The very nature of the art is such that once let there be introduced accidentally or otherwise, a new form or twist of weave or stitch, and a splint differing in color from the other splints, new characteristics of appearance in weave and color would be presented regardless of the desire of the artist, or the effect produced upon the eye.

It was the conscious perception of these adventitious effects, the pleasure they gave, and the desire and determination to repeat them that gave the first great impulse towards the rapid development of the aesthetic nature.

"But it is not to be supposed for a moment that the inception of aesthetic notions dates from this association of ideas of beauty with textile characters. Long before textile objects of a high class were made, ideas of an aesthetic nature had been entertained by the mind, as, for example, in connection with personal adornment. The skin had been painted, pendants placed about the neck, and bright feathers set in the hair to enhance attractiveness, and it is not difficult to conceive of the transfer of such ideas from purely personal associations to the embellishment of articles intimately associated with the person. No matter, however, what the period or manner of the association of such ideas with the textile are, that association may be taken as the datum point in the development of a great system of decoration whose distinguishing characters are the result of the geometric textile construction."

Primitive work was plain in weave, simple and unembellished, and consequently, wholly geometric and extremely monotonous.

As intelligence and skill grew, simple weaves were modified or combined with others, without interfering with perfection of structure or functional uses, and thus a new field opened in the development of decorative tendencies.

FIG. 134. SURFACE EFFECT OF TWINED LATTICE
COMBINATION IN BASKET OF CLALLAM
INDIANS OF WASHINGTON.

With the introduction of color and its addition to either simple or complex weaves an added impetus to this development was given. Hence we may broadly classify the ornamentation of basketry into the following divisions:

1. Ornamentation by simple weave in one color.
2. Ornamentation by a combination of simple weaves in one color.
3. Ornamentation by simple weave in a combination of colors.
4. Ornamentation by combination of weaves in a single color or a combination of colors.
5. Ornamentation by extraneous addition.

"In right angled weaving the figures combine in straight lines, which run parallel or cross at uniform distances and angles. In radiate weaving, as in basketry, the radial lines are crossed in an equally formal

manner by concentric lines.   In other classes of combination there is
an almost equal degree of geometricity."*

In Figs. 127, 128 and 129 we have the forms of simple weave in one
color clearly shown, and Figs. 112 and 21 are types of baskets that
accord with this classification.

By changes in the order of intersection, without changing the type
of combination, we reach a series of results quite unlike the preceding;
so distinct, indeed, that, abstracted from constructive relationships,
there would be little suggestion of correlation.   In the example given
in Fig. 130 the series of filaments interlace, not by passing over and
under alternate strands, as in the preceding set of examples, but by
extending over and under a number of the opposing series at each step
and in such order as to give wide horizontal ridges ribbed diagonally.

This example is from an ancient work basket obtained at Ancon,
Peru, and shown in Fig. 132.   The surface features are in strong relief,
giving a pronounced herring bone effect.

Slight changes in the succession of parts enable the workmen to
produce a great variety of decorative patterns, an example of which

  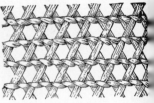

FIG. 135.
**Surface effect in impacted
work of twined combination.**

FIG. 136.
Surface effect obtained by
placing the warp strands close
together and the woof cables
far apart.

FIG. 137.
Surface effect obtained by
crossing the warp series in
open twined work.

is shown in Fig. 131.   The Hopi mat shown in Fig. 124 is also a good
illustration, and another piece, said to be of Seminole workmanship,
is given in Fig. 118.   These and similar relieved results are fruitful
sources of primitive decorative motives.   They are employed not only
within the art itself, but in many other arts less liberally supplied with
suggestions of embellishment.

Taking a second type of combination, we have a family of resultant
patterns in the main distinguishable from the preceding.

Fig. 133 illustrates the simplest form of what Dr. O. T. Mason has
called the twined combination, a favorite one with many of our native
tribes.   The strands of the woof series are arranged in twos and in
weaving are twisted half around at each intersection, inclosing the
opposing fillets.   The resulting open work has much the appearance
of ordinary netting, and when of pliable materials and distended or
strained over an earthen or gourd vessel the pattern exhibited is strikingly suggestive of decoration.   The result of this combination upon a
lattice foundation of rigid materials is well shown in the large basket

*As the major portion of this chapter is compiled from Holmes's mono-
graph, it will be completed without further quotation marks.

presented in Fig. 134. Other variants of this type are given in the three succeeding figures.

The result seen in Fig. 135 is obtained by impacting the horizontal or twined series of threads. The surface is nearly identical with that of the closely impacted example of the preceding type (Fig. 127). The peculiarities are more marked when colors are used. When the doubled and twisted series of strands are placed far apart and the opposing series are laid side by side a pleasing result is given, as shown in Fig. 136 and in the body of the conical basket illustrated in Fig. 139.

In Fig. 137 we have a peculiar diagonally crossed arrangement of the untwisted series of filaments, giving a lattice work effect.

Fig. 138 serves to show how readily this style of weaving lends itself to the production of decorative modification, especially in the direction of the concentric zonal arrangement so universal in vessel-making arts.

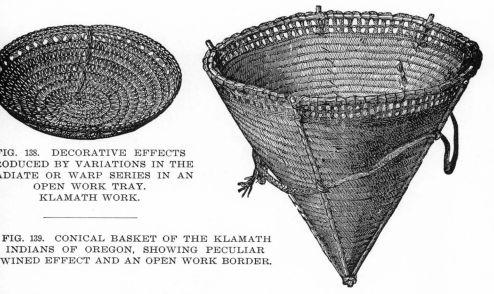

FIG. 138. DECORATIVE EFFECTS RODUCED BY VARIATIONS IN THE DIATE OR WARP SERIES IN AN OPEN WORK TRAY. KLAMATH WORK.

FIG. 139. CONICAL BASKET OF THE KLAMATH INDIANS OF OREGON, SHOWING PECULIAR WINED EFFECT AND AN OPEN WORK BORDER.

The examples given serve to indicate the unlimited decorative resources possessed by the art without employing any but legitimate constructive elements, and it will be seen that still wider results can be obtained by combining two or more varieties or styles of binding in the construction and embellishment of a single object or in the same piece of fabric. A good, though very simple, illustration of this is shown in the tray or mat presented in Fig. 124. In this case a border, varying from the center portion in appearance, is obtained by changing one series of the filaments from a multiple to a single arrangement.

The conical basket shown in Fig. 139 serves to illustrate the same point. In this case a rudely worked, though effective, border is secured by changing the angle of the upright series near the top and combining them by plaiting, and in such a way as to leave a border of open work.

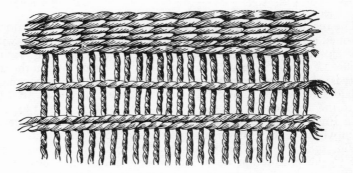

FIG. 140. SIMPLE RETICULATED WEAVE

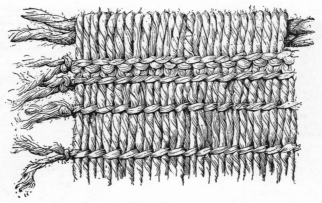

FIG. 141.
PLEASING RESULTS FROM SIMPLE VARIATIONS.

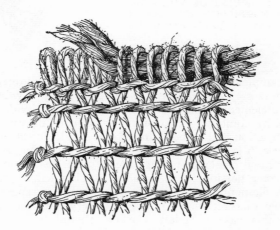

FIG. 142. FURTHER VARIATION.

It may not be out of place here to show three specimens of reticulated weaving bearing somewhat upon this subject. Fig. 140 is a piece of simple reticulated weaving taken from an impression upon an ancient piece of pottery obtained in Tennessee. It will readily be seen that Figs. 141 and 142 are variations, easily made, from the simple form, yet both producing new and pleasing results.

Appended ornaments are not amenable to the geometric laws of fabrication to the extent observed in other classes of ornament. They are, however, attached in ways consistent with the textile system, and are counted and spaced with great care, producing designs of a more or less pronounced geometric character. The work is a kind of embroidery, the parts employed being of the nature of pendants.

These include numberless articles derived from nature and art. It will suffice to present a few examples already at hand.

FIG. 144. CALIFORNIA INDIAN BASKET WITH PENDANTS OF BEADS AND BITS OF SHELL.

FIG. 143. APACHE BASKET WITH PENDANT BUCKSKIN STRANDS TIPPED WITH BITS OF TIN.

Fig. 143 illustrates a large, well made basket, the work of the Apache Indians. It serves to indicate the method of employing tassels and clustered pendants, which in this case consist of buckskin strings tipped with conical bits of tin. The checker pattern is in color.

Fig. 144 illustrates the use of other varieties of pendants. A feather decked basket made by the northwest coast Indians is embellished with pendant ornaments consisting of strings of beads tipped with bits of bright shell. Many others of these may be seen in Figs. 50, 95, 98 to 102, 103, &c.

I have already spoken of color in a general way, as to its necessary presence in art. My object now is to indicate the part it takes in textile design, its methods of expression, the processes by which it advances in elaboration, and the part it takes in all geometric decoration.

It will be necessary, in the first place, to examine briefly the normal tendencies of color combination while still under the direct domination of constructive elaboration. In the way of illustration, let us take first a series of filaments, say in the natural color of the material, and pass through them in the simplest interlaced style a second series having a distinct color. A very simple geometric pattern is produced, as shown in Fig. 145. It is a sort of checker, an emphasized presentation of the relievo pattern shown in Fig. 127, the figures running horizontally, vertically. and diagonally. Had these filaments been accidentally associated in construction, the results might have been the same, but it is unnecessary to indicate in detail the possibilities of adventitious color combinations. So far as they exhibit system at all it is identical with the relievo elaboration.

Assuming that the idea of developing these figures into something more elaborate and striking is already conceived, let us study the processes and tendencies of growth. A very slight degree of ingenuity will enable the workman to vary the relation of the parts, producing a succession of results such, perhaps, as indicated in Fig. 146. In this example we have rows of isolated squares in white which may be turned hither and thither at pleasure, within certain angles, but they result in nothing more than monotonous successions of squares.

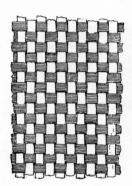  

FIG. 145.
PATTERN PRODUCED
BY INTERLACING
STRANDS OF
DIFFERENT COLORS.

FIG. 146.
PATTERN PRODUCED
BY INTERLACING
STRANDS OF
DIFFERENT COLORS.

FIG. 147. ISOLATED FIGURES
PRODUCED BY MODIFYING
ORDER OF INTERSECTION.

Additional facility of expression is obtained by employing dark strands in the vertical series also, and large, isolated areas of solid color may be produced by changing the order of intersection, certain of the fillets being carried over two or more of the opposing series and in contiguous spaces at one step, as seen in Fig. 147. With these elementary resources the weaver has very considerable powers of expression, as will be seen in Fig. 148, which is taken from a basket made by South American Indians, and in Fig. 149, where human figures are delineated. The patterns in such cases are all rigidly geometric and exhibit stepped outlines of a pronounced kind. With impacting and increased refinement of fillets the stepped character is in a considerable measure lost sight of and realistic, graphic representation is to a greater extent within the workman's reach. It is probable, however, that the idea of weaving complex ideographic characters would not occur to the primitive mind at a very early date, and a long period of progress would elapse before delineative subjects would be attempted.

For the purpose of looking still more closely into the tendencies of normal textile decorative developement I shall present a series of Indian baskets, choosing mainly from the closely woven or impacted varieties because they are so well represented in our collections and at the same time are very generally embellished with designs in color; besides, they are probably among the most simple and primitive textile products known. I have already shown that several types of combination when closely impacted produce very similar surface characters and encourage the same general style of decoration. In nearly all, the color features are confined to one series of fillets—those of the woof—the other the warp, being completely hidden from view. In the preceding series the

FIG. 148. PATTERN PRODUCED BY SIMPLE ALTERNATIONS OF
LIGHT AND DARK FILLETS.

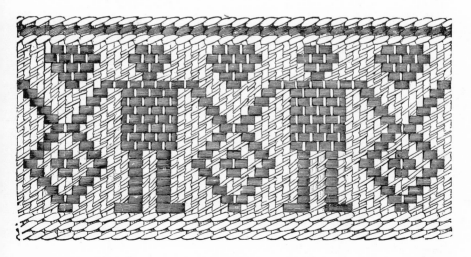

FIG. 149.
CONVENTIONAL HUMAN FIGURES FROM AN ANCIENT PERUVIAN BASKET.

warp and woof were almost equally concerned in the expression of design. Here but one is used, and in consequence there is much freedom of expression, as the artist carries the colored filaments back and forth or inserts new ones at will. Still it will be seen that in doing this he is by no means free; he must follow the straight and narrow pathway laid down by the warp and woof, and, do what he may, he arrives at purely geometric results.

I will now present the examples, which for the sake of uniformity are in all cases of the coiled ware. If a basket is made with no other idea than that of use the surface is apt to be pretty uniform in color, the natural color of the woof fillets. If decoration is desired a colored fillet is introduced, which, for the time, takes the place and does the duty of the ordinary strand. Fig. 150 serves to show the construction and surface appearance of the base of a coil made vessel still quite free from any color decoration. Now, if it is desired to begin a design, the plain wrapping thread is dropped and a colored fillet is inserted and the coiling continues. Carried once around the vessel we have an encircling

FIG. 150. BASE OF COILED BASKET SHOWING THE METHOD OF BUILDING BY DUAL COILING. The base or warp coil is composed of untwisted fibre, and is formed by adding to the free end as the coiling goes on. The woof, or binding filament, as it is coiled is caught into the upper surface of the preceding turn.

FIG. 151. COILED BASKET WITH SIMPLE GEOMETRIC ORNAMENT. WORK OF THE NORTHWEST COAST INDIANS.

line of dark color corresponding to the lower line of the ornament seen in Fig. 151. If the artist is content with a single line of color he sets the end of the dark thread and takes up the light colored one previously dropped and continues the coiling. If further elaboration is desired it is easily accomplished. In the example given the workman has taken up the dark fillet again and carried it a few times around the next turn of the warp coil; then it has been dropped and the white thread taken up, and again, in turn, another dark thread has been introduced and coiled for a few turns, and so on until four encircling rows of dark alternating rectangles have been produced. Desiring to introduce a meandered design he has taken the upper series of rectangles as bases and adding colored filaments at the proper time has carried oblique lines one to the right and the other to the left, across the six succeeding ridges of the warp coil. The pairs of stepped lines meeting above were joined in rectangles like those below, and the decoration was closed by a border line at the top. The vessel was then completed in the light colored material. In this ornament all forms are bounded by two classes of lines, vertical and horizontal (or, viewed from below, radial and encircling), the lines of the warp and the woof. Oblique bands of color are made up of series of rectangles, giving stepped out-

FIG. 152. YOKUT COILED BASKET WITH ENCIRCLING BANDS OF ORNAMENT IN WHITE, RED AND BLACK UPON A YEL-LOWISH GROUND.

lines. Although these figures are purely geometric, it is not imposs-ible that in their position and grouping they preserve a trace of some imitative conception modified to this shape by the forces of the art. They serve quite as well, however, to illustrate simple mechanical elab-oration as if entirely free from suspicion of associated ideas.

FIG. 153. PIMA COILED BASKET WITH TWO BANDS OF MEANDERED ORNA-MENT.

In Fig. 152 I present a superb piece of work executed by the Indians of the Tule River, California. It is woven in the closely impacted, coiled style. The ornament is arranged in horizontal zones and consists of a series of diamond shaped figures in white with red centers and black frames set side by side. The processes of substitution where changes of color are required are the same as in the preceding case and the forms of figures and the disposition of designs are the same, being governed by the same forces.

Another choice piece, from the Pima Indians of Arizona, is given in Fig. 153. The lines of the ornament adhere exclusively to the directions imposed by the warp and the woof, the stripes of black color ascending with the turns of the fillet for a short distance, then for a time following the horizontal ridges, and again ascending, the complete result being a series of zigzag rays set very close together. These rays take an oblique turn to the left, and the dark figures at the angles, from the necessities of construction, form rows at right angles to these. A few supplementary rays are added toward the margin to fill out the widening spaces. Another striking example of the domination of technique over design is illustrated in Fig. 154.

FIG.   154. PIMA   COILED   BASKET WITH ORNAMENT ARRANGED
IN ZIG-ZAG RAYS.

Two strongly marked, fret-like meanders encircle the vessei, the elements of which are ruled exclusively by the warp and woof, by the radiate and the concentric lines of construction. This is the work of the Pima Indians of Arizona.

I shall close the series with a very handsome example of Indian basketry and of basketry ornamentation (Fig. 155). The conical shape is highly pleasing and the design is thoroughly satisfactory and, like all the others, is applied in a way indicative of a refined sense of the decorative requirements of the utensil. The design is wholly geometric, and, although varied in appearance, is composed almost exclusively of dark triangular figures upon a light ground. The general grouping is in three horizontal or encircling bands agreeing with or following the foundation coil. Details are governed by the horizontal and the oblique structure lines. The vertical construction lines have no direct part in the conformation of the design excepting in so far as they impose a stepped character upon all oblique outlines.

Now, as primitive peoples advance from savagery to barbarism there comes a time in the history of all kinds of textile products at which the natural technical progress of decorative elaboration is interfered with by forces from without the art. This occurs when ideas, symbolic or otherwise, come to be associated with the purely geometric figures, tending to arrest or modify their development, or again, it occurs when the artist seeks to substitute mythologic subjects for the geometric units. This period cannot be always well defined, as the first steps in this direction are so thoroughly subordinated to the textile forces. Between what may be regarded as purely technical, geometric ornament and ornaments recognizably delineative, we find in each group of advanced textile products a series of forms of mixed or uncertain pedigree. These must receive slight attention here.

Fig. 156 represents a large and handsome basket obtained from the Apache. It will be seen that the outline of the figures comprising the principal zone of ornament departs somewhat from the four ruling directions of the textile combination. This was accomplished by increasing the width of the steps in the outlines as the dark rays progressed, resulting in curved outlines of eccentric character. This eccentricity, coupled with the very unusual character of the details at the outer extremities of the figures, leads to the surmise that each part of the design is a conventional representation of some life form, a bird, an insect, or perhaps a man.

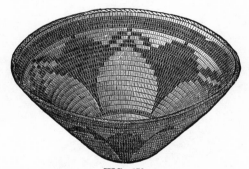

FIG. 156.
APACHE COILED BASKET ORNAMENTED WITH DEVICES PROBABLY VERY HIGHLY CONVENTIONALIZED MYTHOLOGICAL SUBJECTS.

By the free introduction of such elements textile ornament loses its pristine geometric purity and becomes in a measure degraded. In the more advanced stages of Pueblo art the ornament of nearly all the textiles is pervaded by ideographic characters, generally rude suggestions of life forms, borrowed, perhaps, from mythologic art. This is true of much of the coiled basketry of the Hopi Indians. True, many examples occur in which the ancient or indigenous geometric style is preserved, but the majority appear to be more or less modified. In many cases nothing can be learned from a study of the designs themselves, as the particular style of construction is not adapted to realistic expression, and, at best, resemblances to natural forms are very remote. An example is given in Fig. 35. I shall expect, however, when the art of these peoples is better known to learn to what particular mythic concept these mixed or impure geometric devices refer.

The same is true of other varieties of Hopi basketry, notably the common decorated wickerware, two specimens of which are given in Figs. 157 and 158. This ware is of the interlaced style, with radially arranged web filaments. Its geometric characters are easily distinguished from those of the coiled ware. Many examples exhibit purely

FIG. 155. McCLOUD COILED BASKET, WITH GEOMETRIC ORNAMENT
COMPOSED OF TRIANGULAR FIGURES.

FIG. 157. ORAIBI TRAY OF INTERLACED WICKER WEAVING, SHOWING
GEOMETRIC ORNAMENT, PROBABLY MODIFIED BY IDEOGRAPHIC
ASSOCIATION.

conventional elaboration, the figures being arranged in rays, zones, checkers, and the like. It is to be expected, however, that the normal ornament of this class of products should be greatly interfered with through attempts to introduce extraneous elements, for the peoples have advanced to a stage of culture at which it is usual to attempt the introduction of mythologic representations into all art.

Non-essential constructive features.—Now, all the varied effects of color and design described in the preceding paragraphs are obtained without seriously modifying the simple necessary construction, without resorting to the multiple extraordinary devices within easy reach. The development and utilization of the latter class of resources must now receive attention. In the preceding examples, when it was desired to begin a figure in color the normal ground filament was dropped out and a colored one set into its place and made to fill its office while it remained; but we find that in many classes of work the colored elements were added to the essential parts, not substituted for them, although they are usually of use in perfecting the fabric by adding to serviceability as

FIG. 158. ORAIBI WICKER BASKET OF INTERLACED STYLE OF WEAVING, SHOWING GEOMETRIC ORNAMENT, PROBABLY MODIFIED BY IDEOGRAPHIC ASSOCIATION.

well as to beauty. This is illustrated, for example, by the doubling of one series or of both warp and woof, by the introduction of pile, by wrapping filaments with strands of other colors, or by twisting in feathers. Savage nations in all parts of the world are acquainted with devices of this class and employ them with great freedom. The effects produced often correspond closely to needle-work, and the materials employed are often identiceal in both varieties of execution.

The following examples will serve to illustrate my meaning. The effects seen in Fig. 159 are observed in a small hand wallet obtained in Mexico. The fillets employed appear to be wide, flattened straws of varied colors. In order to avoid the monotony of a plain checker certain of the light fillets are wrapped with thin fillets of dark tint in such a way that when woven the dark color appears in small squares placed diagonally with the fundamental checkers. Additional effects are produced by covering certain portions of the filaments with straws of distinct color, all being woven in with the fabric. By other devices

certain parts of the fillets are made to stand out from the surface in
sharp points and in ridges, forming geometric figures, either normal
or added elements being employed. Another device is shown in Fig.
160. Here a pattern is secured by carrying dark fillets back and forth
over the light colored fabric, catching them down at regular intervals
during the process of weaving. Again, feathers and other embellishing
media are woven in with the roof. Two interesting baskets procured
from the Indians of the Northwest coast are shown in Figs. 161 and
162. Feathers of brilliant hues are fixed to and woven in with certain
of the woof strands, which are treated, in the execution of patterns,
just as are ordinary colored threads, care being taken not to destroy the

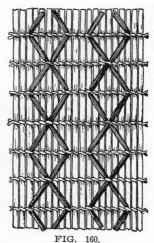

FIG. 159.

FIG. 160.

Ornament produced by wrapping
certain light fillets with darker ones
before weaving. Mexican work.

Ornamental effect secured by weaving in series of dark fillets, forming
a superficial device. Work of the
Klamath Indians.

beauty of the feathers in the process. The richly colored feathers lying
smoothly in one direction are made to represent various figures necessarily geometric.

At a very early stage of culture most peoples manifest decided artistic
tendencies, which are revealed in attempts to depict various devices,
life forms, and fancies upon the skin and upon the surfaces of utensils, garments, and other articles and objects. The figures are very
often decorative in effect and may be of a trivial nature, but very
generally such art is serious and pertains to events or superstitions.
The devices employed may be purely conventional or geometric, containing no graphic element whatever; but life forms afford the most
natural and satisfactory means of recording, conveying, and symbol-
izing ideas, and hence preponderate largely.

An illustration is drawn from a fine example of the basketry of the
Yokut Indians of California. The two figures of Fig. 163 form part of
a spirally radiating band of ornament, which is shown to good advantage in the small cut of the complete basket in Fig. 164. It is of the
coiled style of construction. The design is worked in four colors and
the effect is quiet and rich. A fuller description of this beautiful basket

will be found accompanying Fig. 236. Remarkably similar to this, is an ancient Peruvian basket, woven from rushes. The base and rim of the basket are woven in the intertwined combination, but in the decorated belt the style is changed to the plain right angled interlacing, for the reason, no doubt, that this combination was better suited to the development of the intended design. Besides the fundamental series of fillets, the weaver resorted to unusual devices in order to secure certain desired results. In the first place the black horizontal series of filaments does not alternate in the simplest way with the brown series,

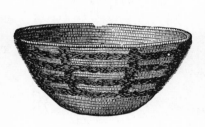 

FIGS. 161, 162. FINE CALIFORNIA BASKETRY, ORNAMENTED
WITH FEATHER WORK.

but, where a wide space of the dark color is called for, several of the brown strands are passed over at one step, as in the head and body, and in the wider interspaces the dark strands pass under two or more of the opposing strands. In this way broad areas of color are obtained. It will be observed, however, that the construction is weakened by this modification, and that to remedy the defect two additional extra con-

FIG. 164. FIGURES ON A YOKUT BASKET.

structive series of fillets are added. These are of much lighter weight than the main series, that they may not obscure the pattern. Over the dark series they run vertically and over the light obliquely.

It will be seen in Fig. 149 that the result, notwithstanding all this modification of procedure, is still remarkably like that of the preceding examples, the figures corresponding closely in kind and degree of geometricity.

The fact is that in this coarse work refinement of drawing is absolutely unattainable. It appears that the sharply pronounced steps exhibited in the outlines are due to the great width of the fillets used.

FIG. 163. CONVENTIONAL FIGURES
FROM A CALIFORNIA INDIAN BASKET.

FIG. 165. HUMAN FIGURE MODIFIED BY EXECUTION IN
CONCENTRIC INTERLACED STYLE OF WEAVING.

That the range of results produced by varying styles of weaving and of woven objects may be appreciated, I present some additional examples. Coiled wares, for instance, present decorative phenomena strikingly at variance with those in which there is a rectangular disposition of parts. Instead of the two or more interlacing series of parallel fillets exhibited in the latter style, we have one radiate and one concentric series. The effect of this arrangement upon the introduced human figure is very striking, as this will be seen by reference to Fig. 165 which represents a large tray obtained from the Hopi Indians. The figure probably represents one of the mythologic personages of the Hopi pantheon or some otherwise important priestly functionary, wearing the charactistic head-dress of the ceremony in which the plaque was to be used. The work is executed in wicker, stained in such bright tints as were considered appropriate to the various features of the costume. Referring in detail to the shape and arrangement of the parts of the figure, it is apparent that many of the remarkable features are due to constructive peculiarities. The round face, for example, does not refer to the sun or the moon, but results from the concentric weaving. The oblique eyes have no reference to a Mongolian origin, as they only follow the direction of the ray upon which they are woven, and the head-dress does not refer to the rainbow or the aurora because it is arched, but is arched because the construction forced it into the shape. The proportion of the figure is not so very bad because the Hopi artist did not know better, but because the surface of the tray did not afford room to project the body and limbs.

In the attempt to reproduce bird or other forms of basketry, strange and marvelous results are obtained—strange in their appearance, marvellous in that any artist, however crude, could see in those results any resemblance to the object she desired to portray. Yet it is in this way complex and singular designs of direct symbolic and ideographic meaning have arisen. Professor Holmes illustrates this with the conventional pattern of a Hopi plaque or tray, Fig. 166. He says:

"We have difficulty in recognizing the bird at all, although the conception is identical with the preceding. The positions of the head the legs and the expended wings and tail correspond as closely as possible, but delineation is hampered by technique. The peculiar construction barely permits the presentation of a recognizable life form, and permits it in a particular way, which will be understood by a comparison with the treatment of the human figure in Fig. 165. In that case the interlaced combination gives relievo results, characterized by wide radiating ribs and narrow, inconspicuous, concentric lines, which cross the ribs in long steps. The power of expression lies almost wholly with the concentric series, and detail must in a great measure follow the concentric lines. In the present case (Fig. 166) this is reversed and lines employed in expressing forms are radiate.

"The precise effect of this difference of construction upon a particular feature may be shown by the introduction of another illustration In Fig. 167 we have a bird woven in a basket of the interlaced style We see with what ease the long sharp bill and the slender tongue (shown by a red filament between the two dark mandibles) are expressed. In the other case the construction is such that the bill, if extended in the normal direction, is broad and square at the end, and the tongue, instead of lying between the mandibles, must run across the bill, total-

FIG. 166. FIGURE OF A BIRD EXECUTED IN COILED HOPI TRAY,
TEXTILE DELINEATION.

FIG. 167. FIGURE OF A BIRD WOVEN IN INTERLACED WICKER
AT ONE SIDE OF THE CENTER.

ly at variance with the truth; in this case the tongue is so represented, the light vertical band seen in the cut being a yellow stripe. It will be seen that the two representations are very unlike each other, not because of difference in the conception and not wholly on account of the style of weaving, but rather because the artist chose to extend one across the whole surface of the utensil and to confine the other to one side of the center.

"It is clear, therefore, from the preceding observations that the convention of woven life forms varies with the kind of weaving, with the shape of the object, with the position upon the object, and with the shape of the space occupied, as well as with the inherited style of treat-

FIG. 167a.—YOKUT WOMAN CARRYING A LOAD OF FRUIT.

ment and with the capacity of the artist concerned. These varied forces and influences unite in the metamorphosis of all the incoming elements of textile embellishment."

As a fitting conclusion to this chapter I commend to my readers the following pregnant utterance:

"The first woman making a change in any natural object for the gratification which it afforded her is the starting point of three evolutions: that of art itself, whether textile, plastic, or musical; of herself in the practice of it, growing out of a mere imitator to be a creator: of the universal or public appreciation of art, of what might be called the racial or the tribal imagination."—Mason.

FIG. 168. TULE RESERVATION WEAVER USING ACORN SIFTER.
Copyright by George Wharton James.

FIG. 169. GRANARIES OF SOUTHERN CALIFORNIA INDIANS.

CHAPTER X.

SOME USES OF INDIAN BASKETS.

Being the chief carrying utensil of the Amerind, the basket, necessarily, has assumed many and varied forms to correspond with the many and varied uses for which it was desired. Hence a multiplicity of forms and uses exist. Among the tribes of Southern California there are bowls, saucers, and flat plaques. Then there are dainty shapes

From The Traveler, San Francisco.

FIG. 170. CAHUILLA, SABOBA, ETC., BASKETS IN THE COLLECTION OF GEORGE WHARTON JAMES.

where the sides narrow toward the top and make a graceful form—an enclosed bowl shape, so common with all California tribes. There is even variety in this "enclosed bowl" shape. Some are made flat at the bottom and then narrow towards the top, with almost vertical sloping sides; others are shaped with an almost flat bottom, the sides rounding out and then narrowing towards the top. This gives the latter the shape of a pumpkin with the top cut off. There are ovals almost flat and also with the sides shaped in the two styles of the circular bowls just described.

Another common form is the milk pan, a most convenient and useful shape. Still another is that of the inverted sugar-cone. This is used by many tribes as a hat, over which the band of the "reda" or carrying net, is placed.

A small bowl-shaped basket, without a bottom, is also placed on the top of their "Ka-wa-wohl" (see Fig. 26)—a granite grinding stone or mortar—thus preventing the seeds, grain or acorns from escaping while being ground or pounded. The basket is fastened to the granite by a layer of pinion gum, which sticks the two almost as perfectly as if they had grown together.

In addition to these: "There are the prettily woven nest for the pappoose; the large plaque-shaped basket on which the Indians gamble with dice made of walnut-shells, halved, filled with brea (tar) into which

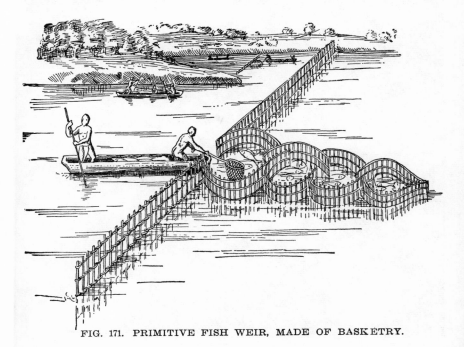

FIG. 171. PRIMITIVE FISH WEIR, MADE OF BASKETRY.

wampum is pressed; the queer conical basket in which burdens are borne on the back; the bottle-necked basket, beloved of connoisseurs; baskets that serve as wardrobes; "pitched" baskets in which water is carried; deep bowl-shaped baskets, in which water is heated for cooking by the throwing in of hot stones; grain sifters, tobacco pouches and many others."

Grace Ellery Channing thus sums up some of the shapes: "Great bell-shaped black and white ones; tall, delicate, vase-like shapes; odd ones like hour-glasses broken abruptly; some small and dainty like a lady's bonbonnierre; others flat and like tiny saucers for sweet-breathed violets."

The cradle has its own peculiar shape, and the harvesting wand is unlike anything else the basket makers have produced. The water bottles of the Desert Indians have their distinctive shape, and the trinket baskets of the Yokut and Poma are entirely different from the yucca floor or sleeping mats of the Pueblos. The kathak of the Havasupai is an improvement upon the wood basket of the Poma, and the exquisite shaped bottle basket of the so-called Mission Indian is a marvelous advance upon the crude willow work of the Hopi.

And all these forms have their motif in the uses to which design or accident led them.

Fig. 171 is a representation, from Hariot, of a fish-weir made of crude basketry and used in prehistoric and later times in Virginia. Slender poles set in the shallow water were held in place by wattling or interlacing of pliable parts.

Teit says the Thompson Indians of British Columbia use their baskets for storage, carrying and other useful purposes. "Large oblong baskets with lids are used for storing food and clothing. Smaller

FIG. 172. CONICAL SHAPED BASKET OF THOMPSON INDIANS.

ones of the same kind serve, for holding sewing materials and trinkets. Their lids slide up and down on a string, which at the same time serves as a handle. Recently the lids have been hinged to the baskets. The most common kind of basket is the conical shape shown in Fig. 172, and is used for carrying. Still another kind which is rounded, or, as the Indian says, nut-shaped, was formerly used for holding water. Round, open baskets served as kettles, the food being boiled by throwing hot stones into it. Such food is generally served in the basket in which it is cooked, and is either supped out of the basket or poured into small bark cups. Still another kind of basket has a flat back, which is made to hang against the post or wall. In shape it is similar to the fish basket used by anglers. Such baskets are used for holding tobacco and pipes, a hole in the center of the lid allowing the pipe-stem to protrude. At one time they were much used for holding bait and fishing tackle, for which reason they were called 'used for bait.' Some Indians

FIG. 173. POMA WITH RUDE WOOD BASKET.

belonging to the Lytton band used the same kind of baskets for saddle-bags."

"Large open baskets made of cedar twigs, of the same shape as those used by the Lower Lillooet and the Coast tribes, were also made by the Lower Thompson Indians. They were used for carrying fish. Very few of them are used at the present day." They are of coarse weave somewhat similar to the crude carrying basket shown in Fig. 173.

It was natural that as soon as basketry became a general art, cradles for the carrying of their babies should be made by the early basket makers. These are of rude willow work. The child is strapped to the main portion of the carrying cradle, and a piece of calico or blanket is thrown over the semi-circular head piece, to protect the child from the fierce rays of the sun. Fig. 174 is one of these cradles, made

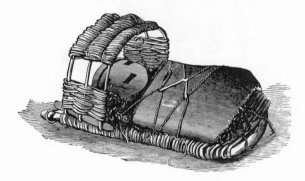

FIG. 174. ZUNI TOY CRADLE AND DOLL.

by a Zuni mother for her child to play with, and a rude, wooden doll may be seen within, strapped exactly as is a child in the real cradle.

In her own poetic fashion Mrs. Carr thus wrote of these baby cradles: "Alone in the forest, or beside some rippling stream, the Indian mother received into her bosom the little brown creature who made her slavery endurable. Its basket nest, cunningly wrought after the fashion of a butterfly's cradle was fastened to a small frame of wicker-work. (Fig. 16.) Taught by the oriole, she lined the nest with down of milk-weed and soft fibres; but prouder or less wary than the bird, she decorated it outwardly with bright feathers and strings of tiny shells. When she travelled the precious basket was strapped to her back, and she never parted with it until the baby died, the empty basket being then hung above its grave. When at home the baby basket was usually fastened to the nearest tree, where, with never a cry, the little bead eyes followed the moving clouds and fluttering leaves into the land of dreams, while the mother moulded her acorn bread in a basket tray, or cooked her dinner in a deep, round basket into which heated stones were thrown to serve the purpose of fuel."

The Modok women make a very pretty baby basket of fine willow work, cylinder shaped, with one half of it cut away, except a few inches at the ends. It is intended to be set up against a tree or carried on the back, hence the infant is lashed perpendicularly in it, with its

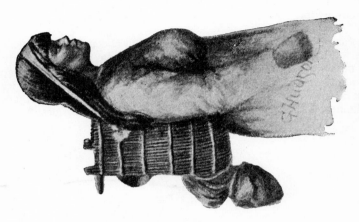

FIG. 175. POMA MOTHER WITH CHILD IN CARRYING CRADLE.

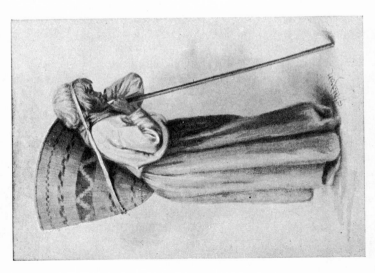

FIG. 176. POMA WOMAN WITH CARRYING BASKET.

feet standing out free at one end and the other end covering its head like a small parasol.   In one, this canopy is supported by small standards spirally wrapped with strips of gay-colored calico, with looped and scalloped hangings between.   The little fellow is wrapped all around like a mummy, with nothing visible but his head, and some times even that is bandaged back tight so that he may sleep standing.   From the manner in which the tender skull is thus bandaged back, it occasionally results that it grows backward and upward at an angle of about forty-five degrees.

The painstaking which the Modok squaw expends on her baby basket is an index to her maternal love.   On the other hand, squaws of

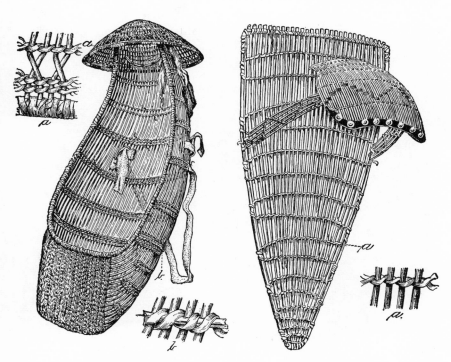

FIGS. 177, 178, 179.   FIGS. 180, 181.
HUPA INDIAN CRADLE BASKET. PYRAMID LAKE UTE CRADLE.

other tribes often set their babies in deep conical baskets, leaving them loose and liable to fall out.   If such a squaw makes a baby basket it is totally devoid of ornament, and one tribe, the Miwok, contemptuously call it the "dogs' nest."   It is among Indians like these that we hear of infanticides.

Figs. 177, 178 and 179 show a cradle basket and methods followed in weaving, of the Hupas of North-Western California.   A slipper-shaped open-work basket of osier warp, and twined weaving constitutes the body of the cradle.   It is woven as follows: Commencing at the upper end, the small ends of the twigs are held in place one-eighth inch apart by three rows of twined weaving followed by a row in which an extra strengthening twig is whipped or sewed in place.   At intervals of two and a half to three inches rows of twined basketry, every alternate series having one of the strengthening twigs, increasing in thickness downward. The twigs constituting the true bottom of the so-called slipper continue to the end of the square toe and are fastened off, while those that form the sides are ingeniously bent to form the vamp of the slipper. This part of the frame is held together by rows of twined weaving boustrophedon. When two rows of this kind of twining lie quite close, it has the appearance of four ply plaiting, and has been taken for such by the superficial observer. The binding around

 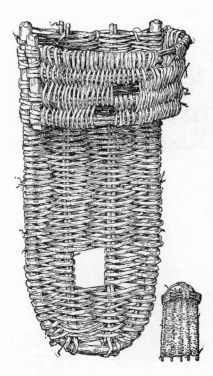

FIG. 182. HOPI WICKER CRADLE WITH AWNING.   FIGS. 183, 184. HOPI WICKER CRADLE WITH AWNING.

the opening of the cradle is formed by a bundle of twigs seized with a strip of tough root. The awning is made of open wicker and twined basketry bound with colored grass.

In the United States National Museum there is a cradle for a new born babe from the McCloud River Indians, of California, belonging to the basket tray type. It is shaped very much like a large grain scoop, or the lower half of a moccasin, and made of twigs, in twined weaving. There are double rows of twining two inches, or such a matter, apart, and nearly all of them are boustrophedon, which gives the appearance of four ply braid.

Figs. 180 and 181 show a Ute cradle from Pyramid Lake, Nevada, with twined weaving, and demonstrates the modifying influences of the nearby California peoples.

Of the cradle baskets of the Paiutis found on the Northern "rim" of the Grand Canyon of the Colorado River, Major J. W. Powell writes as follows: "Mothers carry their babes curiously in baskets. They make a wicker board, by plaiting willows, and sew a buckskin cloth to either edge, and this is fulled in the middle, so as to form a sack, closed at the bottom. At the top, they make a wicker shade, like 'my grandmother's sun-bonnet,' and, wrapping the little one in a wild-cat robe, place it in the basket, and this they carry on their backs, strapped over their forehead, and the little brown midgets are ever peering over their mother's shoulders. In camp, they stand the basket against the trunk of a tree, or hang it to a limb."

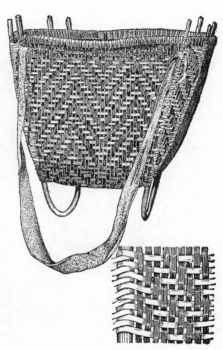

FIGS. 185, 186, 187. SIAMESE WICKER CARRYING BASKETS, BORNE IN PAIRS WITH SHOULDER POLE.

FIGS. 188, 189. CARRYING BASKET OF ARIKARA (CADDOAN) INDIANS.

Fig. 182 is a Hopi wicker cradle made at Oraibi. The important elements it displays are the floor and the awning. The floor is of the ox-bow type, having the bow at the foot and the loose ends projecting upward as in the Yokaia and other California frames. This cradle frame is covered with wicker of unbarked twigs, four rows on the floor and four on the awning. The warp of the floor is formed of series having two twigs each. There is a great variety in the delicacy, the number of warp strands, and the minor details in the Hopi cradle floors. Indeed, while they are all alike in general marks, there are no two alike in respect to patterns.

The awning is still more varied. Fundamentally it is a band of

wicker basketry longer than the cradle is wide, its ends securely fastened to the frame sides by lashings of yucca fibre or string.   Here and
there stitches are omitted so as to effect an open work ornamentation.
An additional strip frequently passes at right angles from the apex of
the awning at the upper edge to the floor of the frame at its upper end,
as shown in the diminutive Fig. 184.

Fig. 183 is a cruder and simpler form made by the same people.
Both styles are in use at the present time, but Fig. 182 is the type of
those most general.

The use of baskets for carrying heavy loads was a natural outcome
of their earliest development.   However the first basket was made, it
would readily be suggested to the most immature and sluggish of minds

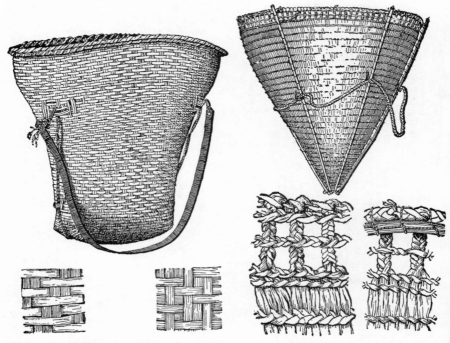

FIGS. 190, 191, 192. CHOCTAW CARRYING   FIGS. 193, 194, 195.
BASKET AND VARIATIONS IN WEAVE.   CONICAL CARRYING BASKET WITH
                                       RODS AND PLAITED HEAD BAND

that a number of small objects could be confined in a large basket and
thus carried to and fro with ease.   Its use for this purpose is world-wide.
Fig. 185 shows a wicker carrying basket, used in the oriental kingdom
of Siam.   It consists of a pole and two baskets.   Each end of the pole
pierces a basket from side to side, holes having been provided for this
purpose.   The material of this structure is split rattan done in wicker
work.   Cords are provided for packing the load and blocks of wood are
attached to the bottom of each basket to protect the weaving.   Figs.
186 and 187, at the bottom of the larger engraving, show how the
bearer carries the two baskets, and also the simple weave of the wicker
work.

Of a style somewhat similiar in shape and general construction to carrying baskets of the Hopi and Zunis, though of much finer workmanship is the old carrying basket of the Arikaras, (Fig. 188). These Indians live in Dakota and are of the Panian or Caddoan stock. The basket is quadrilateral, widest on the top and longer than wide. Four bent poles constitute the frame, each one forming the basis of a side or end. The end ones, much like ox-yoke bows, project below the others to form a rest for the basket. At the top the ends of the poles are held in place by means of a loop. The weaving is diagonal in narrow strips of birch and other tough bark, varying in color, and the method of producing the wavy design is revealed in Fig. 189.

Fig. 190 is a form of carrying basket quite common among the Choctaw Indians of Louisiania. It is a hamper holding a bushel or

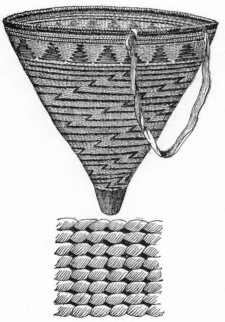

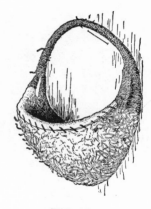

FIG. 199.
Forehead Pad Worn by
the Hupa (Athapascan)
Indians of California.

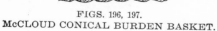

FIGS. 196, 197.
McCLOUD CONICAL BURDEN BASKET.

more, wider at top than at bottom. It is made of the common cane, split and woven by diagonal weaving, as shown in Figs. 191 and 192, the universal method among the Southern tribes of the United States upon all baskets whatever. The head band of leather is attached to the sides of the basket.

Fig. 193 is a conical carrying basket used by the Clallam Indians at Pyramid Lake, Nevada. It shows how the savage inventor converted the soft wallet of the north into the hard cone of the south. The web of the basket is from rushes united by twine weaving, by braiding, and by the plaiting of a single filament, as shown in Figs. 194 and 195. This soft, open net-work is converted into a light but strong cone by the insertion of a hoop into the top and the fixing of six vertical rods at the hoop at equal distances, uniting their ends at the bottom of the cone, and sewing them to the texture of the wallet inside.

Fig. 196 is a burden basket used by the McCloud River Indians of Shasta Co., California. In the Clallam basket just noted, the head band encircles the cone about the middle, raising the load high on the back, after the manner of the Oriental water carriers.

The California woman has abundance of rhus, hazel, willow, pine root, and other rigid material and may decorate the surface with different fern stems, straw, and dyed splint. So she makes her baskets in twined weaving, having rigid switches or small stems for her warp. But in this Central California region there is a device of strengthening the texture not sufficiently explained in the drawing. It is, in fact, the union of what has been called the twined stitch, shown in Fig. 197, with the bird-cage stitch.

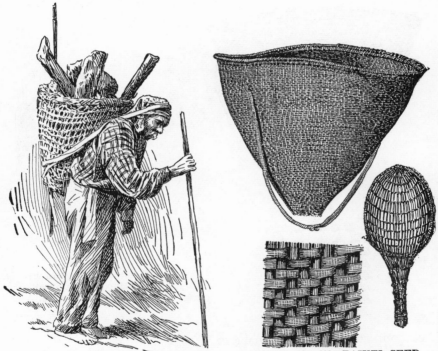

FIG. 198. POMA MAN CARRYING WOOD IN CONICAL BASKET.

FIGS. 200, 201, 202. PAIUTI SEED BASKET AND GATHERING WAND.

There are three elements: 1. The fundamental or vertical warp of twigs; 2. Across this at right angles a horizontal subsidiary warp of twig carried around in the process of weaving, and, 3, a web or weft of twined weaving uniting the two. Dr. Hudson, whose great knowledge has often been drawn on in these pages, calls attention to the fact that all the northern stitches culminate in the Sacramento Valley and parts adjacent, and that the Yokaian stock are very adept at this composite style of texture. The top of this basket is strengthened by a hoop, to which the carrying band is attached. The bottom is strengthened by close weaving.

The Poma Indians use a conical basket for carrying, held on the back in a sling (Fig. 198), the head band of which passes over the carrier's brow. Dr. Hudson once saw an old woman carry three bushels of potatoes in this manner through rain and mud to her home two miles distant. Greater loads are not unusual to the men, and as a consequent result of such customary labor the Poma Indian is abnormally developed in the dorsal and the anterior cervical muscles, besides having a chest magnificent in proportions. This applies also to the Cahuilla, the Havasupai, Paiuti and other Indians, who, like the Poma are accustomed to carry large burdens on the back with the carrying band over the forehead.

Fig. 199 is an elaborately constructed head band worn by the Natano band of Hupa Indians, Athapascan stock, living on the reservation of the same name (spelled Hoopah, however) in Northern California. It consists of a loosely woven, visor-like pad to fit on the forehead, and is

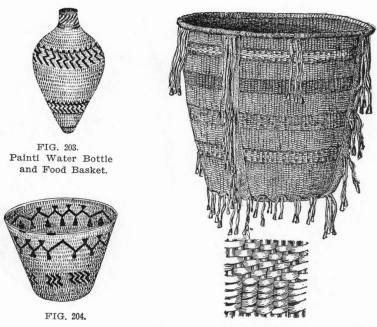

FIG. 203.
Painti Water Bottle
and Food Basket.

FIG. 204.

FIGS. 207, 208. APACHE ORNAMENTED CARRYING
BASKET.

held in place by a rope made of the warp of the pad, sewed with twine made from the native hemp. This apparatus is first placed on the head, and then the head band of the load or of the tracking line is worn over it. It must be remembered that the Hupas are the kinfolks of the Carrier Indians of Canada and Alaska.

Figs. 200, 201, 202, are a Paiuti seed basket and gathering wand. The Paiutis are part of the Great Shoshonean family which occupies the territory from the northern border of Mexico to Costa Rica. This, and all similar baskets of the Paiutis are made of split osiers, rhus stems, and the scions of other plants not identified worked into twined weaving, Fig. 201, leaving a very rough surface on account of the harshness of the material. Once in a while a narrow band of black varies the monotony. But generally the carrying baskets have a uniform hue and texture.

In the days before the advent of the white man the Paiutis and many other kindred peoples were gleaners of all sorts of grass seeds; the women went out with these baskets, stood them on the point behind a bunch of goose foot or other plant, with the fan or wand, Fig. 202, knocked the seeds into the cone until it was full, hung the load on their backs by means of the headband, and carried it home. The contents were winnowed, ground, and cooked by the same industrious women.

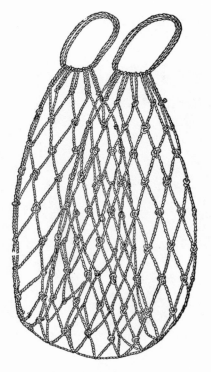 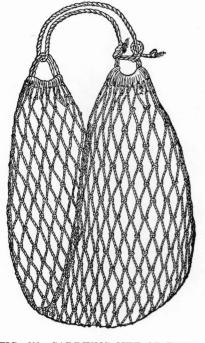

FIG. 205. CARRYING NET MADE OF   FIG: 206. CARRYING NET OR REDA
   AGAVE FIBER, USED BY THE   USED BY THE MISSION INDIANS
   TEMECULA INDIANS OF   OF CALIFORNIA.
   CALIFORNIA.

Even to this day here and there, in isolated regions, one may find the aboriginal women thus collecting seeds. In the mountain valleys near Mount San Jacinto, and on the plateaux surrounding Havasu (Cataract Canyon) where dwell the Havasupais I have often seen this gathering of wild seeds.

Mr. F. V. Coville thus describes the same process: "The Panamint woman, of Death Valley, California, of Shoshonean stock, in harvesting the sand-grass seed (Oryzopsis membranacea) carries in one hand a small funnel-shaped basket and in the other a paddle made of wicker work, resembling a tennis racket. With this she beats the grass panicles over the rim of the basket, causing the seeds to fall inside. When the basket becomes filled she takes it on her back, holding it in place with her two hands brought over her shoulders, or by means of a soft band of buckskin across her forehead."

And he thus describes the gathering of the pine nuts:

"In early autumn the women beat the cones of the pine (Pinus monophylla) from the trees, gathered them in baskets, and spread them out to dry. As soon as the cones had cracked, the primitive

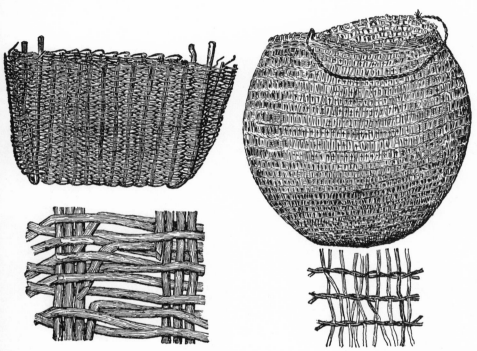

FIGS. 209, 210. HOPI OR ZUNI GATHERING CRATE OR CARRYING BASKET.

FIGS. 211, 212. BASKET FOR CARRYING CACTUS (PRICKLY PEARS) USED BY THE DIEGUENOS (YUMAN) INDIANS OF SOUTHERN CALIFORNIA.

harvester beat out the nuts, raked off the cones, and gathered her crop, which she carried on her back to a dry place among the rocks, where she made a cache for her spoils. When she was ready to serve them she put them into a shallow basket with some coals, and shook the mass around until the nuts were roasted. Thus prepared, she had her lord and her little family either shell and munch them without further preparation, or she ground them in a wooden mortar with a stone pestle, to be eaten dry or made into soup. Every other edible seed this practical botanist gathered and roasted in the same way."

Fig. 203 is of a basket bottle made by Painti Indians, who occupy the western edge of Nevada, near to the Eastern foot hills of the Sierra Nevada. Fig. 204 is of a basket bowl made by the same people. Though the former are intended to be covered with pinion gum to make them waterproof the weavers seem to find delight in working into them various striking and attractive designs, this one having three distinct circles of the conventionalized lightning.

The upper design on Fig. 204 is somewhat unique. It represents the wavy line of mountains and valleys, common with many weavers, but on the summits of the mountains are rain clouds, and reaching down beyond into the valleys are water-courses terminating in lakes.

Figs. 205 and 206 are of redas, or carrying nets, of the Mission Indians of California. The latter is marked Temecula, who are Shoshonean, and the former is of the Cahuilla people who are of Apache stock. Each of these is a strip of open netting with fixed meshes,

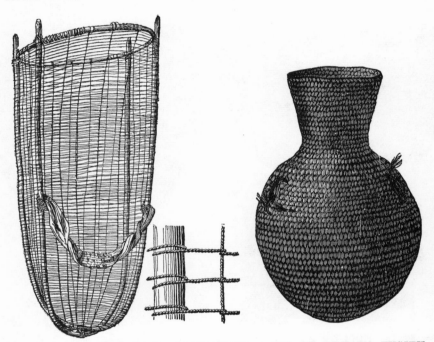

FIGS. 213, 214. CARRYING BASKET, WRAP-
PED WEAVING, USED BY THE MOHAVE
INDIANS OF ARIZONA.

FIG. 217. NAVAHO TUSJEH
OR WATER BOTTLE MADE
BY THE PAIUTIS.

gathered up at the ends into an eyelet or loop like a hammock, and provided with a carrying rope of the same kind. The nets are of bast fibre, probably Apocynum. The knots are sometimes the standard mesh knot, "bowline on a bight," in a nautical phrase, and sometimes square. It is this reda that suggested the net pattern on the rigid baskets woven by the Mission Indians, illustrations of which are given elsewhere.

The Apaches of Arizona make a modified conical basket, handsomely woven and ornamented of which Fig. 207 is a fair example. The material and stitch are precisely those of the Utes, but there are three noticeable features. The basket is oblong, like a northern pack; the surface is decorated by plain colored and checkered bands, and hanging from the top and the bottom are fringes of buckskin, at the ends of which are the false hoofs of deer and bits of tin rolled up. The small square below, Fig. 208, shows how the variations of stitch produce ornamentation effect.

Fig. 209 is a specimen of crude Hopi or Zuni work and is built upon corner bows and warp of three sticks together; the filling is in wicker and the ends are fastened off very neatly by tucking them in, as is shown by Fig. 210.

Fig. 211 is a basket used for carrying cactus fruit and other coarse substances, and is made by the Dieguenos, Mission Indians, of the villages in San Diego County. As will be seen, it is in twined weaving of the rudest sort, a globose wallet, strikingly similar in shape to the great pottery ollas made and used by the neighboring tribes. The noteworthy character about this basket is the occurrence of twined weaving (which is enlarged in Fig. 212) so far south. On the testimony of the basket collections in the National Museum and elsewhere there does not exist a tribe south of this line that practices it.

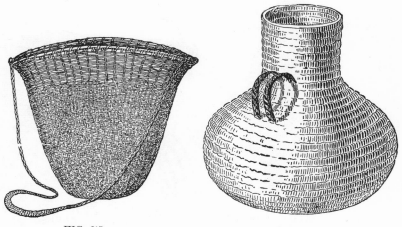

FIG. 215.
CONGO CARRYING BASKET.

FIG. 216.
ZUNI BASKET WATER BOTTLE.

Fig. 213 is regarded by Professor O. T. Mason as one of the most interesting specimens of basketry in the world. It is the carrying frame and net of the Mohave Indians, of the Yuman stock, dwelling about the mouth of the Colorado River in Arizona. They live largely upon the mesquite bean, which they gather, pod and all, and grind for bread. Two poles eight feet long bent in the form of an ox-bow and crossing each other at right angles form the ground w

place by lashing at the bottom and by a hoop a
strong twines of agave fibre pass from the ho
of the framework between each pair of uprigh
rights constitute the warp. The weft is a new t
the Pacific Coast called "wrapped" weaving, a
trated in Fig. 214. A single twine is coiled rou
making meshes into the warp half an inch wide
passes the warp strings or poles, it is simply
The roughness of the agave fibre holds the v

preserves a tolerably uniform mesh. Foster in his "Prehistoric Races" describes the finding of cloth in a mound in Butler County, Ohio, and figures a specimen in which the twines are wrapped in the same manner. The head band is a rag tied to two of the upright sticks. Somewhat similar in weave and material to the rude Hopi work above described is Fig. 215 which is a carrying basket used on the French Congo. In this specimen the common wicker work is used; that is, a rigid warp and a flexible filling.

The kathak, or carrying basket of the Havasupais is well shown in the engraving, Fig. 1. This kathak is woven in the same style as the water bottles of the Havasupais, and from the horse hair loops a broad carrying band of strong raw hide is brought across the forehead. This method of carrying is common with all the Indian tribes of the southwest. It will be noticed that there are two loops or "lugs." The carry-

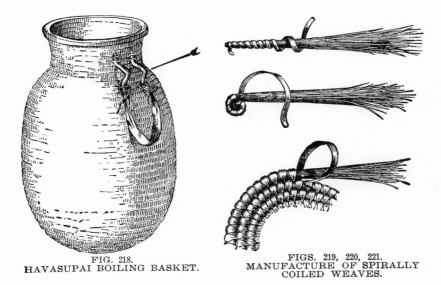

FIG. 218.
HAVASUPAI BOILING BASKET.

FIGS. 219, 220, 221.
MANUFACTURE OF SPIRALLY
COILED WEAVES.

ing band goes from the one on the left around the head to the one on the right, and thus the kathak is held steadily and kept from swinging to and fro as would be the case if but one lug were used.

Most of the Arizona and New Mexico tribes, having to travel over long stretches of almost waterless desert, use water bottles made of basketry. These are manufactured by the Havasupais, Zunis, and the Paiutis of Nevada and Utah. Those of which Fig. 216 is a type are generally made at Zuni. One of the most valued water bottles of my collection is a very old one, made and purchased at Zuni.

Fig. 217 is a water bottle basket, originally labeled by Dr. James Stevens in the National Museum as a Walpi basket. But though purchased at the Hopi village of Walpi this style of basket bottle is made by the Paiutis and by them traded to the Hopi, the Navahoes, and through the latter, to the Apaches. This is the most common form of r bottle found in Arizona. The weave is coarse but firm and and being heavily coated inside and out with pinion gum it is r tight and durable. I have a large number of these Paiuti water bottles in my collection, of all sizes, from a pint to three gallons. What a series of problems confronted the prehistoric woman, when she first began to learn the properties of fire. The roasting of flesh was comparatively easy, but how was she to make water hot, cook the fluid foods she had already learned to make. She invented the boiling

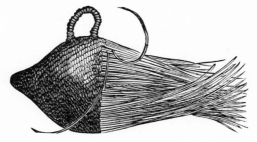

FIG. 222.
Method of Making Havasupai Water Bottles.

basket, into which, after pouring her liquid, uncooked food, she dropped heated rocks, and thus conveyed fire into her pot, instead of her pot to the fire.

Some of the Havasupais still use the boiling basket, and only as late as 1899 I had the pleasure of eating delicious green corn mush

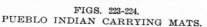

FIGS. 223-224.
PUEBLO INDIAN CARRYING MATS.

FIG. 225.
PUEBLO INDIAN USING
CARRYING MAT.

cooked in this ancient fashion. One of these baskets is shown in Fig. 218. It is bottle shaped, and on its neck two loops are woven, from which depends a rawhide strap handle.

Cushing thus describes the method followed in weaving these baskets, and it is a clear description of most coiled weave. "In the manu-

FIG. 226. INTERIOR OF HOPI HOUSE, SHOWING DOMESTIC USES OF BASKETS.

facture of the boiling baskets, which are good examples of the helix or spirally coiled type of basket, the beginning was made at the center of the bottom. A small wisp of fine flexible grass stems or osiers softened in water was first spirally wrapped a little at one end with a flat, limber splint of tough wood, usually willow (see Fig. 219). This wrapped portion was then wound upon itself, the outer coil thus formed (Fig. 220) being firmly fastened as it progressed to the one already made by passing the splint wrapping of the wisp each time it was wound around the latter through some strands of the contiguous inner coil, with the aid of a bodkin. (Fig. 221.) The bottom was rounded upward and the sides were made by coiling the wisp higher and higher, first outward, to produce the bulge of the vessel, then inward, to form the tapering upper part and neck, into which the two little twigs or splint-loops were firmly woven." See (a) Fig. 218.

FIG. 227. SAUCER-SHAPED BASKET (UNDOUBTEDLY HAVASUPAI).

Fig 222 shows the style of weave followed by the Havasupais in making their basket water bottles. The warp is of unpeeled and unsplit willows of a thickness to correspond to the size the bottle is intended to be. The woof filaments are sometimes split and sometimes not, and either peeled or unpeeled. As soon as the bottle nears completion in weaving, it is covered with a mixture of red ochre and some slightly oleagineous substance, just as painters "prime" a building they are going to paint, with a coating of a mixture of oil, ochre and white lead. Then it is covered inside and out with pinion gum and thus becomes strong, durable and perfectly water tight. Such bottles last for many years and will endure all kinds of hardships.

An annular mat, used for balancing water ollas and other heavy and convex bottomed vessels on the head, is woven by all the Pueblo peoples from the coarse fibres of the yucca (yucca baccata). The fibres are split and plaited as in making a whip. The mats assume different shapes, the two most comon being shown in Figs. 223 and 224. Just as the Irish milkmaid catches up a kerchief or cloth and by a quirk or two converts it into a ring or crown which she places on her head before setting thereon the brimming pail, so the Pueblo Indian throws upon her head one of these mats before lifting thereupon the heavy food-bowl or heavier water olla. The same ring serves also in keeping the jar upright on the floor of her room. Coronado (1540) wrote to the Viceroy in Mexico: "I send your lordship two rolles which the women in these parts are woont to weare on their heads when they fetch water from their wells, as we used to do in Spain; and one of these Indian women with one of these rolles on her head will carry a pitcher of water, without touching the same, up a lather." The method of using them is illustrated in Fig. 225.

FIG. 228. HANDSOMELY ORNAMENTED APACHE BASKET BOWL.

The flat saucer shaped baskets of the Pimas, Maricopas, Apaches, Havasupais and many others show undoubtedly one of the first of all basketry forms. As the artistic faculty increased in power, practice brought increased dexterity and skill, and some of the baskets made before the decadence of the art, (which began with the advent of the Spaniards) are exquisitely beautiful in the perfection of their weave and truly artistic in their designs.

Figs. 227 and 228 might have been made by any of the people above named, although from the finishing border I incline to the belief that 227 is not an Apache, as suggested by Dr. Stevenson, but either a Paiuti or a Havasupai. The Apache and Pima baskets of finest weave, made to-day, are generally finished off with a fine overwrapping stitch as shown in 228. The plaited stitch as I have before described of 227 is common to Navahoes, Havasupais and Paiutis. In an examination of scores of Apache baskets, including the fine collection at the Museum of Natural History, and those in the National Museum I have found but one that is not finished off by the overlapping simple coil stitch. And that one though labeled an Apache and obtained on the Apache reservation is unquestionably a Havasupai brought there by trading or capture.

Murdoch found among the Point Barrow Eskimo small work-baskets (aguma, ama, ipiaru, as they call them), of which Figs. 229 and 230 serve as types. The neck of Fig. 229 is of tanned sealskin, 2½ inches long, and has one vertical seam, to the middle of which is sewed the middle of a piece of fine seal thong a foot long, which serves to tie up the mouth. The basket appears to be made of fine twigs or roots

FIGS. 229, 230. BASKETS OF ATHAPASCAN STOCK FOUND AT POINT BARROW.

of the willow, with the bark removed, and is made by winding an osier spirally into the shape of the basket, and wrapping a narrow splint spirally around the two adjacent parts of this, each turn of the splint being separated from the next by a turn of the succeeding tier.

Fig. 230 was obtained from Sidaru, a small Eskimo village near Point Belcher. The weave of both is similar to that of the Apaches, and, as the owner of Fig. 229 said it came from the "great river" of the South, Murdoch concludes that they were made by the Indians of the region between the Koynkuk and Silawik Rivers, who are of the Tinne or Athapascan family, to which, also, the Apaches belong. They undoubtedly reached Point Barrow through channels of trade or barter.

Large Basket in the Collection of Mrs. Jewett, Lamanda Park.

CHAPTER XI.

VARIOUS INDIAN BASKETS.

A strictly rigid adherence to the various heads of the preceding chapters has been impossible, as the subjects are so inseparably connected. But as far as possible I have sought to elucidate each branch of the subject. The following pages illustrate various types and weaves of basket. They will help the collector and student to a fuller knowledge of the work of the different peoples. Many of the descriptions are given verbatim from Professor O. T. Mason's report.

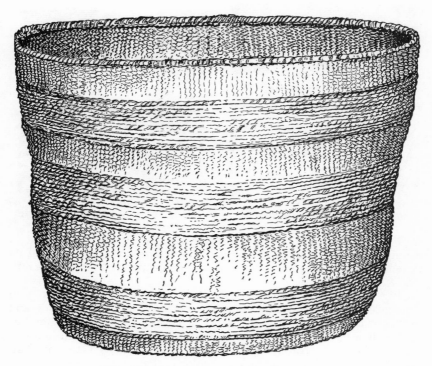

FIG. 232. KLAMATH TWINED BASKET.

Fig. 232 is a twined or plaited flexible basket of the Klamaths, made of rushes and straw. The management of the material is precisely as in wallets made by the Eskimo. The three elevated bands upon the outside are formed by rows of twine set on externally. The border in this case is formed by binding down the warp straws and sewing them fast with traders' twine. By twining a dark and a light colored straw, two dark or two light straws, and by varying the number of these monochrome or dichrome twines, very pleasing effects in endless variety are produced.

Fig. 233 is one square inch of Fig. 232, showing the appearance of the body weaving above and of the ornamental twining below.

Fig. 234 is one of the coiled and whipped baskets of the Hoochnoms, and was collected at Eel River, California, in 1876. It is made of thin strips peeled from one of the ¬oots found in the region. The bottom is started upon a small, flat Turk's-head knot or splint ⅜ of an inch in diameter, and continued in a plane outward 4 inches in diameter before any ornament is attempted. The coils are ⅛ inch in cross-section and there are twenty stitches to the inch. There are three pairs of the ornament on the exterior all alike. The harmony of geometric design produced by inverting the triangles on the alternate sides is much more expressive in the specimen where the brown-black ornament is in contrast with the dark wood color of the body.

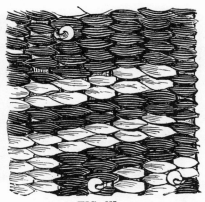

FIG. 233.
ONE SQUARE INCH OF FIG. 232.

FIG. 235.
ONE SQUARE INCH OF FIG. 234.

Fig. 235 is one square inch of Fig. 234, showing the method of coiling with various colored splints. The weave of this basket and its general appearance is much like Fig. 56, fine, smooth, even and beautiful.

Fig. 236 is the inside of a Yokut bowl, one of the finest baskets in existence. It is a truncated cone, sixteen and a half inches wide and seven and a half inches deep. It was collected by the eminent ethnologist, Stephen Powers, in 1875, in California, and now holds an honored place in the U. S. National Museum. The bottom is plain and flat, bounded by a black line. The body color is that of pine root long exposed; the ornaments are in black, straw color, and brown. To understand this complex figure we must begin at the bottom, where five barred parallelograms surround the black ring, with center of brown, and generally four smaller bars of white and black alternating. By a series of steps or gradines this rectangular ornament is carried up to the dark line just below the rim. The spaces in the body color, at first plain, are occupied afterwards by open crosses, and finally by human figures. These human figures are excellent illustrations of that constraining and restraining power of material and environment so ably discussed by Professor Holmes in an earlier chapter. There are eight coils and eighteen stitches to the inch in this work.

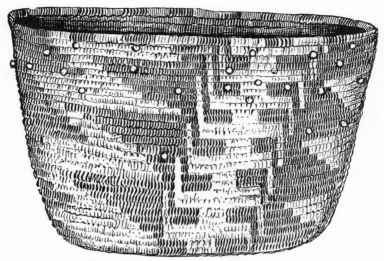

FIG. 234. HOOCHNOM COILED BASKET.
COLLECTED AT EEL RIVER, CALIFORNIA.

FIG. 236. YOKUT COILED BASKET BOWL.

Fig. 237 is a coiled basket bowl of the Cahuillas. The coil is a bundle of yucca or other fibre, and the sewing is done with splints of reed cane, chestnut and black. The lovely cloudy effects produced by the ingenious use of splints of different natural colors resemble those on the Hopi sacred meal trays. The fastening off is simple coil sewing. The ornamentation is a series of crosses arranged vertically and four series of rhomboids inclosing triangles.

Fig 238 is one inch of Fig. 237, showing the multiple coil and the method of stitching.

Fig. 239 presents an inside view of Fig. 237. The black line at the bottom, nearly continuous, incloses a circle in uniform unvarnished color. All the body color above this line is of a shining yellow, varying in shade. The disposition of the ornament is better shown in this illustration than the preceding one.

FIG. 238. ONE SQUARE INCH OF FIG. 237.

Fig 240 is a similarly made basket of the Cahuillas, in which the shading of the body material is, in places, very dark. The methods of making these colored splints is fully explained in the chapter on color. The zig-zag ornaments, an imitative representation of arrow points, are very effective.

Fig. 241 is a jar-shaped coiled basket from the Zuni Indians of New Mexico. This is a very beautiful specimen of coiled ware for this region, in shape, regularity of stitch, and ornamentation in black. It is a common saying among true experts that the pottery-making Indians are not good basket-makers. There is no doubt that this statements is broadly true. Professor Mason suggests that this basket "looks as though it might have come from California." It may have come from the Apaches, for in shape, ornamentation, and, especially in the use of the strip of fibre for "chinking" as seen in Fig. 242, it reminds one of the work of these accomplished basket-makers.

Fig. 242 is a square inch of Fig. 241, showing the use of the chinking fibre and the alternation of white and black stitches.

Fig. 243 is a coiled basket bowl of the Pimas, built on yucca fibre and sewed with rhus or willow. The ornamentation is in red paint and splints dyed black. The border is back and forward sewing to imitate a braid. Its depth is 3 inches.

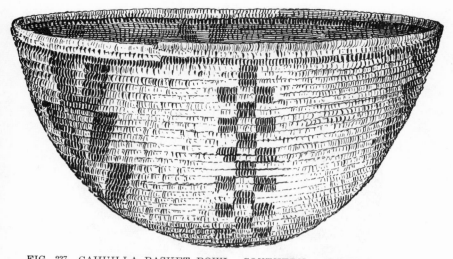

FIG. 237. CAHUILLA BASKET BOWL. SOUTHERN CALIFORNIA.

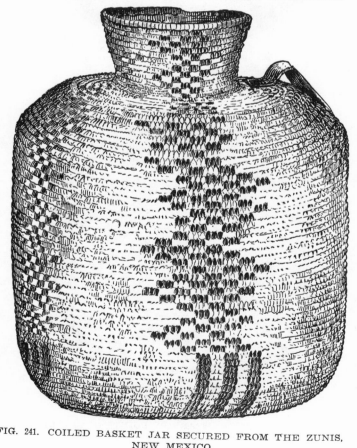

FIG. 241. COILED BASKET JAR SECURED FROM THE ZUNIS,
NEW MEXICO.

FIG. 239. INSIDE VIEW OF FIG. 237.

FIG. 240. A CAHULLA BASKET BOWL.
A REPRESENTATION OF ARROW POINTS IN THE DESIGN

Fig. 244 is a coiled basket bowl of the Pimas, made up on a foundation of yucca, the sewing done with splints of willow or pine. The ornamentation is rude, but exceedingly interesting. On showing it to a Pima Shaman he affirmed that it was made by a woman who had visited a family of the Antelope fraternity in one of the Hopi towns, and that this was her attempt to reproduce the male and female lightning symbols of that fraternity. The male symbols have reached and penetrated the earth, represented by the interior dark circle, and have thereby brought the fire of the sun down to the haunts of men.

Fig. 245 is a coiled Pima basket bowl, similar in structure to Fig. 244. The grecque ornament is worked in with tolerable symmetry. The border has the braided appearance before mentioned and quite commonly met with on Pima baskets, given by forward and backward sewing along the border with a single splint. In this instance the stitch passes backward three stitches of the sewing each time. This is ingenious and effective work.

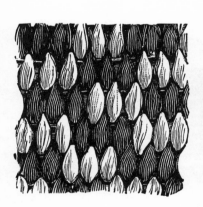

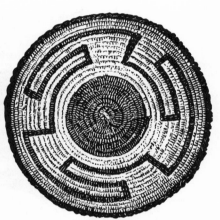

FIG. 242. ONE SQUARE INCH
OF FIG. 241.

FIG. 245. PIMA BASKET WITH
GREEK DESIGN.

Fig. 246 is a coiled bowl of the Apaches, inside view, made upon a single twig. The apparently unsystematic ornament is indeed very regular. Four lines of black sewing of different lengths proceed from the black ring of the center. From the end of all these lines sewing is carried to the left in regular curves. Then the four radiating lines are repeated, and the curved lines, until the border is reached. This is a distinct variant of the Swastika, about which Dr. Wilson has written so learnedly, exhaustively and interestingly. Yet to the Pima woman it was merely a conventionalized representation of a lake with water flowing from it in different directions.

Fig. 247 is an inside view of one of the coiled osier basket bowls of the Garotero Apaches. In every respect of weave and style it resembles Fig. 246. The inclosed triangles alternating with urn patterns constitute the ornamentation. These are conventionalized representations of stone battle hammers and arrow points.

Fig. 248 is a small coiled basket bowl of the Paiutis of Southern Utah and Nevada, made by coiling a splint and thin strip of yucca,

FIG. 244. PIMA BASKET, WITH MALE
AND FEMALE LIGHTNING SYMBOLS.

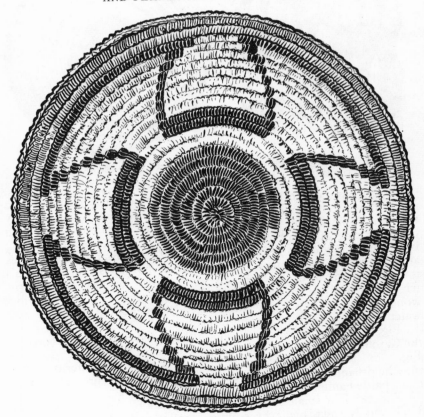

FIG. 243. PIMA COILED BASKET BOWL.

FIG. 246.

APACHE COILED BASKET
BOWL.

FIG. 247.

BASKET BOWL OF THE
GAROTERO APACHES.

FIG. 248.

PAIUTI COILED MUSH
BASKET.

bast, or osier, and whipping them with split osier. The sewing passes over the two elements of the coil in progress and through the upper element of the coil below, looping always under the subjacent stitches. Ornamentation is produced by working into the fabric triangles with strips of martynia or dyed splints. The work is very regular and the texture water-tight. The design represents butterflies.

Fig. 249 is a similarly woven basket. It is founded upon a wooden plug in the center and coiled by means of an osier and a strip of fibre. Its depth is 2½ inches. The work is neatly done, and there is some resemblance in its ornamentation to Fig. 248, yet the steps represent rain clouds.

These baskets (Figs. 248 and 249) are made in the same style and by the same people—the Paiutis—as the so-called wedding baskets of the Navahoes, or medicine baskets of the Apaches, the ornamentation being the only difference.

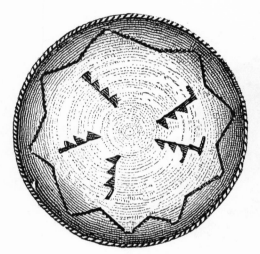

FIG. 249. PAIUTI BASKET.

FIG. 251. ONE SQUARE
INCH OF FIG. 250.

Fig. 250 is a twined basket hat of the Utes or Paiutis of Southern Utah, used by the women either as a hat or a basket. The California women make hats of a somewhat similar pattern, but much finer. The warp twigs converge at the bottom and additional ones are added as the texture widens. The weft splints are carried around in pairs and twined so as to inclose a pair of vertical twigs, producing a twilled effect something like that of the softer ware of the Haidas and Clallams. The border of this twined basket is very ingeniously made. First, the projecting warp sticks were bent down and whipped with splints to form the body of the rim. Then with two splints the weaver sewed along the upper margin, catching these splints alternately into the warp straws below, giving the work the appearance of a button hole stitch. The ornamentation is produced by means of dyed twigs either alone or combined with those of natural color.

The texture of this hat is coarse and rigid, not because the Utes cannot obtain better material, as has been suggested elsewhere, for, now and again, they make baskets as fine as the ordinary ware of the

Yokuts and Pomas. But they are lazy and indifferent generally, and a coarse hat is as good for their purpose as a finer one.

Fig. 251 is one square inch of Fig. 250, showing the method of weaving and administering the colored splints.

Fig. 252 is a twined roasting tray of the Paiutis. The warp is a lot of osiers spread out like a fan. The weaving begins at the bottom by short curves, and progresses by ever widening curves to the outer margin. The rim is made by a double row of the coiled and whipped work. The whole surface is very rough, as in all common Paiuti work, by reason of not twisting the strands when making the twine. There is little or no attempt at ornamentation on this class of objects.

Fig. 253 is a gathering and carrying basket of the same people. It is woven precisely as the hat, Fig. 250, and the roasting tray, Fig. 252. The splints are very fine, but their refractory nature makes the ware coarse. Ornamentation is produced by external twining and by geometric patterns in dyed splints. One Paiuti woman told me that this design was made long, long ago by her mother, as she sat near

FIG. 250. UTE BASKET HAT.

where her husband was making arrow points, and that the triangles are simply these points arranged together in rows of three. Another woman said the design was of the mescal plant from which they obtain one of their principal articles of diet.

Fig. 254 is a harvesting wand of the Paiutis, made of twigs split or whole, bound with yucca fibre. It is a very coarse piece of work, and yet a necessary and useful article. The seeds are struck with this wand into a carrying basket, or Kathak, Fig. 253, and then taken home to be roasted, ground or stored away for winter use.

Fig. 255 is of varied work of the Makah Indians, of the Nutka stock. While this weave is a very simple and primitive one, it is capable of most delicate treatment, and produces exquisite results. It may be called the "fish-trap" style, as it is undoubtedly the lineal descendant of the rude wicker fish-trap.

Figs. 256-7-8 are of the bottle covered with basket work shown in Fig. 255. The ground work is of bast and the ornamentation of red, yellow and black straws sewed on singly after the Makah fashion.

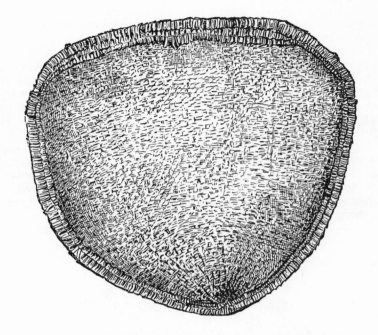

FIG. 252. TWINED ROASTING TRAY OF THE PAIUTIS.

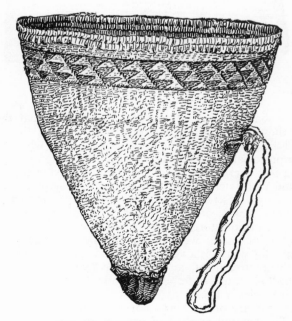

FIG. 253. PAIUTI CARRYING BASKET.

Great numbers of these covered bottles and other fanciful forms are prepared for sale by the Makahs as well as by the Haidas, whose work is similar in external appearance, but not in the method of weaving.

Fig. 257 shows the bottom of Fig. 256, with the radiated warp and the alternation of twined weft with the ordinary in and out weaving.

Fig. 258 is a portion of the side of the bottle, showing the lattice arrangement of the warp, and the twined weft, producing irregular

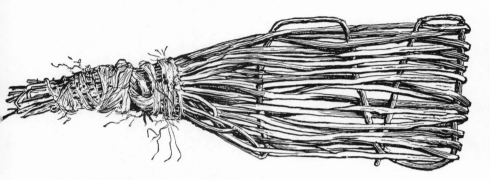

FIG. 254. HARVESTING WAND OF PAIUTIS.

hexagons. This method of producing polygonal meshes, excepting the twined weft, is pursued in great variety and with excellent effect by the Japanese and other oriental peoples.

Fig. 259 is the celebrated "bird-cage" weave of the Makahs. It is a very simple stitch, but exceedingly effective and pretty. It is also used largely by the Clallam Indians of the Salish stock in Washington.

FIG. 255. MAKAH BASKETRY.

FIGS. 256-7-8. BASKETRY AROUND BOTTLE.   MAKAH WEAVE.

Fig. 260 is a carrying basket of this latter people. The framework is a rectangle of large twigs from the corners of which depend four twigs, joining as shown in the figure. To this framework are lashed smaller rods running horizontally and vertically, making a lattice-work with any desirable size of meshes. Finally, spruce-root splints are coiled around the crossings of these lattice-rods. In this particular example the coiling is not continuously around the basket, but on each side separately in boustrophedon, but in the pretty Makah baskets, woven in this style, the coiled thread continues around without break from the beginning to the end of the work. The handles for the attachment of the head-strap are loops of spruce-root cord set on at the corners.

Fig. 261 is one square inch of Fig. 260 and shows the exact disposition of the weave.

Fig. 262 is a fine specimen from the Makahs. It includes the three distinct types, viz.: the plain checker weaving of the Bilhoolas, as shown in Fig. 263, the twined pattern so fully described

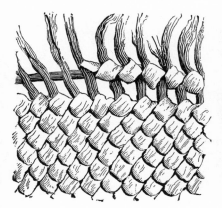

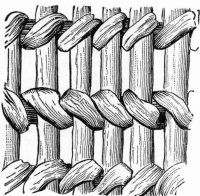

FIG. 259. CLALLAM BIRD CAGE
WEAVE.

FIG. 261. ONE SQUARE INCH OF
FIG. 260.

elsewhere, and also pictured in Fig. 263, and lastly, the bird-cage pattern of the Makahs and Clallams, illustrated in Fig. 249. The ornamentation on this class of baskets, as on the commercial baskets of the Haidas, consists of geometric patterns in black, yellow, drab, reds, blues, etc., colors, many of which are obtained from traders. The straws are dyed and the pattern is alike on both sides.

Interesting as a rude suggestion of this bird-cage basketry pattern is Fig. 264 of a rude carrying or packing basket from Angola, Africa. The bottom is made in form of a mat or head pad. The warp is a series of rods, and the weft is in twined weaving, common in Africa, in Eastern Asia, and in the Pacific States of North America, north of the Pueblo country.

Fig. 265 is a rain hat of twined basketry in spruce-root, from the Haida Indians, reduced to less than one-eighth linear. This is the upper view and shows the method of ornamentation in red and black paint. The device is an epitomized form of a bird, the first step from pictures toward graphic signs. Omitting the red cross on top, the beak, jaws and nostrils are shown above; the eyes at the sides near the top,

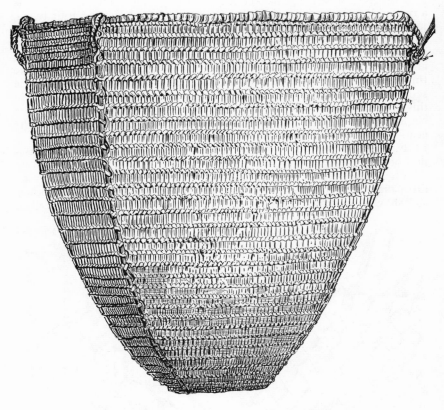

FIG. 260. CLALLAM CARRYING BASKET.

FIG. 262. MAKAH TRINKET BASKET OF FINE WEAVE.

and just behind them the symbol for ears. The wings, feet, and tail, inclosing a human face, are shown on the margin. The Haida, as well as other coast Indians from Cape Flattery to Mount Saint Elias, cover everything of use with totemic devices in painting and carving.

FIG. 263.

FIG. 264. CARRYING CRATE FROM ANGOLA, AFRICA.

Fig. 266 shows the conical shape of Fig. 265. On the inside a cylindrical band of spruce-root is stitched on so as to make the hat fit the wearer's head. A string passed under the chin is frequently added.

Fig. 267 shows the top of this basket hat before painting, with radiating warp, twined weft, and an external twine on its outer boundary.

FIG. 265. HIGHLY ORNAMENTED HAIDA HAT.

FIG. 268. BASKET. USED IN DICE GAMES.

In the dice games of the Arapaho and other tribes, a basket is an essential implement. The players toss up the dice from the basket, letting them drop again into it, and score points according to the way the dice turn up in the basket. The first throw by each player is made from the hand instead of from the basket. One hundred points usually count a game, and stakes are wagered on the result as in almost every other Indian contest of skill or chance. Figs. 268-269 are baskets thus used in dice games. The dice are many and various. Among this tribe they are bone or plum stones. Similar baskets and dice are used by all tribes throughout the West and on the Pacific coast.

FIG. 266.

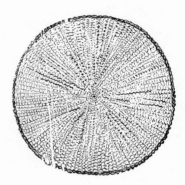

Fig. 267. Haida Hat. Top View Before Painting.

Figs. 104 and 231 are of a large Pauma basket, used as a granary. These immense baskets have long been in use, but few are now to be found. Outside of several Cahuilla homes and at a few other places in Southern California may be seen rude baskets used as acorn store-houses. These are made, however, by twining bunches of willows, in the rudest fashion, and not by any processes of basket weaving, (see Fig. 169).

In Southern California the Indians used to make a basket church. For purposes of worship a circular enclosure was made, tules or willows being woven in basket form somewhat similar to the fences or enclosures found at the village of Saboba to-day. There is still one of these rude basketry churches in use at the Indian village of Santa Ysabel in Southern California.

CHAPTER XII.

SYMBOLISM OF INDIAN BASKETRY.

The recent researches of Fewkes and others have done much to further our knowledge of the symbolism of aboriginal art. Holmes and Cushing long ago demonstrated that there was in this field an almost unlimited fund of unexplored treasure. Little by little we are beginning to reap the harvest of fascinating lore and myth and legend connected with the designs on pottery, basketry, shields, and masks, etc.

As yet basketry symbolism has not had its share of study. In fact, as far as I know, the only articles published upon the subject that have any value are four, one by Dr. Livingstone Farrand, of Columbia University, New York, on the "Basketry Designs of the Salish Indians;" one by Roland B. Dixon in the American Anthropologist on "The Basketry Designs of the Maidu Indians," and two by myself, one in the Traveler of San Francisco, Cal., on "Indian Basketry and its Symbolism," and the other in The Evening Lamp, of Chicago, entitled "Poems in Baskets."

Hence it will be seen that hitherto there have been but few attempts made to penetrate the reserve of the Indian as to the meaning of her basketry designs. It is not easy work, and there are but few fitted to do it. One may live with an Indian basket maker for years and never even know that she attaches any meaning to the designs she incorporates into her work.

The meaning and symbolism of the designs on baskets is certainly one of the most fascinating and important branches of the study, although there are those who emphatically deny that symbolism has any place in the basketry ornamentation of the Amerind. But these persons certainly know little of either the Indian or his methods of work. To all who know him the Indian is remarkable for his poetic conception and equally so for his intense reticence in regard to his inner thoughts. Imagery, symbolism and the picturing of what he sees are habits of his daily life.

That casual observers often arrive at erroneous conclusions as to this and kindred matters all ethnologists and archaeologists well know. For instance: Not long ago I was visiting a tribe of Indians and called upon a lady physician, who, formerly in the Indian service, had lived with this tribe in the capacities of both teacher and physician. When I asked her if she knew anything of the symbolism of their basketry, she said: "No!" and assured me that they attached no meaning, and had no thoughts connected with the designs they incorporated into their work. At the conclusion of my all too brief researches, when I read over to her what I had learned, she confessed that my discoveries were a revelation to her and that never once had a single Indian spoken to her upon the subject, though she was familar with their language, was most kindly received by them and always welcomed to their homes.

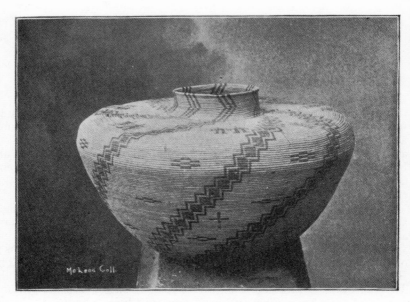

FIG. 270. HEART SHAPED, BOTTLE-NECK BASKET
OF THE YOKUTS. McLEOD COLLECTION.

FIG. 271. THREE BASKETS DEPICTING HUMAN
FIGURES. PLIMPTON COLLECTION.

On this subject Charles Milton Buchanan writes: "The pattern is run at the fancy of the maker. Sometimes the basket maker will possess her own peculiar designs and patterns, which may be recognized anywhere by her tribesmen familiar with her work, and they serve the purpose of a hall mark, revealing at once the identity of the maker. Many of their patterns involve the Greek fret, pure and simple, as well as countless variations worked upon this self-same theme. Then again the barbaric basket maker will attempt to mimic nature with cherry trees, ferns, star-fish, fir-trees, and a thousand and one objects common to their every day life."

The Rev. W. C. Curtis thus writes me upon this subject, referring particularly to the work of the Klickitats and Wascos: "The ornamentation for the most part—as in all the North-west baskets—is conventional; though I have Klickitat baskets with men and horses pictured upon them, also other baskets which depart from the characteristic design in such a way as to make them unique. In the Wascos, besides the conventional designs, (which possibly originated in the desire to imitate waves, mountains and trees on mountains, caves, etc.,) representations of fish, birds, dogs, foxes (wolves or coyotes), deer, frogs, men and women are prominent. Many of their patterns are purely arbitrary, I think, from the beginning, and true knowledge is not served by trying to read into them meaning which the makers never thought of."

The only reliable method of determining the meaning of a basketry design is to obtain a clear explanation from its maker. And this must be done cautiously. With her habitual reserve and fear of being laughed at by the whites, the Indian woman is exceedingly susceptible to suggestion. If you ask her whether her design does not mean this or that, you may with certainty rely upon what the answer will be before it is given. She will respond with a grunt or word of affirmation, and, at the same time, laugh within herself at the folly of the questioner. For, of course, she is "smart" enough to know that if you make the suggestion that the design means so and so, she will be safe if she accept your suggestion.

If the basket is an old one and the maker be dead, one must be content to receive such explanation as the older members of the tribe can give as to the interpretation of its design. Yet it must not be overlooked that the observations of experienced ethnologists insist that these explanations cannot be relied upon. On this subject Farrand says: "It should be noted that most of the designs show variants, and also that what were originally representations of very dissimilar objects have converged in their evolution until the same figure does duty for both,—conditions which result in uncertainty and difference of opinion among native connoisseurs, and consequently, in the conclusions of the ethnologist. Nevertheless, the great majority of the patterns are well recognized under specific names. There are, of course, geometric designs which, so far as all obtainable information goes, are used simply for the decorative value of their lines and angles; but such patterns are usually of great age, and it is quite possible that their representative meaning is lost in antiquity or has only baffled the diligence of the inquirer. The well-known conservatism of the Indian insures the relative permanence of a design, even when its meaning is not recognized."

FIG. 272. COLLECTION OF SOUTHERN CALIFORNIA BASKETS MADE BY THE AUTHOR.

FIG. 273. COLLECTION OF CAHUILLA BASKETS MADE BY MRS. N. J. SALSBERRY AND THE AUTHOR.

He then goes on to state that a Quinaielt basket bore a certain design, a favorite pattern in the tribe, but not the slightest clue to its meaning could be obtained. Its name signifies "standing in the corners of the house," and refers to the fact that in the old days large baskets with this design stood in the corners for the reception of household odds and ends. All informants agreed as to its great antiquity, as well as to the fact that it had doubtless had a meaning at one time, but no amount of inquiry could discover it.

It is not necessary that, in this chapter, I should discuss the growth of the artistic instinct in the Indian, or attempt to show when and how the ideographic art began. That it now actually exists and is exerted in the ornamentation of baskets, there can be no question, but I must not, for one moment, be supposed to affirm that all ornamentation is distinctly and positively ideographic. In his admirable way, Dr. Hudson, when asked as to where the designs of the Indian come from, responded: "Your answer is found in the dentated oak leaf, the angular twig, the curling waterfall, the serrations of mountain tops, and the fins of fish put into conventional form. No artist wants better models than nature's own. Precision in repetition of pattern is a mystery we cannot solve."

(a) SYMBOLISM IN BASKETRY FORMS.

Not only is there a distinct symbolism in the designs woven into the basket, but in some cases the basket itself is a symbol.

Among the Zuni, certain clay water bottles are made in imitation of the human mammae. The pottery maker clearly recognizes a symbolism in these imitative designs. She speaks of water as the milk of adults. The earth is the mother of men, and with water nourishes her children as the mother nourishes her young with the milk from her own breasts. Cushing says he is inclined to the belief that the aperture of this flat-backed, breast-shaped bottle was originally at the nipple, but, being found to leak when furnished with the aperture so low, this was closed. Then, in his inimitable way, the great ethnologist writes: "A surviving superstition inclines me to this view. When a Zuni woman has completed the me-he-ton nearly to the apex, by the coiling process, and before she has inserted the nozzle, she prepares a little wedge of clay, and, as she closes the apex with it she turns her eyes away. If you ask her why she does this, she will tell you that it is a-ka-ta-ni (fearful) to look at the vessel while closing it at this point; that is, if she look at it during this operation, she will be liable to become barren; or that, if children be born to her, they will die during infancy; or that, she may be stricken with blindness; or those who drink from the vessel will be afflicted with disease and wasting away! My impression is that, reasoning from analogy (which with these people means actual relationship or connection), the Zuni woman supposes that by closing the apex of this artificial mamma she closes the exit-way for the 'source of life;' further, that the woman who closes this exit-way knowingly (in her own sight, that is) voluntary closes the exit-way for the source of life in her own mammae; further still, that for this reason the privilege of bearing infants may be taken away from her, or at any rate (experience showing the fallacy of this philosophy) she deserves the loss of the sense (sight) which enabled her to knowingly close the exit-way of the source of life."

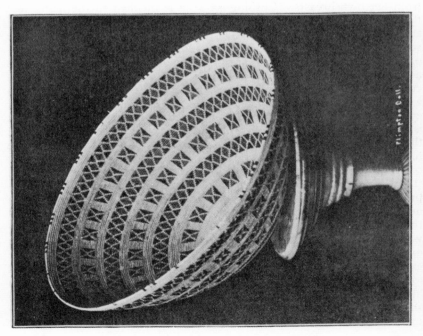

FIG. 274. BASKETRY SPOILED BY VICIOUS IMITATION.

FIG. 275. YOKUT BASKET WITH ST. ANDREW'S CROSS. PLIMPTON COLLECTION.

"The prevalence of the heart shape in the cane baskets of Louisiana is a charming example of Indian symbolism. In their ceremonials baskets were used to hold gifts, and their shape indicated the feeling from which the offering emanated. This is the Indian explanation of the meaning of the shape, but it is interesting to connect it with the realization of animal forms, so strongly marked in the art remains of

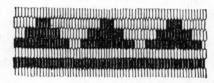

FIG. 276. TYPICAL BASKET DECORATION.

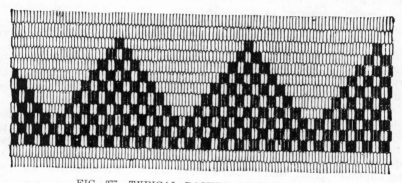

FIG. 277. TYPICAL BASKET DECORATION.

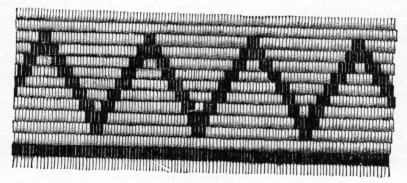

FIG. 278. TYPICAL BASKET DECORATION.

the mound-builders of the middle Mississippi Valley, for it may be some lingering mark of their influence. They represented living forms in a very wonderful way for savages, and though they left only art remains to tell their story, it is one of thrilling interest."—C. S. Coles.

This recognition of a symbolism in the object itself is borne out by Teit in his valuable monograph on the Thompson Indians. He says that lances are often painted with the figure of a skelton. The symbolism as given by the Indians is obvious. Stone war axes represent woodpeckers, the point of the axe to be as powerful in piercing skulls as the beak of the woodpecker the trees.

This symbolism is manifested in the yucca plaques made by the Hopi women of the middle mesa. In accordance with those unwritten laws which are the result of the superstitious fears of the Hopi, singular customs are observed in the "finishing off" of these yucca or amole made baskets and plaques. In those made by marriageable virgins the inner grass is allowed to "flow out," as it were, so that the baskets have an unfinished appearance as shown in the unfinished basket in the weaver's hands, Fig. 108. This is termed the "flowing gate." With married women, capable of bearing children, the ends of the grass are allowed to flow out, but they are cut off about an inch or so from the last stitch of the coil which confines them. This is called the "open gate." In the case of widows and married women, who, for any reason, are incapable of bearing children, the inner grass is "tapered down," and carefully wrapped over with the amole until it is covered and completely finished off. This is called the "closed gate."

It will be obvious that these different methods symbolize the physical condition of the maker of the basket, but the reason for observing these singular customs may not be so obvious. Conversation with several intelligent and friendly Hopis has gradually made clear the thoughts and fears of this superstition. With all the Pueblo people it is a noticeable psychological fact that any fancied resemblance, connection or analogy is taken by them to denote actual relationship and connection. By a process of reasoning, which to us seems as peculiar as it is simple and logical to them, it follows that the virgin basket-maker who closes up the "gate" in finishing the basket renders herself incapable of bearing children. This would mean a life of loneliness and sorrow, for what man would marry a woman incapable of joying his heart with the presence of healthful children? Hence, to preclude the possibility of this dreaded fate, a Hopi virgin is most observant and scrupulously particular to avoid any conscious action, which, by any chance, could be interpreted by the "Powers Above" to denote her willingness to be childless.

The married woman is blessed with children, consequently, while the gate is open, the ends of the grass may be shorter than in the former case, while the barren woman or widow is allowed to "close the gate," —complete the basket—as with her there is no hope of maternity.

As far as my researches have gone these are the only clear instances I have found in which "form" is a symbol, but I am satisfied that further investigations will produce much interesting material in this branch of the subject.

(b) DEVELOPMENT OF SYMBOLISM IN BASKET DESIGNS.

What were the inciting causes that led the aboriginal woman onwards and upwards from the lower plains of mere utility in her basketry to the hill sides of the art, where form, color and pattern display conscious exercise of the art instinct, deliberate thought and plan?

It is possible, as is later argued, that the first steps taken were accidental. In preparing the splints some may have been of a slightly different color from others. When worked into the fabric this difference would be noticed, and, either from curiosity or a desire to imitate, the original effect produced would be duplicated. Once started, the variations produced by color led the weaver along many paths, all of them novel, interesting and pleasing.

Another decisive step was taken when the primitive weaver consciously desired to produce beauty by uniformity of stitch. To prepare the splints so that they were all of exactly the same width, then to weave them according to perfect measurement—this was excellent art training for eye and hand.

This step, combined with the presumed accidental discovery of color values, led to the most wonderful progress. In seeking to imitate the pleasing effects introduced by color the weaver found it necessary to make some kind of measurements. Her eye might generally be relied upon, but as pleasure in accuracy increased she must find some method of absolutely determining where her color work must come in, and where left out. This made of woman, first, a measurer, and then, a counter. Here was the dawn of mathematics to the aboriginal worker. She learned the value of distance, and the inerrancy of numbers.

FIG. 279.

FIG. 280.

The monotony of regular stitches too, taught her further. Each stitch made of splints of uniform size occupies exactly the same area of space; five stitches, five times as much. With these facts clearly in mind she began to alternate her sets of stitches, then to increase or diminish them, and the discovery of geometric figures and designs was the result. Once the geometric door was opened there was no limit to the many and various excursions that could be made. Three white, four brown stitches, ad. lib., produced certain effects. Then on the next round the number was reversed; it was four white and three brown. On the following round five white, and two brown, and so on. And from these simple discoveries she gained pyramids, frets, zigzags, squares, triangles, tetragons, stars, polygons, lozenges, octagons, parallelograms, rectangles, and all the rest, together with their wonderful combinations and relationships.

That Cushing fully accepted this accidental discovery of geometrical design is clear. He says: "There can be no doubt that these styles and ways of decoration were developed, along with the weaving of baskets, simply by elaborating on suggestions of the lines and figures unavoidably produced in wicker work of any kind when strands of different colors happened to be employed together." These remarks are illustrated by the diagrams, Figs. 276, 277, 278, which show typical basket decorations thus discovered.

Accidents of color and design having thus (to change the figure) led her into pleasant meadows where scores of beautiful flowers of simple art awaited her plucking, the aboriginal woman soon began to exercise her own individuality in choosing and planting for herself.

There were certain objects in nature which she wished to copy because they reminded her of certain things; others that were connected with religious worship. At first she imitated these as near as the limitations of her art would allow. Then, as years went on, her successors imitated what she had made, and the design slowly grew away from the original and finally became conventionalized out of all recognition of the object which it was intended to represent.

This was a distinct step forward. It was the birth of ideography or symbolism. Once get the imaginative brain at work, and where was the end? With the Indian there is no end. Her symbolism to-day is wonderful in its profound meaning. There are mythology, religion, worship, poetry and history all woven with busy brain and tireless fingers into baskets which the unversed regard as mere examples of crude and savage workmanship. It is only the things that we love—simple stars though they may be, as Browning puts it—that open their hearts to us, so the learned and the wise have passed by these books of the aborig-

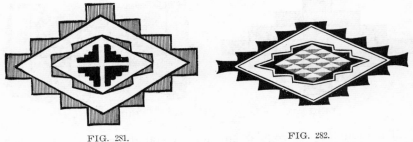

FIG. 281. FIG. 282.

inal woman and having eyes have seen not, ears have heard not, the sweet sights and sounds that were awaiting the simple and the loving.

To the common people of the dark, middle ages, the cathedrals and public buildings were books in which they read many and wonderful things that only the wise of to-day can discern.

What meant Victor Hugo, when he exclaimed "The book has killed the building?" He merely meant to express his belief in the fact that mankind having become accustomed to the easy reading of print, has forgotten the harder reading of stone—of gargoyle, spire, tower, buttress, sculptured figure and carved object. In those typeless, printless, bookless days man stood by the side of a cathedral and read therein and thereupon most of the useful lessons of life. The spires led his thoughts heavenward, the tower symbolized the church which was to connect earth with the heaven-pointing spires; the buttresses spoke of the strength given to the church; while the carved figures of angels saints, pilgrims, demons and devils taught him that while man was a pilgrim here below, devils and saints, demons and angels fought over, around and within him for mastery. Inside the building the dim light, filtering in through the gorgeous colored windows, taught him the rich beauty of the saintly life, though the calm quietude of the place suggested that it was a life of restful gentleness; ascending incense taught him how his fervent prayers should ever be thus subtly arising from earth to the Throne of Grace, and the sweet songs of the choir and melodies and harmonies of the organ bade him sing his songs of thankfulness to the divine and beneficent Being who had given him life and health. These and many other thoughts were inspired in the minds and hearts of the beholders by the great buildings of the bookless ages.

Then, too, man had his poetry—the songs of the troubadours, the ballads of the Border, the Epics of Homer and Virgil—to quicken his intellect and stimulate his soul, and in later days the printed page of poem, song and ballad; of stirring eloquence and vivid enthusiasm. He had and has the sculptured marble of great heroes and beautiful imaginations, and these are books to be seen and read of all men.

But the Indian had not, nor has, any of these. Her only temples are the arched aisles of stately trees and those massive mountain and canyon walls built not by human hands; the only sculptured forms she knows are the wild and irregular carvings of erosion and storm.

Hence, to the woman, living largely in the seclusion of the camp; condemned to be a stay-at-home from the earliest years of the race by the very exigences of the case, her basket-ware, and later, her pottery, became her chief art manifestations, her cathedral, her sculpture, her book, her picture. In them she wrote what civilized peoples transcribed into cathedral, book, picture, and he who would read Indian thought aright must learn to decipher the hieroglyphics of thought written on basketry, just as the antiquarian and archaeologist needed the Rossetta Stone to enable them to read the mysterious inscriptions of the Egyptian obelisks.

But where is the Rossetta Stone of Indian Basketry? Fortunately the writers of these Indian hieroglyphics are not all dead. A few yet remain. Some are still writing, and from what they tell us we are enabled to penetrate some most interesting secrets.

(c) IMITATION AND CONVENTIONALIZATION.

It is impossible to discuss imitation apart from conventionalization. As I have just written, the attempt to imitate naturally produced a conventional design, often far away from the object imitated. Thus conventionalization might be said to be a necessary consequence of imitation. Yet, the first basketry design might have come purely by accident, as Cushing has shown in his "Zuni Culture Growth." The theory is based upon feasible linguistic argument.

In making the stitches with strands of different shades, which, in the earlier days of manufacture, would happen to be used, quaint figures necessarily were produced on the surface of the basketry, by the appearance and disappearance of the discolored splints.

From the haphazard alternations of color doubtless came the first rude suggestions of design, dark and light regularly alternating in bands, and then appearing and disappearing as in Figs. 279 and 280, so that a lozenge shaped series of terraces was produced.

On Zuni pottery these basketry patterns are reproduced as in Figs. 281 and 282, and, that they are veritable basket designs is demonstrated by the name applied to them by the Zuni which is "double splint-stitch-form mark."

From Fig. 284, which shows an unfinished wicker water bottle, it will be seen that the warp strands cross each other in a manner very suggestive to the pottery artist. Indeed, as Cushing states, the name given to this decoration, when seen on pottery, denotes its origin from basketry.

Whether this theory of accidental origin of design be feasable or not, there is no doubt that the exercise of the IMITATIVE faculty was the first important step in the art evolution of the Amerind.

*The Indian is essentially imitative. In the days of his dawning intelligence, living in free and unrestrained contact with nature, his perceptive faculties were aroused and highly developed by the very struggle for existence. He was compelled to watch the animals, in order that he might avoid those that were dangerous and catch those that were good for food; to follow the flying birds that he might know when and where to trap them; the fishes as they spawned and hatched; the insects as they bored and burrowed; the plants and trees as they grew and budded, blossomed and seeded. He became familiar, not

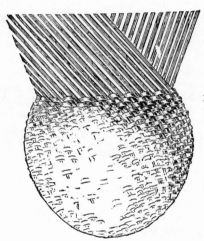

Figs. 285-286. Design on Salish Basket, showing conventionalization.

Fig. 284. Suggestion of design for pottery from basketry.

only with such simple things as the movements of the polar constellations and the retrograde and forward motions of the planets, but also with the less known spiral movements of the whirlwind as they took up the sand of the desert; and the zigzags of the lightning were burned into his consciousness and memory in the fierce storms that, again and again, in darkest night, swept over the exposed area in which he roamed. With the flying of the birds, the graceful movements of the snakes, the peculiar wrigglings of the insects, the tracks of insects, reptiles, birds and animals, whether upon the sand, the snow, the mud, or more solid earth he soon became familiar. The rise and fall of the mountains and valleys, the soaring spires and wide spreading branches of the trees, the shadows they cast, and the changes they underwent as the seasons progressed; the scudding or anchored clouds in their infinitude of form and color, the graceful arch of the rainbow, the peculiar formation and dissipation of the fogs, the triumphant lancings of the night by the gorgeous fire weapons of the morning sun, the

---

* It will be noticed by the critical reader that I vary the sex of the pronoun in writing of the art developement of the Amerind. This is not the result of carelessness, but of purpose. I do not wish any reader to assume that because I use only the feminine when speaking of the weaver, I think the male Amerind had no art developement.

FIG. 287. HARTT'S THEORY OF DEVELOPMENT OF FRET WORK.

FIG. 289. SCROLLS ON PUEBLO INDIAN POTTERY.

FIG. 291. THE FRET OF POTTERY DECORATION, MIDWAY STEP
BETWEEN THE FRET OF BASKETRY AND THE
SCROLL OF POTTERY.

stately retreat of the day king as each day came to its close, all these and a thousand and one other things in nature, he soon learned to know, in his simple and primitive manner and, when the imitative faculty was once aroused, and the art faculty demanded expression, what more natural than that he should attempt, crudely at first, more perfectly later on, the reproduction of that which he was constantly observing, and which was forcefully impressed upon his plastic mind.

Grosse speaks enthusiastically of this faculty of observation of nature and power of imitation possessed by the aborigine, and he commends the accuracy with which the pictorial representations are made. In course of time, however, this imitative faculty became perverted, owing to a mistaken and perhaps mercenary motive, that white men would prefer to buy basketry that contained designs imitated from something pertaining to themselves rather than the Indian. In Fig. 274 examples are given of this vicious imitation. While in themselves an evidence of the imitative faculty, the baskets are to be condemned for the introduction of purely foreign and inappropriate decorative design.

A design once made it would be comparatively easy to copy it. Yet, in copying, variations would necessarily occur, either by carelessness or volition. And here is the next definite stage of conventionalization. The copyist adds to, or takes from, according to her whim or fancy, and thus the design, still retaining its original significance as imitative, loses its purely imitative character, and becomes, by accretion or elimination, a new design.

Anyone of my readers may easily test this unconscious modification of an imitated object. Mr. Henry Balfour in his work on "Evolution of Art" gives a simple, though perfect, illustration. He made a sketch of a snail crawling over a stick and gave it to a friend to copy. The copy he gave to a third, and so on to twelve persons in turn. The result was a drawing of a bird perched on a limb. The designs of the Indian women on their basketry have undergone a similar transformation or evolution. Dr. Farrand, of Columbia University, elsewhere often quoted, gave me a perfect illustration of this in a conventionalized figure he found on the basketry of the Thompson Indians. He saw the hour-glass object (Fig. 285) and when he asked what it represented was told that it was a bird. But he could see no likeness to a bird in this figure, until he was shown, on an older basket, the key to the highly conventionalized design. This was Fig. 286. Here the head and tail of the bird (although crudely drawn) are clearly discernible. By successive stages, deliberately or carelessly, the head and tail were dropped off, but the remaining portion of the figure still stood, a representation of the bird.

A third stage in conventionalization is taken when the weaver volitionally makes changes, in obedience to the growing aesthetic desire within her and thus completely destroys the identity of the new with the old design.

An illustration of this is found in the Tulare basket (so-called) shown in Fig. 275. Here, each alternate circle of the design is composed of St. Andrew's crosses. I have heard people sapiently discoursing on this cross as an evidence of the Christian influence to which the Indians have been subjected In this case the weaver to whom I showed the photograph, and who herself was weaving St. Andrew's crosses into a basket she was then making, promptly replied to my question that it was "rattlesnake." By much questioning and quiet talk I learned the whole secret. If two joined rattlesnake diamonds are split in half a St. Andrew's cross is the result. And though in its new form it bears no resemblance to the snake design, it is still called by that name, and it means exactly the same to her as if it were the original diamond design. For the original diamond-backed rattlesnake designs see Figs. 28, 42, 48, &c.

Last year I purchased a beautiful small basket made by a girl of some eighteen years of age, on the Tule River reservation, on which double diamonds were woven by making the lower borders of the upper row of diamonds form the upper borders of the lower row. This, she said, was her method of representing the rattlesnake, thus affording another instance of mutability of design.

From all that has been said, therefore, it will be apparent to the reader that the author believes that basketry designs, are, or may be, wonderfully diverse in their origin. Some of them are still purely imitative, others are simple conventionalizations, while still others are complex artistic conventionalizations, or conventional designs born of the art instinct.

Nor are these all. As will be shown in a later chapter there are designs that are purely ideographic, that were so contemplated when designed by their makers, and in which the poetry and imagination of the Indian are beautifully enshrined.

(d) THE BIRTH AND DEVELOPMENT OF GEOMETRICAL DESIGNS.

Whence came all the many and diverse geometrical designs found upon Indian basketry? How did they originate? Where? When? By whom invented? Were they brought to this land from some far away foreign shore where art was in a highly developed state? Or, is there some motive power in the human mind, which, working simultaneously in many different regions, evolved the first design from which all others easily followed? I have partially given answer to some of these questionings but the subject is worthy of far more extended treatment than I am now able to give. Yet, it may be that a contribution to this long discussed subject from the standpoint of one of the earliest textile arts known to humanity may be useful in arriving at a satisfactory solution of the problem.

In regard to the development of the Greek fret and the scroll in all their variations, Professor C. F. Hartt, in Popular Science Monthly, Vol. 6, p. 226, advances the theory that ornamental designs follow certain well-defined lines of development owing to the structure of the eye, which finds pleasure in the varying recurrence of these forms. He also argues that in the general course of nature decorative forms began with simple elements and developed by systematic methods to complex forms. Take for example the series of designs shown in Fig. 287. The meander a, made up of simple parts would, according to Mr. Hartt, by further elaboration under the supervision of the muscles of the eye, develop into b. This, in time, into c, and so on until the elegant anthemiom was achieved. The series shown in Fig. 288 would develop in a similar way, or otherwise would be produced by modification in free-hand copying of the rectilinear series. The processes here

FIG. 288. HARTT'S THEORY OF DEVELOPMENT OF
SCROLL WORK.

FIG. 290. The Curvilinear Scroll Modified by Basketry
Becomes the Rectilinear Fret.

suggested, although to all appearances reasonable enough, should not be passed over without careful scrutiny.

In such a theory Mr. Hartt utterly fails to take into account at its true value the imitative faculty in primitive peoples. This is constantly exercised; always has been from the earliest dawning of art strivings, and is still, even in the present day. The scroll has a natural imitative origin. Cushing calls attention to a fact well known to all Indians of the South Western deserts. "Those who have visited the Southwest and ridden over the wide, barren plains, during late autumn or early spring, have been astonished to find traced on the sand by no visible agency, perfect concentric circles and scrolls or volutes yards long and

FIG. 292.

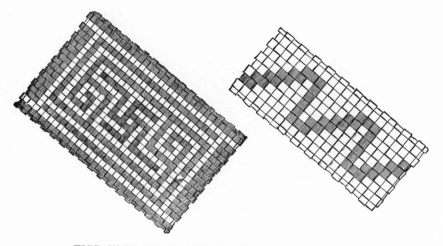

FIGS. 293-294. FRET AND MODIFIED ZIG-ZAG FOUND ON BASKETRY FROM THE AMAZON.

as regular as though drawn by a skilled artist. The circles are made by the wind driving partly broken weed-stalks around and around their places of attachment, until the fibres by which they are anchored sever and the stalks are blown away. The volutes are formed by the stem of red-top grass and of a round-topped variety of the "chenopodium," drifted onward by the whirlwind yet around and around their bushy adhesive tops. The Pueblo Indians observing these marks, especially that they are abundant after a wind storm, have wondered at their similarity to the painted scrolls on the pottery of their ancestors." See Fig. 289.

As basketry was undoubtedly an earlier art than pottery, the artist who desired to imitate these strange desert markings, was compelled by the exigences of the case into the use of the fret. As Professor Holmes well says: "The tendency of nearly all woven fabrics is to encourage, even to compel, the use of straight lines in the decorative designs applied. Thus the attempt to use curved lines would lead to stepped or broken lines. The curvilinear scroll coming from some other art would be forced by the constructional character of the fabric into square form, and the rectilinear meander or fret would result, as shown in Fig. 290."

The only criticism upon these words of Professor Holmes's that I would make is that instead of the scroll coming from some other art it was found by the Indian in nature, as Lieut. Cushing has suggested, and that in attempting to imitate it upon her basket, the Indian woman unconsciously designed the fret.

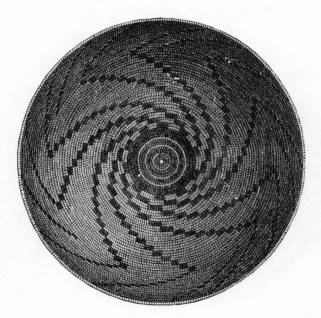

FIG. 295. GEOMETRIC SPIRAL FORM ON APACHE
BASKET

Mr. Holmes calls attention, however, to a self-evident proposition in this discussion, viz.: that though the fret of basketry is a necessary result of attempting to compel the scroll into a woven form, the scroll may easily have been evolved from the fret. And Lieut. Cushing argues that the scroll of pottery is the natural evolution—using Fig. 291, the fret of pottery decoration, as a step between—from the fret of basket decoration.

As ideas began to attach to imitative and conventionalized ornaments, the Indians themselves associated the marks on their baskets and pottery with the marks left on the desert, and, as they believe these latter "to be the tracks of the whirlwind which is a god of such distinctive personality that the circling eagle is supposed to be related to him," these frets and scrolls are introduced as propitiatory offerings.

As recently as August of 1899 I found an example of this among the Havasupais in Cataract Canyon. I purchased a basket from one of my friends and after much persuading she told me that the designs represented the whirlwinds. The general fret design suggests the plateaux and canyons and the inverted pyramids are the whirlwinds as they reach the edges of the plateaux and descend into the canyons. The center design is of a number of small whirlwinds uniting to form one great and powerful one—which brought disaster and death to early members of her family many years ago. See Fig. 292.

That the fret is one of the most ancient of designs is evident from a study of its antiquity and universality. Figs. 293 and 294 are a fret and a modification zigzag found on baskets from the banks of the Amazon.

Fig. 296. Geometric Spiral Form on Pottery, Showing Loss of Accuracy.

As the aesthetic culture of the basket maker slowly evolved, the powers of imitation grew, and the spiral was reproduced even in basketry with an accuracy as wonderful as it is beautiful. In an Apache basket, Fig. 295, this perfect volute is shown, and in reference to Fig. 296 Professor Holmes observes that when the same ornament was copied upon pottery a tendency is observed to depart from symmetry as well as consistency. It is well to note these observations as explaining many similar modifications and variations in design. He says: "It will be seen by reference to the design given in Fig. 296, taken from the upper surface of an ancient vase, that although the spirit of decoration is wonderfully well preserved the idea of the orgin of all the rays in the center of the vessel is not kept in view, and that by carelessness in the drawing two of the rays are crowded out and terminate against the side of a neighboring ray. In copying and recopying by free-hand methods, many curious modifications take place in these designs, as, for example, the unconformity which occurs in one place in the example given may occur at a number of places. and there will be a series of independent sections, a small number only of the bands of devices remaining true rays."

These remarks are especially useful when taken in conjunction with what I have said on the subject of conventionalization of design by carelessness or volition.

In determining the origin of geometric designs I am fully convinced that as far as their appearance on Indian baskets is concerned the exercise of the imitative faculty satisfactorily accounts for them all.

A simple clasification of these designs would give four sources of origin, as follows: Animal, Vegetable, Natural and Artificial (or manufactured) objects.

Before presenting examples of these varied designs, however, it is important that the student recognizes at its full value the thought of the next division of this subject.

(e) DIVERSE MEANINGS OF DESIGNS.

It must be borne in mind that the same design may, and often does, mean entirely different things to different weavers. For instance, the zigzag design seen in Figs. 31 and 36 are clearly conventionalized representations of the lightning. But when the same design appears in the basketry of the Pomas, Mr. Plimpton assures me that Dr. Hudson insists it has no reference to lightning but is the conventional method followed by the Pomas of representing a flowing stream.

When a horizontal series of these rather acute-angled zigzags are made they represent mountains and valleys to the Thompson and many other Indians, and a highly conventionalized variant is shown in the line of broken zigzags in the shape of steps, and of steps arranged in ascending terraces, (see Figs. 298-270, &c.)

In the basket held in the hands of Pedro Lucero, Fig. 305, are a number of circles connected with lines. The explanation given of these is that they represent the villages of the Saboba people, connected by ties of blood and friendship. According to Teit the same sign used by the Thompson Indians represents two lakes connected by a river.

The cross, according to Teit, represents to the Thompson Indians the crossing of trails. Among the Yokuts it generally represents a battle, and among the Wallapais and Havasupais it is a phallic sign.

On this subject Dr. Farrand writes of the Salish designs: "Snake designs are widely used, but in many cases are indistinguishable from other similar patterns, and exhibit the confusing process of convergent evolution. The typical snake or snake-track pattern among the Salish Indians generally, is a simple zigzag, vertically arranged, but this often represents lightning as well; and, unless the artist himself is at hand to tell what he had in mind at the making, there is practically never unanimity of opinion among the authorities. Investigation of the significance of color has thus far borne little fruit in this region, though it is not impossible that it may have a determinant value in just such cases as this. The snake zigzag may also be placed horizontally, but in that event is often identical with the mountain pattern representing a mountain chain."

The diamonds of Fig. 302, to the Quinaielts, represent roughly the shape of the flounder. This is a common and well recognized design of that tribe. Yet among the Cahuillas, Rosario Casero showed me the

FIG 297. BASKETS OF HIGHLY CONVENTIONALIZED DESIGNS IN PRIVATE COLLECTION OF W. D. CAMPBELL.

FIG. 298. BASKETS MADE BY SALISH STOCK INDIANS.

same design and said it represented the leaves of the trees that grow by the side of one of their springs.

Among the designs of the Salish Stock (The Thompson Indians) is one exactly the counterpart of Fig. 292 (except for the inverted pyramid). This represents a snake, yet in the Havasupai design represented it means the plateaux and canyons of the region in which they live. The same design is seen around the top of the basket to the right in Fig.

FIG. 299. SALISH BASKETRY.

48. This is made by a Mono, and she herself explained that it was in imitation of the fences of the white man.

(f) DESIGNS OF ANIMAL ORIGIN.

These are numerous, and are found in the work of all the basket makers. First and foremost are the human figures.

Fig. 271 represents three most beautiful and rare baskets in the Plimpton Collection, San Diego, Cal. These interestingly reveal the

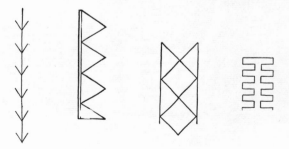

FIGS. 300-301-302-303.

various modes of presenting the human figure. The upper basket, oval in shape, was made by a Wichumna of the Yokut tribe. She was living in one of the upper reaches of King's River in Kern County. Here the figures are those of dancers, holding hands, some wearing feathered kilts. I showed the photograph of this basket to an intelligent weaver, and she informed me that it represented a "big dance," something the weaver desired to celebrate and keep in memory, as the kilted figures were possibly those of the Shamans, many of whom were present. The crosses were copied from the Pictured Rocks of the locality, and, taken in conjunction with the great dance, the presence of so many kilted Shamans or medicine men, and the explanation given that these crosses represent battles, she assumed that this was a memorial basket made by a woman who witnessed the dances held in honor of certain decisive victories won by her people. Above the dancers is the diamond-back rattlesnake pattern beautifully woven.

FIG. 304. ONE OF DAT-SO-LA-LEE'S MASTERPIECES.

The basket to the left is by a Tulare weaver, and shows the general method followed by this people to represent the human figure. In the border above are the St. Andrew's crosses before referred to.

The basket to the right is an old Inyo County basket, purchased in Lone Pine from a Paiuti woman by Mr. A. W. De La Cour Carroll, an enthusiastic basketry collector, who has secured some choice specimens. It shows the oldest type of human figure known to these Indians and offers a singular contrast to both the other designs.

The large basket, Fig. 80, is evidently a dance basket, used to represent a circular dance, and may be a Yokut, a California Paiuti, or an Apache. This latter people often make a circular dance basket the design of which represents the Havasupai Thapala or Peach Dance. This is supposed to bring good luck to the maker and her family, as the Thapala Dance is associated in her mind with the abundance of the harvest of the Havasupais when she, as a visitor, was feasted on corn, melons, squash, pumpkins and other good things.

In the chapter on "Basket Forms and Designs and their Relation to Art" is shown a Hopi presentation of the human face (see Fig. 165) and on the Apache basket, Fig. 105, many human figures are woven. In the basket marked No. 10 in Fig. 272, Rosario Casero, the Cahuilla weaver, represents girls using the skipping rope in which the figures are strikingly realistic. Such designs as these are important as they show a high stage of geometrical conventionalization, imposed by the materials used in weaving, and, at the same time, as close an imitation of the originals as the limitations of weaving allowed. This subject has been fully discussed elsewhere.

In two of the baskets of Fig. 28 dancing Shamans are shown.

In the Thompson Indians' designs Farrand shows several most interesting ones of human heads. In all of them the mouth is open, and in one case the teeth are represented. This design is practically shown in Fig. 298, on the lower right basket. It requires some imagination to see, in this highly conventionalized design, which is simply two of the plateaux and canyon design of Fig. 292, placed face to face in a perpendicular, instead of a horizontal position, the representation of a human face and yet that is the explanation given by its weaver. It is well to compare this with the graphic representation on Fig. 265.

In Figs. 28 and 48 hunters are seen in the quail design basket, and in the beautiful Yokut bowl of Fig. 52 are well made human figures. These are similar to the ones found in Figs. 164 and 236 and two of the baskets of Fig. 58. But in Fig. 72 there are decidedly novel presentations of men and women. The men are differentiated from the women by being taller and in the exaggerated form of their "divided" garment, the split of which is made to reach far up beyond the waist, even to the bottom of the chest. The women stand straddling so that their spread-out skirts are made very imposing. In Fig. 79 basket No. 3 has a number of human figures, who stand hand in hand in a circle. These are undoubtedly dancers, and Fig. 149 is a "stitch" representation of similar figures showing how the lines of geometricity are imposed by the splint stitch upon the weave. In Fig. 105 many of the men stand with the left arm upraised and the open palm presented. This is signal, or sign-language for "halt," and is the hunter's sign of success, he having "halted" all the deer that came near him on the occasion of his excursion. Human figures will also be seen on the beautiful McLeod basket, Fig. 270.

Perhaps the most common design in California baskets is that of the diamond-backed rattlesnake. In its simplest and purest form it is well shown in Fig. 48 (the basket to the right) and Fig. 52. Here there can be no mistaking the design. It is also very clear in Fig. 275, the circles alternating with the St. Andrew's crosses, which, as I have before explained, are an evolution from the rattlesnake design. Other manifestations of this design may be seen in Figs. 3, 4, 15, 28, 42, 48, 52, 58, 74, 79, 271, 275, and 297. In Fig. 42 the Saboba weaver called this "rattlesnake," yet it is very much like the design in Fig. 305, which represents the villages of the Saboba people joined together by ties of kinship and amity. Farrand pictures a somewhat similar design, with double lines, however, which represents to the Thompson Indians lakes connected by a river.

Another common California and North Pacific region design is that of the quail. The distinguishing feature of this design is the plume, which appears something like a rude sketch of a golf club and is invariably shown in vertical square-tipped appendices to parallelograms or triangles, which represent the bodies of the birds. This design is seen in the center bottom basket of Fig. 28 and the basket to the left in Fig. 48; also in Fig. 164. The best representation is in Fig. 52. A highly conventionalized form is shown in Fig. 234, and it is possible that on basket 49, in Fig. 97, is still another highly conventionalized form. In Fig. 234 some of the plumes are placed upside down to correspond with the upright ones opposite. In basket o, Fig. 297, one of the beautiful baskets of the Campbell collection, an unusual quail design is shown. This is a so-called Tulare basket, and represents large ponds or lakes, near which quail abound. Basket No. 2 of Fig. 79, also in the Campbell collection, shows the quail plumes and a highly conventionalized mountain design, down or through which the water flows.

It is no uncommon thing to find fine baskets ornamented with the plumes themselves, many of them being used in the ornamented shi-bu of the Pomas.

Birds of different kinds, beside the quail, are often represented. The large center basket of Fig. 170, on the bottom row, was made by Felipa Akwakwa, at Cahuilla, and the large diamonds, she said, were flying geese. In Fig. 155 the inverted triangles that run around the upper part are said to be flying geese. In Fig. 81 the upper basket to the right is said to be a flying bird, as is also the highly conventionalized design on Fig. 156. The bottom basket to the right, in Fig. 96, has a design much like the quail designs, but Dixon says he was told by the Maidus that this represents flying geese, though in the design figured by him the appendices are triangular instead of square, as in Fig. 96. Figs. 166 and 167 are bird forms explained by Holmes. Elsewhere, in speaking of the evolution of design I have quoted Farrand. In Figs. 46, 262 and 78 the hour glass bird design is clearly shown. In the large basket of Fig. 297, of Poma weave, No. 4, the central design is a highly conventionalized calyx of a flower, but the main design is of birds, somewhat similar to those pictured by Farrand. Dixon pictures a zig-zag design something like the two shown in Fig. 77 and explains: "It is said to signify the patch of white seen on each side of the bird." It is known as the "duck's wing."

The flying bats of Fig. 306 are readily distinguished.

In Fig. 27 in the Apache basket to the right on the bottom row, and in basket No. 2, Fig. 79, are several butterflies, and in Figs. 53 and 248 are also butterfly wings.

In the Hopi basket, Fig. 61, is a highly conventionalized design which I have been told represents both the dragon fly and the bee.

Clusters of flies are represented in the round basket in the center of Fig. 45, and in Fig. 86. The center design of Fig. 237 is also a fly cluster.

The spider-web design, so important to the Hopi, is shown in their baskets in Figs. 34, 81 and 114, and is also represented in the Apache basket in Fig. 27 (the bottom to the right), and in the Agua Caliente basket in the hands of the weaver, Fig. 55.

In the bottom basket to the right of Fig. 170 and the bottom to the left of Fig. 73 are different representations of the track of certain earthworms.

In the upper row of the design of the basket to the left in Fig. 78 are several animals, possibly reindeer, and in Fig. 105 both deer and elk are shown.

In Fig. 272 the keen-eyed may see a basket marked 15. This was made at Cahuilla, and represents the four feet and claws of a bear, put in star fashion, with a design on the sides representing the sharp saw teeth of ursa major.

Fish are often found represented on he baskets of the North Pacific Coast and Alaska Indians. In Fig. 46 the basket at bottom to the right shows the glisten on the rolling waves, through which fish (represented by the diamonds) are seen to be swimming. See also Fig. 302 and the comments in section e of this same chapter, where the use of the diamond to represent fish is discussed.

I have an interesting Havasupai basket in my own collection, the design of which is much like the horizontal zig-zags seen in Figs. 76 and 196. These zig-zags, however, all start from near the center, and at the beginning of each is a sort of imperfect parallelogram, which is clearly a head. The weaver told me that these were four plumed serpents, and that the basket was used to carry the sacred meal which was sprinkled at a certain shrine, the serpent being the guardian of their water sources.

(g) DESIGNS OF VEGETABLE ORIGIN.

Farrand and Dixon picture few designs of vegetable origin. The former found an acute zig-zag which was said to represent a plant with fern-like leaf, end view. A somewhat similar design is shown in the top basket of Fig. 28. Dixon pictures a flower, brake, vine, pine cone and bush. In Fig. 56 the design on the last basket but one to the right was said to be pine cones piled one above another, but it is a very different design from that pictured by Dixon.

Trees are represented in the singular design of the Alaska basket to the left, on the bottom of Fig. 45, and the seventh basket from the left of Dat-so-la-lee's work, Fig. 56, also represents trees. In Fig. 63 the Chemehuevi weaver represents a tree, stem and leaves, and Fig. 300 is a conventionalized representation, quite common in Southern California, of the twigs shooting out from the trunk of a growing tree. It is generally placed around the basket, instead of perpendicular, as in Fig. 63.

In Fig. 196 the upper circle of the design is of trees. In Fig. 170, on the second row from the bottom, and the second basket from the left, is a basket I bought in Saboba. It was made by Juana Apapos while on a visit to Cahuilla.

The design shows mountain benches and towering peaks, and deep, depressed valleys. A tiny spot of white will be seen in most of these "valleys" These represent the water pools and ponds that accumulate below the ground. Over the valleys are great, overhanging, black, double triangles, and for some time she hesitated before declaring these to be crude representations of the large trees that grow on Mounts San Jacinto and San Gorgonio. With a deprecatory laugh she exclaimed: "I made the first too big and it didn't suit me, but I made all the others like it."

Beautiful flower designs are often found in the basketry of Southern California. In Fig. 80 the design of the basket to the left is of the calyx of a flower, and a similar beautiful design is shown in the fourth basket from the bottom on the left in Fig. 170. This same basket is seen clearer in Fig. 273, No. 11. The designs on the two baskets at the extreme right and left of Fig. 103 are similar to what Dixon pictures as a flower design. It consists of broad-based triangles, each row from the base to the top containing successively larger triangles.

Dixon also figures a fern design somewhat similar to basket No. 8 in the Campbell collection, Fig. 297. It is the common brake (Pteris aquilina), and the points are intended for the pinnae of the ferns, but, he adds, "the meaning of the bars in the central stripe is not yet clear." Accepting the Poma interpretation this design represents the ascending steps of the mountains, and the central stripe is of water flowing down.

In Fig. 170 the second basket from the bottom on the left has a beautiful design worked in brown. Its maker told me it represented the waving leaves of corn, as they were bowed over in the wind. Basket No. 5 in Fig. 272 is an exquisitely worked Agua Caliente, representing the base of the yucca, and Fig. 303 is a common design showing the pointed leaves of this desert denizen.

(h) DESIGNS OF NATURAL ORIGIN.

In the realm of nature, aside from the animal and vegetable kingdoms, the aboriginal artist found the motive for many of her most effective and interesting designs. In the exercise of the imitative faculty she could not fail to be led into imitating those things that most impressed her, hence we find designs of mountains, lightning, rainclouds, the streams, etc., in great profusion.

Perhaps the most common design of all basketry is the zigzag, both horizontal and perpendicular. As before shown, this may represent lightning, mountains, waves, flowing water or the ripples in the streams, according to the individual taste of the weaver. In Fig. 31, however, we have a solid basis to rest upon, in the antelope altar of the Hopis. Here the zigzags are assuredly of the lightning, connected with the rain clouds. In Fig. 244, also, we have a design said to be the male and female lightning. In Fig. 15 is the bottom of a saucer-shaped basket, just below the Ute seed-wand, on the right, and this is of the conventionalized lightning pattern. In the top basket of Fig. 28 is a design either of lightning or mountain and valleys, and in the basket just below the left is a highly conventionalized pattern, which Dr. Hudson says is the ripples on the water. The Havasupai basket held by the woman in Fig. 36 (the largest basket there) is undoubtedly of the lightning, as both the holder and a Havasupai to whom I submitted it said the same thing. In the basket to the left of the weaver in Fig. 49 is the descending lightning, and this same pattern is seen in Figs. 56, 74, 87, 203 and 204. Zig-zags that are as likely to represent the ascending steps of the mountains as lightning are shown in Figs. 73 and 196. The difficulty of determining between the two is well illustrated in Fig. 106, the interpretation of which I obtained from an Apache.

The upper chevron is the conventionalized lightning pattern. The lower chevron represents the mountains and intervening valleys, and the black line reaching from each valley to the common black circle center, shows how the waters accumulate in the valleys and from thence go to feed the great waters at the center of the earth from which all springs originate. This black line and center cannot be seen in the engraving.

Fig. 62, however, is certainly of the mountain and valley design, as its Wallapai maker so informed me. The Sacred Navaho Basket, Fig. 27, as I have before explained, represents the mountains and valleys of the upper world and also of the under world. Fig 227 is an indifferent imitation of this design and means the same thing.

The two top baskets in Fig. 46 represent mountains and valleys, with lakes, and the Washoe design of Fig. 204 is interesting because of its complexity. It shows mountains and valleys, and on the summits of the mountains the inverted pyramids are rain clouds. Reaching down below the valleys are water courses terminating in lakes.

Fig. 51 is a fine Poma basket and the zigzag is that of mountains and valleys, as is also the design of Fig. 188. The Saboba design of Fig. 170 (second basket from left of second row from bottom) has been fully explained.

Perhaps one of the best of the highly conventionalized mountain and valley patterns is shown in the large basket No.1 of Fig. 79. Here trees are represented growing both on the heights and in the plains. Fig. 151 clearly shows mountains and valleys, and the black patches are pools or lakes of water.

The ascending steps or terraces of the mountains are often shown, however, in an entirely different manner, and Fig. 86 is a type of this design. Here the ascent is gradual, but certain. This design appears in Figs. 48, 164, 236 and 270, and in a modified form in Figs. 28, 52, 92 and others. Some weavers contend that this represents flowing water, and in the case of such designs, as on the basket to the right in Fig. 76 claim that water flowing down the mountain sides is represented. This latter is a common Poma design.

In the top center basket of Fig. 58 is a volute design which represents mountain steps, and this is also said to be the design of the large basket dimly seen to the right in Fig. 57. The center upper basket of Fig. 298 is clearly a mountain step design. From what has here been said it will be seen that only the weaver herself can determine which design represents mountains, and which flowing streams. The large center basket of Fig. 28, the left basket of Fig. 48, the large basket of the second row from the top of Fig. 58, the large shu-set to the left of Fig. 74, the shu-set on the right of Fig. 76, the two to the left of Fig. 92, and the design on the body of Fig. 155 are all said, by some weavers, to represent flowing streams and the sunshine ripples upon the water. On the bottom basket of Fig. 76 and the body of Fig. 196 are rippling streams.

In the Apache and Pima baskets are to be found many and varied manifestations of a design that has undoubtedly the same motive. Dr. Wilson regards this design, in some of its forms, as the Swastika, and there is no doubt as to its likeness to this well-known and world-wide sign or symbol. The constant recurrence of this design in some form or other, so interested me that I made enquiry of a number of weavers, both Apache and Pima, and always with the same result. Water is their greatest desideratum. This design represents the source of the water supply in the great central figure, and the geometrical lines leading out from this central reservoir are the winding and meandering streams. Excellent examples of this design will be found in Figs. 27, 120, 246, 82, 57 and 75, and when I showed a Pima weaver the photograph of Fig. 58 she insisted that the designs of several of those were of the same origin.

The difference between this "water-source" design of the lakes can be seen by comparing the foregoing with Figs. 46, 78, 151 and 204 in all of which lakes are said to be represented.

In the two bottom baskets in Fig. 46 waves are said to be shown. In the one to the left one weaver said the diamonds were flounders, or some other flat fish, and that waves and flounders alternated, but another insisted that the wavy lines were mountains and valleys and the hour-glass design, which makes the diamonds, was of a bird; (see remarks of Farrand's on the bird design, earlier in this chapter).

Rain clouds often appear, but in varied forms. In the sacred Navaho basket, Fig. 29, clouds, heavy witl. rain, are represented. Fig. 31 shows the rain clouds of the Hopi Antelope Altar. In Fig. 36, the basket of the woman whose head is most bowed shows the Havasupai design for the rain cloud, a kind of terrace, more like a mountain than a cloud. The same design is seen in Fig. 25, and the peculiar geometrical design of Fig. 35 is said to be a Hopi representation of rain clouds. In showing Fig. 120 to one Pima weaver, she claimed that the funnel-shaped figures on the rim are the rain clouds, which send rain to the earth, there to meet the streams that flow from the water source in the interior of the earth.

Connected with rain are the rainbows and these are seen in the second basket from the bottom on the right in Fig. 170. This was made by a Cahuilla woman. The same basket is seen in Fig. 272 and is No. 18.

Stars are not uncommon. In Fig. 57 a Mescalero Apache has made a star in the basket I have marked M, and in Fig. 75 is an Apache star. In several Cahuilla and Agua Caliente baskets the star is seen. See Fig. 272, basket No. 8, and Fig 307.

In Fig. 119 Dat-so-la-le represents the up-darting beams of light of the rising sun, and in Fig. 304 the ascending heat waves, or the light of early morning rising from behind the serrated mountain summits.

(i) DESIGNS OF ARTIFACT ORIGIN.

The most common of designs gained from manufactured objects is that of the arrow point. This is met with in a thousand and one ways. The ingenuity of the weaver seems to have been exercised to the utmost to produce variations upon this single theme. On the top basket of Fig. 27 is a row of arrow points, and they appear in Figs. 56, and the smaller designs of Fig. 247. Fig 240 is made entirely of arrow points, and basket 16 of Fig. 272 is the same. Baskets Nos. 1, 3, 4, 9 and 10 of Fig. 273 and No. 1 of Fig. 297 are all of arrow point design. Farrand pictures a Salish arrow point design exactly like that seen on Fig. 299.

Of almost as common occurrence is the "reda" or net design. This carrying net was one of the earliest premonitions of basketry, hence it is not strange that it should be frequently incorporated into modern work. In Fig. 15 the basket below the topmost one has this design, as has also the basket in the hands of the weaver, Fig. 47. Two of the baskets of Fig. 49 are net designs, and the one to the right of the weaver is well shown in Fig. 172. In Fig. 121 the net is shown with a number of articles inside. Baskets No. 11, of Fig. 272, and No. 13, of Fig. 273 are both of this "reda" pattern, the former from Agua Caliente and the latter from Cahuilla.

In Fig. 247 the wife of a warrior wished to represent stone battle axes as well as arrow-points, and Farrand figures one of a somewhat similar motive.

The cross occasionally appears. It may represent a star, a place of battle or slaughter, (either of men or animals), the crossing of trails, or a phallic sign. It will be seen in Figs. 59, 86, 105 and 270.

Twice weavers have told me that they intended to represent fences. The upper design in the basket to the right of Fig. 48, and the two upper and two lower designs, enclosing the St. Andrew's crosses, of the basket to the right in the middle row of Fig. 28 show these representations.

The small basket on the top to the left of Fig. 170 was made by Juana Apapos, at Saboba. She said it represented the time "a great many snows ago, when, here in Saboba, and she was a very little girl, the old men and women came together and sat in a rude circle and there played a game with sticks, which they stuck in the sand within the circle. As they won or lost the sticks changed hands, and some would have many and some few."

The players are represented in the oval at the bottom of the basket and four of the sticks, standing upright, are shown above it, while eight more are at each end and four more at the other side.

(j) BASKETS WITH MIXED DESIGNS.

It is scarcely necessary here to dwell in detail upon the fact that in many baskets the design is complex. There are mountains, valleys, canyons and trees in one, and streams, quail, hunters, trails and butterflies in another. Examples of this complexity in design are seen in Fig. 28, where the rattlesnake design and dancers are found in one basket, and flowing water with ripples, quail plumes and human figures are in another. The baskets in Figs. 46, 48, 52, 53, 57, &c., serve to illustrate further. I am satisfied that, ultimately, it will generally be found that this complexity is not purposeless, or merely imitative, but that these various signs or symbols are placed in juxtaposition for some reason clearly in the mind of the weaver. When we are able to interpret these mixed designs as the weaver herself does we shall be a long step nearer the goal of knowledge which will reveal the Indian to us, not the dumb, unintelligent, unimaginative, unreligious character we have too long regarded him, but as a mentally alert, intelligent, observant, imaginative, poetic and religious being, whose mental operations it is both interesting and instructive to study.

FIG. 306. DESIGN OF FLYING BATS ON CAHUILLA BASKET.

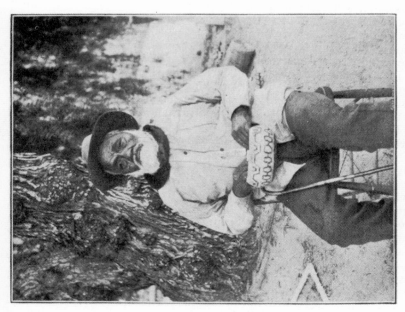

FIG. 305. POETIC DESIGN ON SABOBA BASKET.
Both photos copyright by George Wharton James.

CHAPTER XIII.

THE POETRY OF INDIAN BASKETRY.

No collector will need to be told of the charm and delight that are to be found in each "fine" basket. One's emotional nature is aroused and quickened again and again, as new beauties are observed in form, color and design.

But the greatest source of delight in basketry, to my mind, is to be found in the, as yet, almost untouched well of symbolism; the poetry, the religion, the superstition woven by the humble Amerind into her basket.

Capt. J. G. Bourke in his "Apache Campaign," speaks of Indians of that tribe who "are happy in the possession of priceless sashes and shirts of buckskin, upon which are emblazoned the signs of the sun, moon, lightning, rainbow, hail, fire, the water-beetle, butterfly, snake, centipede and other powers to which they may appeal for aid in the hour of distress." And he might have added to this that the women, in their basketry, incorporate exactly the same signs for the same purpose. Many of these signs and symbols are to be found in the Apache collection of baskets in the American Museum of Natural History, New York. They were donated to the museum by Mr. Douglas, of the Queen Copper Company, and were collected from the Apaches on the San Carlos Reservation, Arizona, by a trader there.

I have but few illustrations to elucidate this idea, yet these are sufficient to demonstrate the existence of the highest faculties of the soul. These, too, will serve to stimulate others to a true and full interpretation of designs that otherwise have little or no significance. Farrand speaks of certain Thompson designs which represent the dream visions of the weavers. Could we get at a full statement of these visions how instructive and interesting they might be.

It was from the basket held in the hands of Jose Pedro Lucero, Fig. 305, that I gained my first sight into, and delicious draught from, this deep poetic well. Lucero's wife was one of the few basket makers left at Saboba, near San Jacinto, California, and in this basket she wove the legendary history of her people. The story told was as follows: "Before my people came here they lived far, far away in the land that is in the heart of the setting sun. But Siwash, our great god, told Uuyot, the warrior captain of my people, that we must come away from this land and sail away and away in a direction that he would give us. Under Uuvot's orders my people built big boats and then, with Siwash himself leading them, and with Uuyot as captain, they launched them into the ocean and rowed away from the shore. There was no light on the ocean. Everything was covered with a dark fog and it was only by singing as they rowed that the boats were enabled to keep together.

It was still dark and foggy when the boats landed on the shores of this land, and my ancestors groped about in the darkness, wondering why they had been brought hither. Then, suddenly, the heavens opened, and lightnings flashed and thunders roared and the rains fell, and a great earthquake shook all the earth. Indeed, all the elements of earth, ocean and heaven seemed to be mixed up together, and with terror in their hearts, and silence on their tongues my people stood still awaiting what would happen further. Though no voice had spoken they knew something was going to happen, and they were breathless in their anxiety to know what it was. Then they turned to Uuyot and asked him what the raging of the elements meant. Gently he calmed their fears and bade them be silent and wait. As they waited, a terrible clap of thunder rent the very heavens and the vivid lightning revealed the frightened people huddling together as a pack of sheep. But Uuyot stood alone, brave and fearless, and daring the anger of 'Those Above.' With a loud voice he cried out: 'Wit-i-a-ko!' which signified 'Who's there;' 'What do you want?' There was no response. The heavens were silent! The earth was silent! The ocean was silent! All nature was silent! Then with a voice full of tremulous sadness and loving yearning for his people Uuyot said: 'My children, my own sons and daughters, something is wanted of us by "Those Above." What it is I do not know. Let us gather together and bring "pivat," and with it make the big smoke and then dance and dance until we are told what is required of us.' "

So the people brought "pivat"—a native tobacco that grows in Southern California—and Uuyot brought the big ceremonial pipe which he had made out of rock, and he soon made the big smoke and blew the smoke up into the heavens while he urged the people to dance. They danced hour after hour, until they grew tired, and Uuyot smoked all the time, but still he urged them to dance.

Then he called out again to 'Those Above:' 'Witiako!' but could obtain no response. This made him sad and disconsolate, and when the people saw Uuyot sad and disconsolate they became panic-stricken, ceased to dance and clung around him for comfort and protection. But poor Uuyot had none to give. He himself was the saddest and most forsaken of all, and he got up and bade the people leave him alone, as he wished to walk to and fro by himself. Then he made the people smoke and dance, and when they rested they knelt in a circle and prayed. But he walked away by himself, feeling keenly the refusal of 'Those Above' to speak to him. His heart was deeply wounded.

But, as the people prayed and danced and sang, a gentle light came stealing into the sky from the far, far east. Little by little the darkness was driven away. First the light was grey, then yellow, then white, and at last the glittering brilliancy of the sun filled all the land and covered the sky with glory. The sun had arisen for the first time, and in its light and warmth my people knew they had the favor of 'Those Above,' and they were contented and happy.

But when Siwash, the god of earth, looked around and saw everything revealed by the sun, he was discontented, for the earth was bare and level and monotonous and there was nothing to cheer the sight. So he took some of the people and of them he made high mountains, and of some, smaller mountains. Of some he made rivers and creeks and lakes and waterfalls, and of others, coyotes, foxes, deer, antelope, bear, squirrels, porcupines and all the other animals. Then he made out of other people all the different kinds of snakes and reptiles and insects and birds and fishes. Then he wanted trees and plants and flowers, and he turned some of the people into these things. Of every man or woman that he seized he made something according to its value. When he had done he had used up so many people he was

scared. So he set to work and made a new lot of people, some to live
here and some to live everywhere. And he gave to each family its own
language and tongue and its own place to live, and he told them where
to live and the sad distress that would come upon them if they mixed
up their tongues by intermarriage. Each family was to live in its own
place and while all the different families were to be friends and live as
brothers, tied together by kinship, amity and concord, there was to be
no mixing of bloods.

Thus were settled the original inhabitants on the coast of Southern
California by Siwash, the god of the earth, and under the captaincy
of Uuyot."

In the basket the circles representing the villages of the Sabobas
are seen, and the link that binds them together. Above this design
is the representation of the mountains and valleys in which their villages were located, and peeping over the latter may be seen figures
which represent sun, moon, evening and morning star, etc., which
assured the simple-hearted Sabobas that "Those Above" had not de-
serted them.

I once found another basket at Saboba with stitches and cross
stitches upon it, making a criss-cross design that seemed as if it could
not be imitative, conventionalized, symbolic or ideographic. Yet as I
talked with Juana Apapos, its maker, a bright, witty, elderly woman,
I was convinced that it had its meaning. For a long time she parried
all my questions, with the Indian's dread of being laughed at or derided,
but, at length, convinced that I should not ridicule her she said that
"over and over again when she was weary and tired, and angered at
the subjection of her people to the rude and domineering whites, as
she lay down at night, her eyes wandered to the 'long path of gray light
in the sky'—the milky way—and she felt she would like to pass away,
to die. Then her spirit would walk on this path of light with 'Those
Above,' and from thence she could look down upon the white people
in the sorrows she hoped would come upon them for their wicked
treatment of her people."

The mingled pathos, indignation and anger with which she said
these things showed the deep current of feeling which possessed her,
though she was living among surroundings of poverty and squalor,
and had a physiognomy that, to the general visitor to her village, contained nothing but the low, grovelling, animal, and sensual.

This criss-cross pattern was her method of representing the milky-
way.

Some years ago I sought to find the meaning of a similar design
upon a certain Zuni head-dress, worn in one of their mystic dances.
At last, after pledging myself not to laugh at the answer, I was asked
what the white man called that "up in the sky, all same sprinkled with
white ashes," and when I explained it was "the milky way," I was
informed that that was the meaning of the design that had so puzzled
me, thus revealing a keen observation of the heavens in Zuni as well
as Saboba.

Another most fascinating basket is the one held in the hands of
the woman in Fig. 307. It is well known to all who have studied the
facts and fictions of "H. H.'s" wonderful novel "Ramona," that the
pages that describe the shooting of Alessandro by Jim Farrar are based
on fact. Indeed, taking the Indian's side of the story, they are literally

FIG. 307. RAMONA AND HER STAR BASKET.
Copyright by George Wharton James.

FIG. 308. COLLECTION OF DR. C. C. WAINWRIGHT, SAN JACINTO, CAL.

true. The woman of this part of the story is still living at the village of Cahuilla, in the San Jacinto mountains, where "H. H." located the scene as it transpired in her novel. For some years I have known Ramona, and on several occasions have photographed her. On my last visit to Cahuilla, in the summer of 1900, I purchased several baskets from a weaver, one of which had a large star in the center. When I asked her for an interpretation of this design she said she did not make the basket and therefore knew nothing of the weaver's thought. But though I urged her she refused to tell me who made the basket. That afternoon Ramona came to my wagon to tell into my graphophone the story of the shooting of her husband. While I prepared the machine she looked over the various baskets I had bought, and, suddenly, darting upon this star basket, breathlessly asked me where I had bought her basket. "Your basket, Ramona?" I queried. "How is it yours? I bought it from Rosario." "Ah!" she replied. "It is mine, I make it, then I sell it."

The next day when I went down to her little cabin I took the basket with me, but she would tell me nothing of it until later. Then I learned the interesting story, which was somewhat as follows:

"Sometimes I cannot sleep when I lie down at night. I see again that awful man coming over the hill with his gun in his hand and I hear the shot as he fired at my husband. Then I see him pull his revolver, and hear his vile curses, as he shot again and again at the dead body. And I look up into the sky and my face is wet with tears and I try to think of what the good padre tells me that I shall some day go up there somewhere and be with Juan again. I hope so, for I love the stars, and when I begin to think of being up there my sorrow ceases and I am soon asleep."

"But," I asked, "why did you sell the basket, Ramona? If it gave you comfort, why didn't you keep it?"

"Ah!" she replied, "I wait a long, long time. I want to go many times, but I no go. I stay here. I no want to stay here. I grow tired waiting. Basket say I go, I no go. Basket heap lie. I no like'em, so I sell 'em," and with a despairing gesture she threw the basket away from her, as if she had thrown away all hope of ever reaching her poor murdered husband in the region of "the above" which the good priest had endeavored to describe to her. Poor Ramona, she is not the only human being who has grown weary of the battle and conflict of life and longed to depart hence.

The basket into which the old Indian woman is gazing, shown in Fig. 306, is more interesting than at first sight one would suppose. The design represents flying bats. These nocturnal pests had gained access into the sleeping room of the old woman and were "sucking her breath away," so that she would soon die. She made the basket to hold the propitiatory offerings that she intended to give to the powers who controlled the bats, in order that they would heed her prayer, and keep the vermin away from her. With naive simplicity and perfect faith she assured me that since she had made the offerings in this specially designed basket the bats had ceased to trouble her.

Fig. 308 represents a portion of the collection of Dr. C. C. Wainwright, of San Jacinto, Cal. On the large carrying basket, in which the doctor's little son would sit while I was making the photograph, are a number of concentric rings, which diminish in size as the bottom of the basket is reached, and there give place to a single dot. With touching pathos the maker said she intended that the lessening circles should describe the diminishing power and numbers of her people. Said she: "When my people first came here they were under the direct smile and approval of 'Those Above.' They were a great people and the large circle represents their power and influence at that time. But as the years rolled on the Padres (Spanish missionaries) came and they took away first one, then another of the privileges of my people until they were reduced to this size, and this, and this, (pointing to the diminishing size of the circle). Thus, when the Mexicans drove out the Spaniards, they were too weak to fight with and overcome them; so once again their power was curtailed and this circle represents their diminished grandeur.

Then the Americans came and finished the demoralization begun by the Spaniards, and now this tiny circle represents my people, and soon, alas! very soon, nothing will be required but this dot to represent a once proud and great race that surrounded the earth."

FIG. 269. BASKET USED IN DICE GAMES.

CHAPTER XIV.

BASKETS TO BE PRIZED.

If from what I have written or quoted in the foregoing pages there has not been enough said to show that there are some baskets which have peculiar and distinctive claims, nothing that I can now write will have any effect. It is is merely to more fully emphasize what is there written that this chapter finds place.

Broadly it may be said that the baskets most highly prized by intelligent collectors are the older specimens of the work of all the Mission Indians, the Yokuts, Pomas, Klamath, Haida, Salish Stock, Makah and Attu peoples of the Pacific coast, and of the Apaches, Chemehuevis, Hopi, Havasupais, Pimas and Paiutis in Arizona and thereabouts.

Individual tastes vary, necessarily, but no one can look upon such baskets as those of the Campbell private collection, pictured in Figs. 15, 79 and 297, or those of the Plimpton collection, Figs. 27, 28, 45, 46, 50, 51, 52, 53, 74, 76, 77, 86, 87, 271 and 275, or the Wilcomb collection, Fig. 94, or the one selection from the beautiful McLeod collection, Fig. 270, as well as many others herein pictured, and not see that their makers displayed exquisite taste in shape, conmate skill in weave, artistic conception in ornamentation, and, if the exact colors could be reproduced, an appreciation of the harmony of colors that few Americans can surpass.

Baskets of this class are prizes, and well selected collections contain specimens of all the weaves thus typified.

Mrs. Carr thus wrote of the charm of old basketry: "Jacinta, one of the last surviving neophytes of Father Junipero Serra's flock, was brought to Pasadena in 1888, with all the materials and implements of basketry, to assist in illustrating it during an Art Loan Exhibition. Passing up the nave of the Library Building, where Navaho blankets and the fine Crittenden Collection of Indian Curiosities from the Gulf of California to Alaska, attracted attention, the dim old eyes of Jacinta fell upon the display of basketry. It was touching to see her interest aroused as she gradually recognized her own work, which she took from the shelves, fondling it with her small brown hands, as a mother would linger over the playthings of a dead child. Whenever the crowd diminished, Jacinta was seen examining her treasures, which were woven early in the century. It is scarcely to be expected that such a collection will ever again be gathered, as since that time the State has been ransacked for baskets in the interest of Eastern and foreign collections and of speculators for their artistic value. There yet remain a few valuable private collections in the possession of owners notably interested in the perpetuation of this beautiful art. There is an indescribable magnetism attaching to them altogether different from any other feminine property. Collectors and dealers find it harder to part with them than with articles of far greater value, and reserve certain favorites for the elect among customers, who are likely to cherish them."

The true passion of the basket collector is made the theme of a charming little story in Scribners for August, 1890, by Grace Ellery Channing-Stetson. It opens "Sixteen in all. Five large ones, two small queer ones, four medium, three with the Greek pattern, the little brown one, and this beauty." Then comes the sting. The proud collector is told that she "has as fine a lot of baskets now as anyone in the valley, saving only old Anita. Ah! if the Senorita could see hers—!" Yes, indeed, hers was three feet high and "fine"—he cast a disdainful glance at the baskets about her—"you have nothing like it, Senorita. But that is not all. Where the pattern goes there are feathers—woodpeckers' feathers woven in, all of the brightest scarlet—oh, far gayer than these!" Or, as the collector's true cavalier described it: "Its majesty would stand, I think, about three feet high. It was very quaintly shaped. It was the finest I have ever seen. There was a beguiling, mellow-brown tone to the whole, which attested its honorable age, and a most seductive pattern climbing about its sides. But there was something more—a gleam of scarlet about it which gave it character."

And the ten interesting pages tell us how, finally, Anita's basket did come into the possession of the ardent and infatuated collector.

Dr. Hudson says: "There are ten graded rules governing a 'basket crank' in estimating the value of a Poma basket. Given in the order of their importance they are: weave, symmetry of outline, of stitch, of thread, delicacy of thread, material, pattern, ornamentation, general effect and size. Size is properly placed last in the list, because a shibu's diameter is seldom greater than fifteen inches. However there is a most rare specimen in a Chicago private collection, which measures nine feet in circumference, and for which was paid $800." I believe this is now in the Field Columbian Museum.

CHAPTER XV.

THE DECADENCE OF THE ART.

What are the causes that have led to the rapid decadence of the art of basketry? There can be but one broad answer, and that is the iconoclastic effect of our civilization upon a simple-hearted people. The Amerind is not far-sighted. His reasoning faculties are not ,as highly developed as ours. A basket takes weeks, months, to make. It sells for few or many dollars. One dollar will buy several tin, copper, or brass utensils that serve all the practical (or utilitarian) purposes of the baskets, even better than the baskets themselves. Hence the utilitarian forces the aesthetic to the wall; drives it from the field, and the basket disappears.

In the high noon-days of the art, the woman had several distinct motives to urge her to the highest endeavor. The basket was her battle-field. In it she won her triumphs or suffered her defeats. To be the best weaver of her family was the height of her early ambition, to be the head weaver of her tribe, the aim of her mature life, and to be recognized as the leader of leaders of other tribes, the satisfaction of the highest possible life ambition. Then, too, in her ability as a weaver, a keen-sensed woman saw other advantages than the mere gratification of personal, family or tribal ambition. To gain the high approval of others meant an increase of power and influence. To be a good weaver was of practical advantage, just as to be an accomplished piano player, conversationalist or housekeeper, is an advantage to a young lady among civilized peoples. Men, ever and always, whether white or red, are looking for wives, and a wife that can do something better than other women possesses a charm and a power those others do not possess. This law operated forcefully among the simple Amerinds where there were fewer opportunities for the manifestation of power and ability than are possessed by the civilized. To be a good weaver, therefore, meant plenty of suitors, and the woman of many suitors has greater opportunities of choice than she who has few at her feet.

Of course there would always be those who did the best they could in order to gratify the dawning and growing aesthetic sense. These were the true artists; the true preservers of the ideals; the constant setters-up of standards which their less artistic friends eagerly sought to reach, for the more practical advantages I have suggested.

And this was the condition of the art when outside influences began to be felt; first Spanish, then Mexican, Russian, French, English, American, in speedy succession. The over-powering of the esthetic by the utilitarian I have already shown. Side by side with this destructive spirit has grown up another equally demoralizing. That is the spirit of mere commercialism, alas! so prevalent among so-called civilized peoples, and that John Ruskin wrote so powerfully, indignantly, and, at times, pathetically, against. How many men and women in shop and factory, mill and foundry, labor with definite love for their work? Far too few. In cases without end it is merely drudgery; so many hours to get through with somehow, with as little expenditure of energy as possible. Ten hours work mean, not so much progress in my art to my own and my employer's advantage, but so many dollars and cents. This spirit has begun to possess the Amerind weaver. She no longer does her work fondly and with true love. It matters not what, to her, she uses in her ware so long as she can make something that will sell. Durability, beauty, artistic form, harmony of coloring, following her own ideal fancies, these things mean nothing. The main questions are: "Will it sell?" and "For how much?" As a result we see the wretched aniline dyes desecrating aboriginal work, and tom-fool imitations of white men's designs &c., taking the place of the old worshippings at Nature's shrine.

Indeed, as Dr. Hudson well expresses it: "During the wet season, when food and work are scarce, the majella is forced to weave salable baskets in order to support her family. Her heart is not in this task, but improvidence or gambling has dissipated the earnings of last season. What was once her grandmother's chief delight has now become a labor, for she knows that when her work leaves her hand it contributes another pleasure to the white man, or coin to his pocket. To what extent our artistic world concurs in this belief she little knows.

All (Indian) baskets correctly may be classified under just two heads—baskets made to sell and baskets not made to sell. An expert in this line can detect the difference at ten feet; even a novice will note it on slight inspection. It matters not what weave is employed, the most difficult or the coarsest, whether it be a basket of use or a gaudy ti, old or new, the counterfeit will expose itself to the initiated. Do not believe for a moment that a majella will furnish you goods of as fine a class as she makes for herself. She invariably infers you know nothing of quality, and charges in proportion to the breadth of your ignorance or length of your purse, maybe both. She is no fool; for more than a whole generation she has been a pupil in our school of finance and deception. She has blood in her veins very similar to ours, else her complexion strangely misinterprets. Why not grant her the law-given privilege we have always enjoyed, of taking all she can in safety? However, you may depend upon it,though the price may appear exorbitant, you will get value received, if labor, eye-taxing labor, is taken into consideration.

To a "basket crank" a salable basket possesses no attractions. Inferior material, faulty patterns, spaces between stitches, exposed ends of threads, each and all proclaim carelessness, and when an unsymmetrical outline is added to these, his cup of contempt overflows. Deterioration in basket excellence must be expected in the decadence of their makers. If there is any one cause more responsible than others for this inferiority it is the rapacity of the basket speculators. Four years ago, when the Mendocino Indian basket first made itself known and appreciated by lovers of the unique, a speculator came up from San Francisco to investigate. Within a radius of six miles from Ukiah there lay five rancherias, and it is said by their inhabitants that this man bought, or rather pilfered, two thousand baskets during his brief stay. His ideas of barter were models and marvels of simplicity and effectiveness. Entering a native "shah" he would select whatever could be found to suit his taste, despite the loud protests of the owners, and what could not be purchased at his own price was seized upon as lawful plunder, and a few small coins thrown upon the floor left the

only visible evidence of his unwelcome visit. His depredations extended north as far as Covelo, where fortunately his true merits were
recognized and rewarded by the government agent, who promptly
kicked him out of the reservation. These raids have been occasionally
repeated with rapidly decreasing success. The Indian, after all his
treasure has gone, has realized his own simplicity and cowardice.

The lesson has proven severe, mentally as well as financially, for
with those rare old family heirlooms the incentive to weave similar
ones has disappeared. There are a few specimens in private collections
of weaves once well known and much used by the Pomas that have
now become obsolete. Of all this mongrel brood there are only seven
"majellas" that still emulate the examples of their grandmothers in
conscientious, skillful weaving. Work from their hands is altogether
a different affair from baskets made to sell, being planned, woven and
finished with but one object in view, personal use. These constitute the
class referred to, baskets not made to sell, and hard indeed must be her
straits before parting with them. A stranger never sees them; even
confidence in those she knows and respects must be strong before her
treasures are allowed inspection.

Before you lies the subject most interesting to the majellas' mind,
and, next to her animate children these beautiful products of care and
patient labor are nearest her heart. Hold up this plate-shaped basket
in a favorable light; from bottom to rim a sheen of gold and purple is
reflected like the plumage of some rare tropical bird. She calls it
"doowy pekah," or moon basket. Surely the idea is pretty, and the
effect consistent, though the colors may not be artistically correct.
The greenish plumes of the summer duck are woven in so closely
that no glimpse of the sustaining mesh can be seen, making a soft uniform back ground for zigzag lines of the more brilliant woodpecker.
All is blended like pigment from a deft brush; the rim is encircled
with a row of wampum, under whose snowy edges droop the pride of
our valley quail. Pendants of strung beads tipped with polished bits
of abalone shell complete the effect, and no suggestion s needed by
our imagination in finding their originals in the twinkle of stars.

"How many ducks' heads are in this, Guadaloupe?"

Nine fingers are extended in answer.

"How many kartot (woodpecker)?"

Both hands are raised thrice and still two fingers more."

In Fig. 69a on page 70 I have introduced a photograph of some
girls of the Yokut nation, at the Tule River Reservation, California,
whose parents have insisted upon their learning the art. As I have
before remarked elsewhere, the young women and girls often refuse
to learn, hence the art is rapidly dying out. But the mother of the
three girls here shown, when I spoke to her upon the subject, said
in effect: "No! I don't want my girls to grow up ignorant of one of
the arts that my ancestors learned in the years when the world was
young. Too many young girls go wrong because they don't have the
right kind of work. Mine shall learn to make baskets as I can. (And
she, by the way, is one of the best weavers on the reservation.) These
girls hold specimens of their own work, and some of their baskets I
now have in my own collection; they show care and a keen appreciation of color and design.

CHAPTER XVI.

HOW THE ART MAY BE PRESERVED.

It would be a calamity to Indians and whites alike if the industrial art of basket making were allowed to die. Intelligent, concentrated effort can save it, and in its salvation a greater good can be done the Indians than by a century's distribution of rations and supplies. Let the Indian know that she must be self-supporting; let her know that every basket made according to her own highest traditions can find a ready market at a reasonable price; let systematic efforts be made to encourage the mothers to teach their daughters, and the daughters to learn from their mothers; teach meddlesome traders, teachers, and missionaries that true art does not consist in substituting gaudy aniline colors for the Indians' own dyes; teach the Indians themselves the worth of their own dyes and methods of work, and then let them receive just compensation for their labor, and the art will be saved.

A friend of mine not long ago asked a lady missionary to the Indians if she encouraged her dusky flock in the work of basket making, and confessed herself almost paralyzed at the answer: "No, indeed! I never encourage them in any except the Christian arts."

And this wise "saver of souls" then expatiated on the saving power of delicate embroidery and such like work as compared with the heathen industry of basket making. The idiotic twaddle and sanctimonious nonsense of such people is too foolish for condemnation were it not that, to the undiscerning Indians, they represent the best elements of the white race.

On every reservation; in every school under the control of the government, arrangements should be made instantly to gather together all the old majellas and give them adequate compensation for teaching the young girls all the various branches of the art. The materials used; the proper time to gather them; the best methods of preparing them; the various mineral and vegetable dyes; the best mordants; the various styles of weave; the many and varied shapes; the sources and origins of the wonderful diversity of design; all these things should be taught. Then let intelligent white people study the subject and suggest improved methods of growing, harvesting and preparing the necessary material. Let scientific culture direct new methods of securing the permanent and beautiful colors of the native dyes; and then leave the Indian alone to follow the bent of her own mind, as far as shape, design and symbolism are concerned. It would not be long, were these suggestions carried out, ere there would be a revival of the art; a true renaissance, from which Indian and white would alike profit—profit in more important ways than the merely financial, good though that alone would be.

CHAPTER XVII.

HINTS TO THE COLLECTOR.

In bringing my labors to a close, (which to me at least, have been exceedingly interesting) I shall be pardoned if I give a few more hints which may be useful to collectors in addition to those generally scattered throughout the work.

Experience has long demonstrated that that collector who purchases his baskets from dealers is likely to be misinformed even as to the simplest matters regarding his acquisitions. And this is not to be wondered at. There are few dealers who have either the time, opportunity or desire to personally study the weavers in their own homes. The field occupied by the basket weaver is a large one and it would require a lifetime to thus familiarize one's self with every detail. Hence, all the spirit of commercialism will allow the dealer to do is to gather as much lore as he can from those who collect the baskets for him, and retail it out to his customers with greater or lesser accuracy as his memory or imagination prompts.

One great difficulty that often arises to confuse the young collector is what might be termed the "emigration" of the basket. As I have shown in writing of the so-called "Apache medicine basket," also known as the "Navaho Wedding basket," the basket is made neither by Apache or Navaho, but by Paiuti. It came into the hands of the former by trading. Yet it is often found in good collections labeled: "Made by a Navaho," or "An Apache basket made in Southern Arizona," both of which labels are wrong and misleading. I have also found many Havasupai baskets, which, having been bought from the Hopi (or Moki) were labeled as belonging to and made by the latter people.

Great care, therefore, must be exercised in determining the manufacture of a basket. Let it be known (if necessary) from whom it was purchased, but at the same time, do not let the purchaser make the assumption that because it was purchased from a certain tribe it was therefore made by that tribe.

In the chapter on symbolism I have shown the only true spirit that should possess the collector in gathering information in regard to the designs of desirable baskets. Go always to original sources for information. Don't inject your interpretation into the brain of the weaver, but let her tell you her own idea. This means patience and diplomacy, but the time and energy spent are generally well repaid.

Discourage, wherever possible, the introduction of vicious elements into the art, such as those pictured in Fig. 274. Discourage the use of aniline dyes. The Indians would not use them did they not think white purchasers preferred them. On my last visit to the Havasupais I refused to buy any basket that bore any other than their own native colors. When brought to me I pointed to the strips or patches colored with native dyes and exclaimed "Ha-ni-gi"—good, but gave a frowning and emphatic "Ha-na-to-op-o-gi"—bad—to every intrusion of a foreign color. I know a few such lessons as this would remedy the evil among that people and I should be glad to know of similar discouragement offered elsewhere. Then again, it is well never to purchase a basket that is evidently made for sale only. Where the maker of a basket has a definite use for the work of her hands it means something to her more than a mere money-getting proposition. Something of herself, her life, her thought, is put into that which she expects to use in her home life. Just as that expectant mother who sews upon the diminutive garments that are to clothe the little stranger upon his arrival adds more than mere stitches to the linen and woolen stuff, so does the Indian woman to the basket that is to form part of her household equipment. A trained eye can generally tell, and keen fingers feel, the difference between a basket which has this personal factor connected with it, this sentiment, and the collection of mere coils and stitches which represents a certain number of dollars. In work of the former character the individuality of the maker is more likely to be shown; the mode of thought at the time of making the basket. It is thus that the symbolism of the design has meaning and reality. It reflects the mind and heart of the weaver at the time of its weaving. The result of this is that its decorations are purely Indian. They are not made to please white men; they are the expressions of the Indian women's thought, hence there are no letters or words or numbers or anything that denote a mere anxiety on the part of the maker to catch the eye of the prospective purchaser. This latter spirit means the degradation and ruin of the industry. Hence to the real collector everything that savors of the spirit of destruction of the art is religiously eschewed.

The more the intelligent and conscientious collector studies his baskets the more they will mean to him. Question them and they will tell you many things. As you sit alone with them they will bring up pictures of forest, desert, canyon and village, where humble huts shelter simple and poetic people—people who are as yet "near to Nature's heart." They will tell you of art and religious aspirations and longings, of a Nation's struggling from the lower to the higher. They will reveal the steps of progress, and the methods followed by our own ancestry as they evolved from savagery to civilization. Thus the student is led to a keener appreciation of the solidarity of mankind, and to a fuller apprehension of that doctrine, which, properly understood and lived, is to be man's salvation, viz.: The universal brotherhood of mankind and the consequent fatherhood of God.

CHAPTER XVIII.

BIBLIOGRAPHY OF INDIAN BASKETRY.

BOOKS.

All the Reports of the U. S. Bureau of Ethnology, Washington,. D. C.

All the Reports of the Smithsonian Institution and the U. S. National Museum, especially "Basket-work of the North American Aborigines," by Otis T. Mason, Smith. Inst. Report, 1884. Part 2, pp. 291-306 and plates I to LXIV.

"The Human Beast of Burden," by O. T. Mason, in Report of U. S. National Museum, 1887.

"Primitive Travel and Transportation," by O. T. Mason, Report of U. S. National Museum, 1894.

All the reports of the U. S. Commissioner of Indian Affairs.

"Navaho Legends, by Washington Matthews, American Folk Lore Society.

"The Thompson Indians of British Columbia," by James Teit, Memoirs of the American Museum of Natural History, Vol. 2., part 4.

"Basketry Designs of the Salish Indians," by Livingston Farrand. Ditto, Vol. 2., part 5.

"Woman's Share in Primitive Culture," by Otis T. Mason.

"The Beginnings of Writing," by Walter James Hoffman.

"The Beginnings of Art," by Ernest Grosse.

H. H. Bancroft's Histories.

Journal of American Ethnology and Archaeology, Vol. 4. "The Snake Ceremonials at Walpi," by J. Walter Fewkes.

"Old Missions and Mission Indians of California," by George Wharton James.

"Ramona," by H. H. Jackson.

"A Century of Dishonor," by H. H. Jackson.

"Tribes of California," by Stephen Powers.

JOURNALS, MAGAZINES AND NEWSPAPERS.

Scribner's Magazine, August, 1890. "The Baskets of Anita," by Grace Ellery Channing.

The California Illustrated Magazine, October, 1892. "Among the Basket Makers," by Jeanne C. Carr.

American Anthropologist, October, 1892. "A Study in Butts and Tips," by Washington Matthews.

Overland Monthly, June, 1893. "Pomo Basket Makers," by Dr. J. W. Hudson.

American Anthropologist, October, 1893. "The Navaho," by A. M. Stephen.

American Anthropologist, April, 1894. "The Basket Drum," by Washington Matthews.

Harper's Bazar, September 1, 1894. "Indian Baskets," by Eliza Ruhamah Scidmore.

"The Lost Art of Indian Basketry," by Olive May Percival. Demorest's Family Magazine, February, 1897.

Journal of American Folk Lore, April-June, 1899. "Hopi Basket Dances," by Dr. J. Walter Fewkes.

The Traveler, San Francisco, Cal., August, 1899. "Symbolism in Indian Basketry," by George Wharton James.

Harper's Bazar, Nov. 11, 1899. "Last Industry of a Passing Race,' by Ada Woodruff Anderson.

San Francisco Chronicle, December 3, 1899. "The Art of a Passing Race."

The House Beautiful, February, 190c. 'Aboriginal Basketry in the United States," by Claudia Stuart Coles.

American Anthropologist, April-June, 1900. "Basketry Designs of the Maidu Indians of California," by Roland B. Dixon.

"The Hudson Collection of Basketry," by Otis T. Mason.

Outing, June, 1900. "The Hopi Snake Dance," by George Wharton James.

"Types of American Basketry," by O. T. Mason. Scientific American, N. Y., July 28, 1900.

The Evening Lamp, Chicago, Ill., September 8, 1900. "Poems in Indian Baskets," by George Wharton James.

The Cosmopolitan, October, 1900. "How Indian Baskets are Made," by H. M. Carpenter.

Brief reference to Indian Baskets in "Irish Letter" in Lady's Pictorial, London, Nov. 3, 1900.

The Outlook, January 12, 1901. "Indian Industrial Development," by Mrs. F N. Doubleday.

"The Technique of Amerindian Basketry," by O. T. Mason. Paper read before the A. A. A. S., Baltimore, Dec. 27., 1900, and printed in American Anthropologist, January-March, 1901.

The House Beautiful, April, 1901. "Indian Pottery," by George Wharton James.

Outing, May, 1901. "Indian Basketry," by George Wharton James.

Good Health, June, 1899. "Industries of the Navahoes and Mokis."

New York Tribune, Sunday, Dec. 9, 1900. "Hopi Basket Dance."

Sunset Magazine, San Francisco, February, 1901. "Among the Mono Basket-Makers."

Southern Workman, Hampton, Va., August, 1901. "Indian Basketry."

Sunset Magazine, San Francisco, November, 1901. "With Some California Basket-Makers."

The Chautauquan, September, 1901. "Indian Basketry in House Decoration."

Literary Collector, New York, January, 1902. "Ideas in Indian Baskets."

Ladies' Home Journal, 1902. "The Charmed Indian Baskets."

P. S.---Since this book was written the Second Part of the Seventeenth "Annual Report of the Bureau of American Ethnology" has been received. In it Dr. J. Walter Fewkes has an elaborate and fascinating monograph in which the designs on the ancient pottery of Tusayan are fully described. The reader interested in Symbolism will find a rich treat and a fund of new information in this work.

APPENDIX.

The first edition of this book was issued in the latter part of April, 1901. Before September the whole edition was exhausted and a second imperatively called for. I am glad, therefore, to seize the opportunity to add new and interesting material, both in illustrations and descriptions, that has recently become available.

DIXON ON "BASKETRY DESIGNS OF THE MAIDUS"— In the April-June, 1900, number of the American Anthropologist there appeared an interesting article by Mr. Roland B. Dixon, entitled: "Basketry Designs of the Maidu Indians of California." These people are before referred to on page 57. By the courtesy of Mr. Dixon and the authorities of the American Museum of Natural History, where

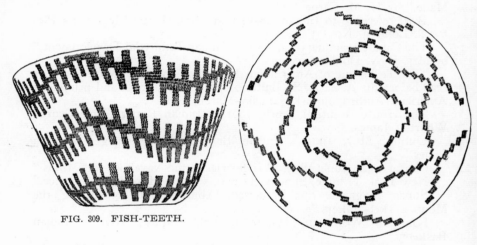

FIG. 309. FISH-TEETH.

FIG. 310. EARTHWORM.

the baskets enshrining these designs are exhibited, also of Mr. F. W. Hodge, the managing editor of the Anthropologist, I am herewith privileged to present to my readers the engravings and descriptions.

Says Mr. Dixon: "In the series of forty baskets nearly two dozen different designs are used. For about twenty of these satisfactory explanations have been obtained up to the present, and these may be divided for convenience of treatment into three classes—animal designs, plant designs, and those representing objects such as arrow-points, mountains, etc.

"One of the simplest and clearest of the many designs belonging to the first group is that known as fish-teeth (figure 309). The execution of this pattern is rather irregular, and it is somewhat difficult to determine whether it was intended to have the crossbars opposite each other or alternating. Looking at the basket from below, the resemblance to the wide open mouth of a fish is rather striking.

"A little less obvious in its meaning is the earthworm on a basket from the same locality as the last. In this (figure 310) the worm is represented by a succession of parallelograms, linked together by the corners, to form a sinuous chain running around the basket. The separate parallelograms here are said to stand for the segments of the earthworm's body.

"Of very frequent occurrence on baskets from Sacramento valley and the foothills is the design representing the quail (311). In this the characteristic feature is the plume on the quail's head, shown here by the vertical square-tipped appendices to the parallelograms which are meant for the bodies of the birds. The quail-plumes themselves

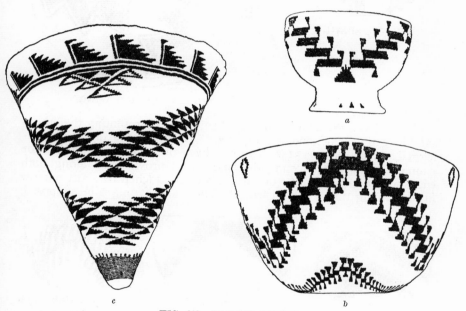

FIG. 312. FLYING GEESE.

are used at times in the decoration of the feather-baskets, being woven in while the basket is being made, and standing out all over when done. The use of the bird's plumes does not, however, seem to have been restricted to baskets which had the quail design.

"Two other designs are representations of birds, the "geese flying" and the "duck's wing." One form of one of these designs (figure 312 c) is apparently meant for a flock of geese in flight, their triangular order being well shown in the arrangement of the points of the design. The other two forms (figure 312 a, b), said also to be "geese flying," are not quite so clear as the first. That numbered 312 b is curiously like the quail pattern already described, except that the appendices are triangular instead of square; it is possible that these may refer to the feet of the goose seen just as the bird lights (?). The design known as the "duck's wing" (figure 313) is more or less doubtful in its meaning. It is said to signify the patch of white seen on each side of the bird.

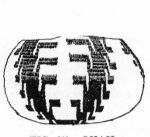

FIG. 311. QUAIL.

FIG. 313. DUCK'S WING.

"Very clear in their meaning are the designs representing the "thousand-legged worm" and the raccoon. The millipede or "thousand-legged worm" (figure 314) is shown by a broad band of solid color running in a zigzag around the basket and provided all along both edges with a great number of small triangles attached by short narrow lines, forming thus a sort of fringe. These are, as might be supposed,

FIG. 314. MILLIPEDE.

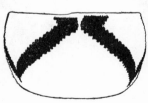

FIG. 315 RACCOON.

FIG. 316. GRASSHOPPER LEG.

the many feet of the millipede. The characteristic feature of the raccoon design (figure 315) is in the peculiar curve of the band of color which runs around the basket. This is said variously to stand for the stripes of the animal, or for the os penis; in either case the intent of the pattern is clear.

"Rather less realistic than the foregoing designs is the grasshopper pattern, found on a small basket from Genesee (figure 316). This might more properly be called the grasshopper-leg pattern, as this is the part of the insect which is represented. Apparently the longer bars are the legs, and the shorter bars at right angles to the former are the "feet" (?). Classed with the animal designs for convenience is the pattern known as the eye (figure 317). This is represented simply by a hollow rhombus or diamond.

"Turning to the second group of designs, those representing plants, it is evident that here the number of different patterns is considerably less than in the first group. On a number of baskets is found a design of which the only explanation that could be obtained was that it was "just a flower." This design (figure 318) consists of rows of broad-based triangles, each row from the base to the top containing success-

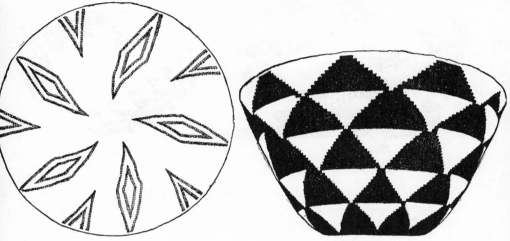

FIG. 317. EYE.   FIG. 318. FLOWER.

ively larger triangles. In the specimen figured the design is not perfectly regular, but the pattern is sometimes made with great regularity, and the triangles arranged in a kind of whorl, giving a curious effect when the basket is seen from below. The triangles here represent the separate petals of the flower.

"The common brake (Pteris aquilina) is represented by the design shown in figure 319 from a basket from Mooretown. The points in this are intended for the pinnae of the fern, but the meaning of the bars in the central stripe is not yet clear. Closely resembling this pattern is one from the Konkau (figure 320), but of this I have not been able to obtain a reasonable explanation. Very similar also is the design said to depict the vine (figure 321). In this the spiral character of the pattern as it winds around the basket is the twining of the vine about a pole, while the points are the separate leaves as they stand out on either side.

"One of the most effective plant designs is that of the pine-cone, used by the people of the higher Sierras. In this design (figure 322) the realism is quite marked, the broad, pyramidal form and the horizontally directed points being strikingly like the large and strong-spined cones of the digger and yellow pines. Although the digger pines grow in large numbers on the foot-hills, no specimens of this design were seen except in the higher portions of the mountains. What is apparently the same figure cut in two is represented around the upper edge of the large pack-basket on which the full design is shown.

"Similar to the cone, but differing in that it has a solid center, is the pattern found on a basket from Big Meadows (figure 323). This is regarded as the representation of a bush, growing high up in the mountains, and apparently rather rare, as I was unable to get a specimen to identify the plant.

"Of the designs representing objects belonging to the third group

FIG. 319. BRAKE.

FIG. 320.

into which the different patterns were divided, that of the feather is by far the most important. It seems to occur in several different forms. The simplest of these, perhaps, is shown in figure 324. The

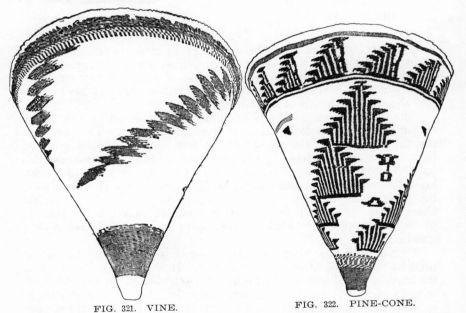

FIG. 321. VINE.

FIG. 322. PINE-CONE.

characteristic feature of the design appears to be the notched or saw-tooth edge, in imitation of an old custom of thus notching the arrow-feathers by burning. In figure 325 the design appears in a slightly different form, the notched "feathers" being arranged in points around the basket. A variation of this design is shown in figure 326, where the interior of the point is filled with a somewhat elaborate pattern, and again in figure 327, where this interior pattern is different in each point. There is reason to believe that these isolated triangles are meant to represent flint arrow-points, a design which alone is very frequently met. The association of the arrow-point with the

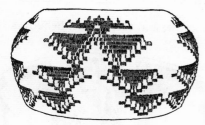

FIG. 323. A BUSH.

FIG. 326. FEATHERS.

arrow-feather would not be an unnatural one, and till further evidence is forthcoming it may be considered that in the designs shown in figures 326 and 327 there is a combination of the feather pattern with the flint arrow-point.

"The flint arrow-point as it occurs alone is seen in figures 328 and

FIG. 324. FEATHERS.

329. The triangles which make up this figure are linked together in a way different from those making the feather designs, and the longer axes of the triangles or rhombuses are vertical instead of horizontal.

"The simple circular band of color surrounding the basket is said to be a path or trail (figure 322). It does not seem to be of very frequent occurrence, and in all the specimens seen is a complete circle, without the gap so common on baskets and pottery from the Southwest, as also among some of the California tribes, of which the Yuki may be taken as an example.

"A rather elaborate composite design representing mountains and clouds (figure 330) is shown on a basket from Big Meadows. Here the mountains are represented as a range in perspective, the short vertical lines being trees growing on the slopes. Above these mountains, and running all around the upper edge of the basket, is a zigzag line signifying clouds floating over the summits of the mountains."

Mr. Dixon also states that "the knowledge of the designs is almost exclusively confined to the older women, the younger generation knowing only very few."

That this is a fact all close observers know, and therefore it behooves

FIG. 325. FEATHERS.   FIG. 327. FEATHERS.

those who are interested to work with greater energy than ever to obtain as speedily as possible the meaning of all existent designs. The

FIG. 328. FLINT ARROWPOINTS.

drive, rush, pressure and materialism of our modern civilized life is rapidly changing the character of the thought of the Indian. In the old days she had opportunity for quiet meditation upon the objects of nature to which her attention was arrested, but now the utilitarian (falsely so-called) and commercial spirit forced upon her afford little time for such cogitation. The new race of Indians, therefore, is growing up as unpoetic, unsentimental and unromantic as their severest censors could wish, and only by the prompt adoption of such methods as I have elsewhere suggested can this evil condition be averted.

FEAR IN DESIGNS—Speaking of the zigzag design of one of his baskets, Mr. A. W. de la Cour Carroll says: "It has been said that the Indians do not imitate in their designs anything that creates fear within them. This is an error. These Indians (the Paiutis and Shoshones) are much afraid both of lightning and snakes, and in the photograph you see the lightning design (so explained to me by its weaver, the widow of the last chief of this district), and I have two or three baskets in which the diamond back rattlesnake and the long blacksnake are shown."

FIG. 329. FLINT ARROWPOINTS.   FIG. 330. MOUNTAINS AND CLOUDS.

SOUTH SEA ISLAND BASKET—In a letter received Sept. 20, 1901, a gentleman writes me: "While in Nantucket this summer I found in an old curiosity shop a basket brought to this country from the South Sea Islands by an old Nantucket captain who died forty years ago. The basket is of the weave and shape of your Fig. 104, page 105. It was ornamented around the edge with white rings (ivory?) like your Fig. 41, page 46, and there are also arrowhead patterns on the side done in these same white rings which were not sewed on, but carried on thread woven into the texture."

CAHUILLA WEAVER—Fig. 331 is a pathetic picture to me. I made it some years ago in Cahuilla. To see this old woman almost helpless, halt, and slowly going blind, and yet anxious to work as long as she is able, is truly piteous, and it contains a lesson of sturdy independence that it would be well for many a white woman to learn. The old women are the only basket makers at Cahuilla, the young women preferring to do less laborious work even though it bring them less money.

BENHAM COLLECTION—Fig. 332 is of a Pima weaver, brought by Mr. J. W. Benham from the reservation in Arizona to the Pan-American Exposition, in Buffalo, N. Y. Here she plied her awl and wove her baskets in front of a tule hut, exactly as she does when in her native Arizona home. Thousands came and watched her dexterous fingers as they wrapped the willow splints around the grass of the inner coil, and saw the design worked in by means of the martynia or cat's claw. Object lessons of this nature are exceedingly valuable. They give opportunity for the gaining of definite and accurate knowledge of the Indian woman's skill, and demonstrate not only how perfectly the figures of designs are mapped out in her active little brain, but how easily she leads her fingers to compel the splints to reproduce that which she mentally imagines. It would be a good thing for art students, whether of the beaux arts, or the textiles, etc., to study a num-

From the Southern Workman.

FIG. 331. A CAHUILLA WEAVER.

FIG. 332. PIMA WEAVER AT PAN-AMERICAN EXPO SITION.

FIG. 333. PIMA BASKETS IN THE BENHAM COLLECTION.

ber of such Indians as this engaged in their art work in their own simple, natural, untrained fashion.

Fig. 333 is of six Pima baskets in the Benham collection. Here the geometrical designs predominate, only the one to the right having human figures. As I have before explained the weavers state that most of these meandering fret, zigzag, swastika and similar motifs have their origin in flowing water.

Fig. 334 is of Apache baskets also in the Benham collection. Here the superiority of the Apache over the Pima weave is very evident. In the two baskets to the right a similar motif is presented in the design to many of the Pimas, viz., a central water reservoir from which streams flow out in various directions.

The center basket is a fine large specimen of a shape dear to the heart of the Apache weaver. It used to be her granary in which she stored acorns, corn, grass or other seeds. It was large and commodious and built for use and wear, consequently combines strength with its utility of form. As the esthetic instinct grew, the decorative principle demanded greater scope in the treatment of the designs, and simple bands gave place to more complicated and expressive symbols.

Fig. 335 is a magnificent specimen of one of these Apache baskets. It stands about four feet high and contains many thousands of stitches. In shape it is almost perfect, and the designs are most striking, though I am unable to give the weaver's interpretation of them. The steps that ascend from the bottom are mountains, and the same design with the two descending lines upon them are mountains upon which the rain is falling. On either side of these the connected diamonds sometimes represent the rattlesnake. The upper band below the net-work design is the conventionalized mountain and valley pattern.

Mr. Benham has called my attention to a method of his own in determining which are Pima and which Apache baskets. He says that in the examination of many hundreds made by these two peoples he has never known the sign to fail, viz., that in the Apache weave there is a ridge in each coil which denotes the presence of three splints of about equal thickness, while the Pima weave lacks this distinguishing mark.

In Fig. 337 are various baskets in the Benham collection. No. 5 is a well made and colored Oraibi (Hopi) sacred meal tray, while No. 6 is a Mashonganavi (Hopi) yucca plaque of star design, most accurately and beautifully worked out.

Fig. 338 is interesting mainly as it shows several striking designs on Oraibi (Hopi) wicker-work plaques. On the left is a distinct representation of a Katchina, one of the totemic, ancestral divinities of the Hopi, to whom much of their worship is addressed. They might be termed "lesser divinities" of this people of many gods, for they do not hold so high a place in their regard as do the gods which personify the powers of nature. Three other of these baskets in Fig. 338 represent the mythical thunder bird, a creature of whom Dr. Fewkes has written most interestingly in his recent monograph on Ancient Hopi Pottery, published in the Reports of the Bureau of Ethnology.

The star design in the Mashonganavi plaque to the right is effective and well worked out.

DAT-SO-LA-LE—Fig. 340 is of Dat-so-la-le (whose name, I am told, is pronounced to rhyme with Charley, emphasis on the "la"), the

FIG. 334. APACHE BASKETS IN THE BENHAM COLLECTION.

FIG. 335. LARGE APACHE BASKET IN BENHAM COLLECTION.

FIG. 337.   VARIOUS BASKETS IN THE BENHAM COLLECTION.

FIG. 338.   BASKETS, MOSTLY ORAIBI, IN BENHAM COLLECTION.

Washoe weaver of The Emporium, Carson City, Nevada. She is engaged in the making of her basket, No. 24, a beautiful three-colored specimen, the design of which is purely Indian and beautifully poetic. On the top of the basket the homes of the Indians are represented; in the designs below are four different signs, representing nests and young and old birds flying. The meaning is: "When the birds and their fledgelings leave their nests and fly away the Indians will move to new homes." This basket contains over 50,000 stitches, woven thirty to the inch and occupied six months in the weaving. Of the basket to the right, at her feet, the following legend is given: The "tower"-like part of the design represents certain families and their descendants. The squares or parallelograms, with triangles on each side and darting rays top and bottom, represent certain sacred rites or degrees. Below these are seen four lozenges, which denote four chiefs. Dat-so-la-le explains that there are four chiefs of the Washoes who receive the four "degrees," or pass through the four stages of certain societies, ere they are recognized as of full power or authority, and these four acquire this right of initiation by inheritance, only those descended from former initiates being eligible. This basket contains over 45,000 stitches and is woven 29 to the inch.

KERN COUNTY, CALIFORNIA, WEAVERS—There are a number of fine basket makers in Kern County, California. No attempt, as far as I know, has yet been made to study these people to get at definite knowledge as to their tribal relationships. The baskets they make are of the Yokut type, and I doubt whether there is any real difference in their manufacture, materials or designs. Dr. J. W. Hudson, whose admirable writings about the Pomas have been largely drawn upon in the preceding pages, is now, at the present time of writing (end of September, 1901), gathering baskets and other Indian material from the aborigines of this country for the Field Columbian Museum, and there is reason to hope that he will ere long enlighten our ignorance by one of his luminous and carefully prepared monographs.

McLEOD COLLECTION—Undoubtedly the best collection of Kern County baskets now in existence is that of Mr. E. L. McLeod, of Bakersfield, Cal. With a keen love of the beautiful, Mr. McLeod has always been attracted by the charms of fine baskets, so, for many years he has been adding to his store. Living in close contact with the Kern County Indians, he has had unusual opportunities for selection and choice, and the result is a collection that is at once the delight, envy and despair of all who see it. To merely catalogue his baskets would be to fill up many pages of this work. A score or more are really typical baskets and ought to have both pictorial and fully written description, and, should the interest in the subject demand a third edition of my modest book, I hope I may be able to secure these for that edition.

One basket, however, of the McLeod collection has already been pictured and described in these pages (see Fig. 270, page 188). Another illustration of the same basket is also presented in Fig. 122a.

This is one of the most interesting baskets I have ever seen. In color it is a rich cream, with the designs worked out in red and black, the whole mellowed by time into that indescribable but so real charm that only expert collectors can fully appreciate. It is 16 inches across and 9 inches high. The neck is 5 inches across. When Mr. McLeod first heard of it and saw it, it was being used as a water receptacle by its owner on Paiuti Mountain, Kern Co. For four years he visited its owner and endeavored to purchase it without avail. At last, succumbing to the dazzling vision of several handsful of silver spread temptingly before her, the owner reluctantly parted with it. Before doing so, however, Mr. McLeod learned from her that the basket was made by a Christianized woman early in the last century. The priest had so pictured to her mind the life of Christ and the Apostles that she wove them into her basket. From Fig. 122a it will be seen that on the top there are thirteen human figures depicted, and that ten of these are in pairs, standing side by side. Then one figure is in a division alone,

FIG. 340.   DAT-SO-LA-LE, THE WASHOE WEAVER.

while the other two figures are together, one a little below the other. With an ingenuity that is striking in its simplicity and effectiveness the weaver thus placed Judas, the betrayer, in a solitary and separate place, while the beloved disciple, John, is with Christ but not equal to him, being placed a little behind him.

Another interesting basket in Mr. McLeod's collection is a baby cradle, a type in itself. I purchased a similar cradle two years ago at the Tule River Reservation. It is simple and primitive, yet effective. A forked stick is found, with the arms of the fork extending some two or three feet from the fork itself, and gradually widening out. At the terminus of the two arms the sticks are about a foot and a half apart. Across these divided arms lesser sticks are placed and lashed to each arm. Upon these cross sticks peeled willow shoots are placed, twined around the topmost cross stick, and bound together by twenty-five cross stitches. Thus a rude carrying cradle is formed, which I have never seen elsewhere.

Another basket that its owner prizes highly is a very old and dilapidated looking specimen, that none but the really scientific collector would be more than casually interested in. This is a very ancient specimen excavated from a cave in the Cuyama Valley, which is located between Bakersfield and Santa Barbara, Cal. It is made with tules for warp and a fibrous hemp for woof, and was lined inside and out with asphaltum. It is of the twined weave, with alternate bands where two splints instead of one are twined, as a decorative device. It is 15 inches high. When found it was entirely collapsed and out of shape and was only restored by the exercise of great care. As much barley was put inside as it would hold, and this was then soaked in water. How old the basket is none can tell, for there have been no Indians in the region where it was found for fully fifty years.

Another basket of Mr. McLeod's demonstrates the impossibility of any other than the weaver determining the meaning of the design. It shows a large number of St. Andrew's crosses radiating from the center of the basket. The explanation given by the Monos and Yokuts of the St. Andrew's Cross has already been given, but this weaver said she was imitating the flight of a flock of butterflies that came from the valley to tell her of the arrival of spring. And as the basket is held at a little distance and in the proper light the fidelity of the design to the object depicted is remarkable. There is a deep poetic pathos in this design. The old woman who made it lived about a hundred miles away from Bakersfield, high up in the mountains in the forks of the creeks that go to make the Kern River. After a long weary winter it would seem like a glimpse of a new and beautiful world to have these butterflies come into vision, and, thankful for the joy the sight of them gave to her, the grateful woman thus expressed the inner emotions of her heart. So I see joy, gratitude and thankfulness in this design.

But there is an added pathos in the fact that in August of 1901 a waterspout fell in the mountains above this poor old weaver's solitary hut, and as the torrents dashed down and met at the forks, the frail structure, with its inhabitant, was swept down the canyon, and though Indians and a few whites both searched, the body has never been found. Perhaps she is now enjoying many butterflies, in a land where flood and destruction are unknown. According to a careful estimate made, reckoning from the known dates of events in which she participated, she must have been over 118 years old when the storm waters thus washed out her life.

BRAIDED BORDER STITCH—It will doubtless be recalled what I have said about the "herring-bone" finishing stitch found on Navaho, Paiuti and Havasupai baskets. Mr. McLeod has a basket, bought at Lake Tahoe some years ago and made by a Washoe Indian, that has this same finishing stitch. This opens up the question as to whether the Washoe uses this stitch, and, if so, from whence did she obtain it, or, is it another instance of independent origin? Mr. A. Cohn of The Emporium, Carson City, writes me that there is a

Washoe squaw now living who uses this braided finish. Mr. Benham also informs me that he occasionally purchases a basket from an Apache weaver who makes the same stitch.

It is not at all unlikely that the Navaho tradition of the origin of this stitch locating its first usage with this people is, so far, correct. Accepting this, it would be easy to explain its existence among all the other weavers. The Paiutis on the north, the Apaches on the south and the Havasupais on the west, all have dealings with the Navahoes, and their baskets are found interchangeably among the three tribes. The Washoes and Paiutis are neighbors, in western Nevada, and it is not at all unlikely that some Washoe weaver, visiting her Paiuti sister, learned the art by watching the latter as she continued her work while gossiping with her visitor.

From Mr. McLeod I learn that the Kern County Indians are mainly Yokuts and Paiutis. The presence of these latter Nevada Indians in this region, so far away from their original habitat, has been already fully explained. The Yokuts originally possessed the land. They made a great rendezvous of Fort Tejon, both before and after its occupancy by the whites.

MONACHI WEAVERS—Above Kernville, in Mountain Meadows, are a few Monachis, who are excellent basket weavers. To what tribe these belong I do not know. They may be Shoshones, Monos or Yokuts. Mr. A. W. De la Cour Carroll writes me of the Monachis being formerly on the eastern slopes of the Sierra Nevada. He says "there is scarcely a Monachi left. This tribe used to make the Monachi Valley their summer hunting and fishing ground, but now there is not one family left."

DIFFICULTIES IN COLLECTING—There are some people who funnily imagine that all those who collect baskets from the original weavers are after the type of the scoundrel described by Dr. Hudson on page 227. The following letter may interest some readers and show to others that the Indians are fully alive to the value of their wares. A friend had purchased for me a basket from the wife of the chief of a California tribe. It was as yet unfinished. The price, finished, was to be $10. One day he received this letter, doubtless dictated by the weaver and written by her son, a lad of some 13 years. I give its original spelling, etc.:

"Dear Sir: I am gone to tell you of about the basket. the basket worth $15. He is little big. I put 1 inch more I think. I sell the basket $15.00.

from yours."

My friend refused to pay the $15, and a few days later another collector came along and gladly took it for $16. He writes: "You see that it is almost impossible to get a basket unless you stand right over it. The Indians will not set a price until they have finished a basket. Then the fellow who is there and will give the most gets it." This, of course, refers to finely woven baskets, some of which are almost as beautiful as any ever made.

On this subject of "New versus Old" baskets, Mr. Cour Carroll says: "The old baskets are scarcely now to be had, but if of equally fine work I like the new as well, for time will bring the ripe desired tinge."

This suggests that Mr. Cour Carroll has found in his experience, west of the Sierra Nevadas, what I have found among the Yokuts, Pimas, Apaches, Havasupais and Paiutis, viz., that there are still a few weavers who do as good work as ever was done. Few, indeed, these are, yet they do exist, as is further shown by the work of Dat-so-la-le.

MONO WEAVERS—In the February number of "Sunset," published in San Francisco, I wrote of some Mono weavers and baskets. Here I found baskets of exquisite shape, color, weave and design, and by kind permission of the Southern Pacific Co., I am privileged to republish both illustrations and descriptions.

"Just below the Yosemite valley, east and south, a nation of aboriginal basket-makers is to be found. One of the counties of California, as well as a noted lake, are named after them—the Monos. Little by little the lands owned by their ancestors have been stolen from them, and now they are driven in every direction higher and higher into the mountains. With an indifference to their rights that is very different from the passionate rebellion of such people as the Apaches, they have allowed themselves to be dispossessed of their homes, and have climbed away further from the white man. Doubtless the reason for this seeming indifference is to be found in the fact that there is plenty more valuable land in the higher Sierras which they can use for their simple pastoral wants.

Not long ago I visited this people with a desire to see what could be learned of them before they entirely disappeared from the ken of white men. Leaving the line of the Southern Pacific at Fresno, I drove up into the heart of the Sierras, past the great flumes and lumber yards at Clovis, where millions of feet of lumber annually are floated down from the mountain heights; past great vineyards; past sites made famous by gold-hunters in the "days of '49"; up, and ever up, until a most beautiful and charming retreat was found in Burr valley. Here, once the home of the Fresno Indians, white men have planted apples, plums, pears, peaches and other fruit trees; acres and acres are sown to grain, and, when I arrived, the clatter of the harvester and the hum of the thresher filled the whole valley with their welcome sounds.

A few miles over the ridge, and the first of the Mono Indian rancherias was found. Perched on the steep sides of a mountain, near a spring, the little cluster of huts was observed as we approached over the ridge. Houses of rude lumber, not much larger than good-sized dry-goods boxes, with here and there a "ramada," or shack of brushwood, formed the dwelling places of these people. The major portion of the inhabitants were gone into the San Joaquin valley to cut peaches and pick grapes, so our investigations here were somewhat limited.

The following day, however, we pushed along over the mountain sides, down into a shut-in valley, and then on and up, over steep and difficult trails until a large settlement was reached. Here we were in the veritable home of the Monos. They are seldom visited, and white people are a rarity. Here we spent several days, watching the Indians at their crude farming, grinding of acorns, preparing the meal, making "bellota," or as they pronounce it, "viota" or acorn bread, peeling the

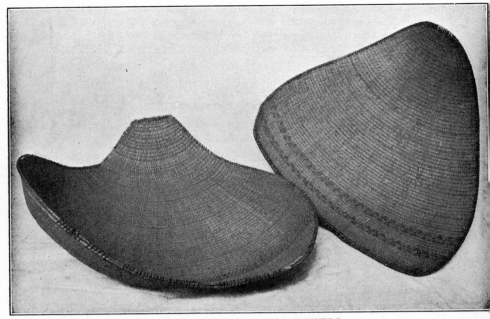

FIG. 342.   MONO FLOUR SIFTERS.
In the Collection of George Wharton James.

FIG. 344.   MONO INDIAN MUSH BASKETS.
(Collection of George Wharton James.)

roots for basket-making, dyeing the strands, and finally making the exquisite basket-work for which they are justly famed.

Watch one of the women at work, pounding acorns. It is not an easy task. The "pounder" is a heavy piece of granite, and the "mortar" is a hole hewn out of a great granite boulder that rests under a tree. The shade is grateful, for the sun is hot and the work arduous. Raising the pestle as high as her arms can reach the woman brings it down with great force upon the acorns until she deems them pounded enough. Then the meal is placed in the sifter, a peculiar shell-shaped

FIG. 343. MONO INDIAN BASKETS.
(Collection of George Wharton James.)

piece of basketry, (see Fig. 342,) and that part of the meal that is not fine enough goes through the pounding process anew.

Now the meal is prepared, but before it can be used for food it must be so treated that the horribly bitter and strong taste will be taken from it. A large bowl-shaped cavity is made in the sand or gravel, and in this is placed a piece of canvas or cloth of some kind to act as a strainer. The acorn meal is now well mixed with water in which a little lye has been placed. This mixture is then poured into the canvas, and, as the water seeps away, the acorn meal is left in a kind of mushy state, but much nearer to food than it was before. This paste is thrown into baskets, large and beautiful specimens of their labor. When enough moisture has evaporated to permit, the paste is cut up into short strips, placed on canvas, boards, or anything that will answer the purpose, and put out into the sun to dry.

FIG. 345. MONO INDIAN BASKETS OF RATTLESNAKE DESIGN.

One would think by this time it would be ready for use. Not at all. It has to undergo two more processes before it can be eaten. First, it must be pounded again into meal. Then it needs to be cooked. A large fire is made. Into it are cast a large number of good-sized stones. While they are becoming heated, the acorn flour is mixed with water and well stirred with a peculiar-looking stick, one end of which has been bent to form an oval loop.

You wonder what the loop is for, and your curiosity is soon satisfied; for, with dexterous movements, the woman uses this looped stirring-stick to pick up a red-hot rock from the fire and convey it to the basket where her mixture of acorn meal and water stands. Hissing and sizzling, the rock drops into the basket, and the stick is now used with vigor to stir the liquid. Another and another heated rock is brought, and by this time the thin, watery gruel is changed into a cooked, glutinous, thick mush. This is poured out into another basket, or, after the rocks are taken out, is allowed to remain in the cooking basket, and it is now ready to be eaten, or to undergo further processes. If it is to be made into bread it is again dried, again pounded, and then is mixed with water, as ordinary flour, made into small cakes and baked on heated stones. But to the white man it is a poor and disagreeable substitute for his own wheat bread, although to the Monos it is, perhaps, their staple article of diet.

To gather the acorns and transport them over the steep mountain trails is no easy task, and this is entirely the work of the women. With a large carrying basket, shown in the frontispiece illustration, and the basket to the left in Fig. 343, the patient and hard-working "lady" of the household will carry a load ten or a dozen miles, heavy enough to stagger many a hearty and stout-looking man.

To call this Indian woman a lady seems strange and out of place, I know, does it not? And yet, do you know, the term is absolutely appropriate and true. For, are you aware—and I give John Ruskin as my authority—that a lady is a laf-dig—loaf-maker or provider; she who makes the loaves for the household? The Mono woman, therefore, in the original and true sense, is a real lady, and, as such, should be honored and respected.

Few people on looking at one of these women would recognize an artist, a poet, a profound religionist. And yet she is all these. On page 54, fig. 48, the woman from whom I bought four baskets is pictured. The basket she holds is a beautiful creation. The colors of many of these bottle-necked designs are as harmonious and pleasing to the most cultured chromatic taste as the finest dress made under the direction of Worth, and the weaving is as regular and perfect as if done by machinery. In shape, too, it is artistic, symmetrical and perfect. It was made to be a little household treasure basket, and the design is an embodied prayer.

After I had purchased this and the weaver sat looking at it with regretful longing that her necessities were such that she was compelled to part with it for the white man's money, I could imagine her thoughts lifted to Those Above that they would not deem her sacrilegious in selling that which she had intended as a perpetual prayer."

One of the baskets of Fig. 48 is now in the Wanamaker collection and is pictured in the article entitled: "What Baskets Are to the Indian," which appeared in Everybody's Magazine for November, 1901. It will also be observed in the frontispiece of this volume. The design is of the diamond-backed rattlesnake, the commonest of Mono designs, and dancing Shamans, or Medicine Men. The weaver told me that the diamond design is a prayer of propitiation to the powers that control the rattlesnake, which abounds in the region, so that her husband,

Photo by George Wharton James. From the Southern Workman.

FIG. 346. THE HILL COLLECTION.

her children and herself may not be bitten as they wander to and fro in the snake-infested districts.

On the upper basket of the frontispiece several flowing streams are depicted in the zigzags below the rattlesnake pattern, and, standing above each zigzag to the left, is the conventionalized form of the quail plume. This informs the beholder that there are plenty of quail to be found near these streams.

The carrying baskets represent the conventional design for hills and valleys, the steep mountain summits of the "Sierra"—the Saw Teeth— being intended. Another conventional design pictured on the second basket from the right in Fig. 344 represents hills and valleys lower down in the mountains, where valleys are broader and hills not so pointed.

In the basket to the right of Fig. 345 the rattle of the rattlesnake is represented. The small basket in front in Fig. 343 is especially interesting to the collector. The woman from whom I purchased it informed me that it was made by her grandmother, hence it must be very old, possibly a century or more. It represents water flowing down the steep slopes of a mountain, the latter represented by the steps, on which are plenty of quail, represented by the quail plume, one of the common and most beautiful designs of the Sierra Nevadas.

THE HILL COLLECTION—Fig. 346 is a portion of the collection of the daughter of Thomas Hill, the well-known artist of the Yosemite Valley. Here is quite an interesting variety and they add no inconsiderable element of attraction to Mr. Hill's always attractive studio at Wawona. The largest basket, perched high in the corner, is one of the carrying baskets. Its size and capacity can better be understood by glancing at Fig. 167a. I think it is Hudson, elsewhere quoted, who says that if one compares the carrying capacity of the "kathak" with that of the wheelbarrow, everything is in favor of the former. It is, indeed, truly wonderful the great burdens the women will carry in these simple and primitive carriers. The photograph, Fig. 167a, shows a Yokut woman of Tule River Reservation in California, with a load of figs and peaches. The basket is suspended on a broad band of rawhide across the upper forehead. It is such a load as few men would care to carry far, and yet this woman carried it for nearly two miles before she reached her home, and was most obliging and patient when I asked her to kindly allow me to photograph her. And this two miles was not on a level road. It was a steep hill, where no man that I know would have cared to push a wheelbarrow. The lightness combined with strength, too, manifested in the weave of these baskets is remarkable and is well worthy the attention of those who regard the Indian as an incapable.

But to return to Fig. 346. The careful observer will note Hopi plaques of both Mashonganavi and Oraibi weave, dice basket or plaque, baby cradles, hats, trinket baskets, mush bowls, unpitched water bottles, and seed sifters. Most of them are baskets collected in the Sierra Nevada region, and were woven by Yo-ham-i-ties, Monos, Yokuts and Paiutis.

YOKUT AND PIMA NAMES—On the Tule River Reservation the bowl shaped baskets are called Ku-tsou and the bottle necks, Oza. The baskets of these weavers are invariably of natural colors, white,

FIG. 348. ALEUT BASKETS IN THE FROHMAN COLLECTION.

FIG. 348A. SALLY BAGS IN FROHMAN COLLECTION.

black and red. The white material—squaw grass, willow and the like —is all termed "ho-put," while the black, the martynia, is "mo-noch-koot." The red splints are made by peeling the bark from the roots of the red bud, and are called "annup."

The Pima name for a bowl basket is "wah," or almost two syllables, thus "hu-ah." The "cat-tail" is largely used by these weavers as the material or core of the inner coil.

WATER BOTTLES—A Nevada correspondent writes to me in regard o the shape of the water-bottles, such as pictures in Figs. 203 and 222. Somewhere I have written that this shape undoubtedly originated in a sandy country so that it could be stuck in the sand and be thus kept upright when not being carried. He says: "Our Nevada Indians tell me that it is made in this particular shape so that should it fall it will always "right" itself, thereby saving whole or part of its contents. Water is one of the scarcest things on the Nevada deserts and every drop is esteemed precious. This shape basket is used when traveling. For home use they make a flat-bottomed vessel."

FROHMAN COLLECTION—Mrs. J. Frohman, of Portland, Ore., is an intelligent collector, especially of the baskets of the Northwest. In her collection are to be found all the varieties, and the accompanying engravings give some idea of the scope of her endeavors. Fig. 348 shows a number of Aleut baskets, and Mrs. Frohman writes as follows:

"The Aleutians are from the Islands of Attu, Kesega, Makushin, the most remote and isolated of our possessions. In these little sea-girt islands, scarcely more than a stepping-stone to Asia, we discover the finest weavers in the world of basketry. The barabas or homes of the Aleuts are sodden huts, for they are literally made of sod. The roof is gay with brilliant flowers during the long days of their brief summer, but in winter it is inconceivably damp and dreary in the interior of the barabas, and it requires many months of scanty light to construct a single basket. Luxuriant grass springs up while the sunshine lingers, and this is gathered, dried and split many times. The finest baskets are perfectly round, having covers, holding about a pint, and others much larger, have no covers, are round and not so fine. The weave of the small ones is so fine as to closely resemble gros grain silk, the number of stitches to the square inch being almost double that of any other Indian basket. No dyes are used and only a little ornamentation of colored silk thread or worsted is deftly introduced. The feather of the eagle is also sometimes interwoven with each stitch. Many of these Indians have died off in the last year and only a few of a once flourishing tribe are left. Measles and whooping cough cleaned out entire villages, and Aleutian Island baskets will soon be a thing of the past."

In Fig. 349 are seen a large variety of Alaska baskets in the Frohman collection. They are mainly made on Yakutat Island and are of great beauty. The shape is unvaried, being round, rarely flaring, but of many sizes. Spruce roots and grasses in the dull natural green or dyed brown and black were originally used. But the Indian of to-day loves not the labor of securing her own inimitable dyes, but she does love color, so she substitutes the easily-obtained aniline dyes. Hence happy is that present day collector who can find a basket of this type

FIG. 349. ALASKAN BASKETS, MADE ON YAKUTAT ISLAND, IN THE
FROHMAN COLLECTION.

in the original lovely old browns over which the genuine connoisseur raves and rhapsodizes.

Many of these baskets are of a small size, convenient for the holding of household or personal treasures, and they are provided with lids. It is a quaint conceit to place pebbles in a most skillfully constructed hiding place within the lid. The rattle of these gives warning to the owner when any one would purloin the treasure.

The three front baskets in Fig. 351 are highly prized specimens in the Frohman collection. The one to the left is a beautiful old Yokut bottle-neck, and the design clearly indicates a dance. The one to the right is of the rattlesnake design, and both are bordered with quail plumes. The center basket is a Klikitat, known to be 75 years old, of perfect weave and design.

Fig. 352 shows several interesting old Haida hats similar to the one described on page 183, and pictured in Figs. 265 and 266. These are Potlatch hats made by the older generations of the Haidas, and were and still are worn in dances. The making of them is now a lost art. The present generation know nothing whatever of making them. Each one is painted with the totemic design which represents the tribe to which the dancer belongs. The two lower ones are Bella Bella Siwash hats, worn by British Columbia Indians.

Fig. 353 represents two Klikitat weavers and a number of their baskets in the Frohman collection. Of this weave and its people Mrs. Frohman sends me the following, which supplements the information given on page 53:

"These rare and beautiful baskets are made by the different tribes belonging to the Shahaptian linguistic stock. The derivation is Salishan. Their habitat was along the waters of the Columbia and its tributaries, from the Cascade Mountains on the west to Bitter Root range on the east, or what is now eastern Washington and Northern Idaho.

"The Klikitats have been styled the 'Iroquois of the Northwest.' They were marauders and robbers. The very word Klikitat means robber.

"Two of their favorite haunts in times gone by were the Cascades and The Dalles or long narrows of the Columbia. They were a constant menace to the trappers and voyagers from the foundation of the Pacific Fur Co. in 1811, and continued to worry the pioneers until they were subdued by the Yakima war of 1856.

"They went down to the ocean on the west, carrying the wild hemp, dried and twisted into neat bundles. This was much sought after by the coast Indians for fish net, and they gladly gave in exchange their wampum or dentalia, a small shell collected in those days at Nutka. The wampum was the money or circulating medium, and Alexander Ross said in 1814 three fathoms of it bought ten beaver skins.

"When the Klikitats procured firearms, bows and arrows were soon out of date and making beautiful arrow heads became a lost art.

"So also when buckets superseded baskets, basket making to them became almost a lost art."

A description of the materials used is found on pages 76, 77.

Now Mrs. Frohman: "After these preliminaries, that ran through weeks and months, were arranged, the weaver seated herself upon the

FIG. 351. FINE YOKUT BOTTLE-NECK, KLIKITAT, HAIDA, AND ALEUT BASKETS
IN THE FROHMAN COLLECTION.

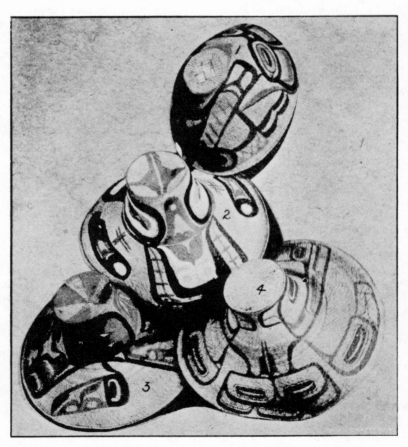

FIG. 352. POTLACH HATS OF THE HAIDAS. IN THE FROHMAN COLLECTION.

ground either by a spring or stream and began to work by taking a small bunch of these water-soaked roots which, when tightly compressed, were about the size of a lead pencil. She began at the bottom of a basket by making a coil and tightly lashing it with a soaked thong of spruce root, each time piercing the stitch in the preceding row with the bone awl, threading the spruce through, and tightly drawing it in place. She thus succeeded in making a lockstitch, water tight, so that if it were possible to draw out the coil the basket would still preserve its shape. This coiling and whipping continued with the spruce alone until the bottom was completed, for the ornamentation seldom, if ever, appeared on the bottom. When the last coil of the bottom was made, then the ornamenting or decorating began. A strip of the grass was laid on and lashed in place, then turned back and lashed again, each time being held in place by the all-important spruce thong. This lapping back and forth gave it the name "imbricated." Every time a stitch was made it took the circuits of the spruce whipping to hold it in place, each time following the puncture made by the awl. This renders it exceedingly hard work, one round of a large basket or three of a small one being considered a hard day's labor for an experienced basket maker.

"The figures of the designs are always triangular or angular, never round, in the original shapes, as to the Klikitats the circular figure mean civilization. The baskets are always round and are carried on women's backs by a broad strap passed around the forehead or across the chest. When gathering berries the woman throws them over her shoulder into the basket. The Indians say the berries keep sweeter in these baskets, and as they are water tight there is no loss of juice."

On Clatsop Plains, in Oregon, there resides Mrs. Machelle, the last of the Clatsop tribe, nearly 100 years old, who still occupies herself in weaving baskets. Says Mrs. Frohman, in speaking of her work: "One cannot fail to be impressed by the rare and skillful combination of beauty and utility in these baskets, and their wonderful adaptability to the Indians' various needs. The dwellers of the North Coast obtain their food from the sea, so the weavers make a loosely woven cedar bark receptacle for their fish, both fresh and dried. The open mesh of the clam-basket, of a coarse grass, permits the sea water to escape as the weary digger trails home across the sands at dawn."

Another of the weaves that is growing rarer as the years go by is that of the Skokomish, barely referred to on page 53. These Washington weavers have gradually decreased in number until now the tribe is almost extinct. A fine specimen in the National Museum is pictured in Fig. 78, and in Fig. 354 are four others in the Frohman collection. On all of these specimens will be noticed what might almost be called the sign manual of the Skokomish, viz., the circle of dogs on the upper part of the basket. No matter what other design is incorporated into their work, this symbol invariably is used at the top. This fact opens up an interesting field for investigation which it is to be hoped some local enthusiast will later explore.

Of the few good Skokomish weavers left, Sarah Curly is said to be the best, and she will work only when the weather is damp and rainy, as she says otherwise her grasses crack and split.

Fig. 355 shows several fine Thompson River baskets, similar to those described on pages 79 and 147. These are interesting specimens, varying in shape and design, but all useful and attractive.

GATHERING INFORMATION—Those who are interested in the preservation of accurate knowledge of Indian baskets and their weavers can do good service in their respective localities by recording such particulars as the following blank calls for, verifying the answers given by one weaver by comparison with those given by others. Only by persistent endeavor can reliable information be obtained. The blank is one prepared and sent out by Professor Mason, of the Smithsonian Institution, to whom lovers of basketry owe so much.

BASKET WORK OF AMERICAN INDIANS.

Tribe................., Location of Tribe....................
Plant,

       Scientific name ....

       Common name ....

       Indian name ....

How prepared ....

How woven ....

Legend. ....

Specimen in Collection of ....

FIG. 354. SKOKOMISH BASKETS IN FROHMAN COLLECTION.

In addition to these particulars I always endeavor to obtain the name, Indian and American, of the weaver, and her photograph where possible, either while weaving the basket or when it is completed. This photograph should always include the material used and the tools, and the actual processes of weaving. For instance, the Hopi weavers invariably place their splints in a blanket full of moist sand, in order to keep them pliable. It adds much to the scientific value of the photograph if this sand blanket is shown.

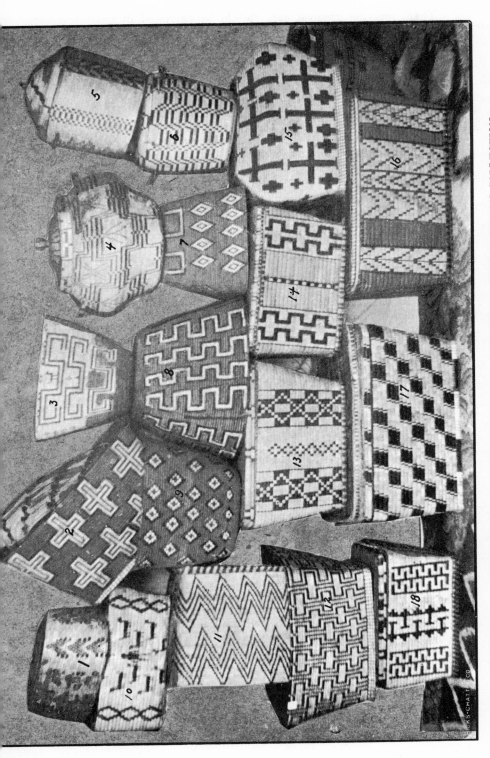

Then, too, the greatest care should be exercised in obtaining the tribal name of the weaver. The Yokuts have a number of sub-tribal names, and one is apt to get confused, unless he is persistent in questioning and requestioning, directly and indirectly, on this particular.

Under the head of "How Prepared," much valuable information can often be obtained. The gathering of the material as described by Dr. Hudson on pages 80-81 ; the stripping of the bark, or splitting up of the willow, how done, and a description of the tools used, if any, (see page 85); the dyeing processes for the different colors, especially where native dyes and processes are followed; the materials used in the extraneous decoration of such baskets as the "moon" and "sun" baskets of the Pomas; all these legitimately come under that head.

Then, too, careful attention to the methods of weaving may often reveal interesting facts. I am told that there are three different methods of procuring the "herring-bone" or braided finishing stitch of the Navaho wedding basket. Some use three splints, others two, and still others but one, and yet to the casual observer there is not the slightest perceptible difference in the result.

The importance of gaining the weaver's own interpretation of the legend cannot be too strongly emphasized. A short time ago a friend purchased a beautiful basket and brought it to me in New York. She knew the weaver well, a Cahuilla Indian, the wife of Juan Costello, but had not herself secured the meaning of the design. At her suggestion I wrote to a gentleman, who kindly visited the camp for the purpose of gaining the information. I quote his reply in full as an interesting confirmation of what I have before written: "My questions of the Indians at the time of the receipt of your letter happened to be directed to an old woman at Juan's camp, who, I thought, was the maker. She, who was his mother, told me, through Juan's interpretation, that it was patterned after some rock form on the desert side of the San Jacinto Mountains; it is doubtful if she understood my query or I her answer. To-day I went to the camp and did my best to learn from Juan's wife, by the use of my limited Spanish and the chary use of English of her little girl, more about it, expecting the same information. She drew figures upon the ground of the leaves of what she called 'mescal,' idealized, for they did not have the broad base and point of the plant she referred to. I called her attention to some plants along a road we knew, the Agua Americana, four of which are just now maturing gigantic flower stalks, and this plant was what she meant, and the girl, said her mother, not the grandmother, made the basket you refer to. It is a little odd, isn't it, that they apply the name of the distilled product of the juice, 'pulque,' to the whole plant, but 'mescal' was the name used for it. You can take your choice of the answers obtained, but I think the leaves of what we call the 'Century plant' was the model for her design."

This is undoubtedly the proper interpretation, as "mescal" is the word commonly applied by all the Indians of the Southwest to this plant, also to a food which they prepare from the cooked leaf fibres.

INDEX.